Hope you enjoy this.

Maria & Richard

MALAYSIA NO PROBLEM LAH!

Four Years in Malaysia
and
Southeast Asia

A Diary

by

Maria and Richard Yates

McClain PRINTING COMPANY
Parsons, West Virginia 26287
1994

International Standard Book Number 087012-523-0
Library of Congress Catalog Card Number 94-90263
Printed in the United States of America
Copyright ©1994 by Maria and Richard Yates
Colorado Springs, Colorado 80920

DEDICATION

to

Our Family and Friends

Whose Encouragement

Made Our Adventure Possible

Especially to Maria's father

Ralph W. Phillips

and

In Loving Memory

of

Mildred and Harold Yates

With Special Thanks
to
Our Editors and Proofreaders

Suzanne Gustat
Ralph W. Phillips
Joan Shull

Text for this manuscript is based on trip diaries kept by Richard and letters written by both Richard and Maria. Narration is by Maria.

TABLE OF CONTENTS

FOREWORD

Living and working in Malaysia from 1987-1989 and again from 1991-1993, we witnessed dramatic political, social, and environmental changes. Malaysia, a country in a hurry to develop and compete, is eager to gain recognition in the emerging new world order.

The IU/MUCIA/ITM[1] students have performed outstandingly at American Universities. As future leaders, we trust their cross-cultural experiences will have changed them in ways that will benefit Malaysia and mankind.

Our diaries provide insight into the struggle between old and new value systems. Malaysians desire "the good life." The dilemma facing the government and foreign investors is to find ways to preserve the environment and culture that is so much a part of Malaysia's charm.

This volume compares life in Malaysia from 1987-1989 with parallel experiences during 1991-1993. Dates at the beginning of chapters and different type faces for the text identify the time periods. Inevitably the rapid change will continue so that visitors in the future will experience a country vastly different than the one we describe.

The phrase "No problem lah!" is a commonly used expression in Malaysia. The first two words are self-explanatory. "Lah" is an intensifier which is frequently added to words, phrases, or sentences to indicate optimistic attributes. Unfortunately, it is often used to cover distinctly pessimistic attitudes.

---

[1] Indiana University/Midwest Universities Consortium for International Affairs, Inc./Mara Institute of Technology. See glossary.

"And so I am home in America. A traveller returns, but he is never the same; he returns, and what he returns to is new. And if he comes from an outpost of the British Empire, and from jungles and swamps, and from Eastern languors and tropical calm, then a traveller returned is momentarily confused by life in the U.S.A." Agnes Keith, <u>Land Below the Wind</u>

INTRODUCTION

OFF THE HIGH DIVING BOARD: 1987-1989

30 JULY, 1987—Comfortably settled on a Boeing 747, we were racing the sun toward Hong Kong. Somewhere over the Pacific we lost a day. How did we get ourselves into this situation? Just hours before we had said goodbye to family, friends and a comfortable life in Munster, Indiana, to pursue our dream of living and working in Southeast Asia. I'm reminded of years ago when friends talked me into climbing the ladder to the high diving board. The rules said you couldn't climb back down so, since I couldn't stay up there forever, I had to jump. In October 1986, Richard asked me what I would think about moving to Malaysia. I said, "Sounds great . . . where's Malaysia?" We had a vague idea Malaysia was near Indochina or Thailand. We learned a lot about Malaysia in ten months of anticipating and preparing for the move and during the time we called Malaysia home, but on that day in July 1987, the laughter, tears, frustrations and satisfactions of learning about and adjusting to life in Asia, along with travel adventures, were still ahead of us.

MUCIA is a consortium of midwestern universities involved with a cooperative education project in Malaysia. Malaysia sends more students to the United States than any other country and a few years ago decided these students would be more successful with two years of college preparation by U.S. faculty before going abroad. In 1985 the first groups of MUCIA faculty went to Shah Alam to collaborate with Institut Teknologi Mara in establishing a

1

campus there. Students earn a two-year associate degree from Indiana University and finish their education at a U.S. campus. In the fall of 1986 Richard applied to teach math at the Shah Alam campus and we began the climb up the ladder to our diving board. We passed inspection but in January were told there were no openings in math. We resigned ourselves to waiting a semester or a year and then in April received a letter offering Richard a position starting August 1. Suddenly the dream was to become reality and we had four months to put our lives in Munster on hold and get organized for a move halfway around the world.

Peninsular Malaysia, the size of England without Wales, is the continuation of the isthmus shared by Thailand and Burma. The west coast is washed by the Indian Ocean and the Straits of Malacca, and the east coast is warmed by the South China Sea. The Kingdom of Kedah is mentioned in Chinese and Sanskrit writings as far back as 600 to 700 A.D. Portuguese, Dutch, Japanese, and British all occupied Malaysia for a time, but on August 31, 1957, the independent Federation of Malaya was created. Malaysia was formed in 1963 and is made up of thirteen states, eleven on the peninsula and two on the island of Borneo. Singapore originally belonged to the federation but withdrew in 1965.

The climate is tropical with temperatures ranging from 70 to 95 degrees and 100 inches of rainfall per year. There are northeast and southwest monsoons and dry seasons. The northeast monsoon inundates the east coast, washing out roads and bridges, destroying houses, and taking lives. Each year the people patiently rebuild. These rains, stopped by a mountain ridge bisecting the peninsula, have less effect on the west coast. The southwest monsoon is also obstructed by a central ridge of mountains in Sumatra after dropping most of its moisture there on the west coast. In Shah Alam it rained every few days year-round. The longest dry spell we experienced was nine days. The heat and the mosquitoes were both worse during the dry spells.

Orang asli, the indigenous people, live in the jungles. Bumiputra[2] are Muslim and considered the native Malays. People from south India were brought in to work on the rubber plantations and railroads. Chinese came because of trade advantages. The population includes a substantial number of Eurasians, a result of British, Portuguese, and Dutch occupation. The official

---

[2]Malaysian word meaning "sons of the soil." See glossary.

language is Bahasa Melayu[3] and the official religion is Islam. However, Mandarin, Tamil, and English are spoken, most major religions are represented, and the mix of racial and religious backgrounds gives Malaysia a rich cultural heritage.

In many ways Malaysia is not a third world country. The government actively encourages industrial development and the overall standard of living is higher than that found in many Southeast Asian countries. Unfortunately, the desire to compete overshadows the need to preserve the environment. By the time controls are imposed on cars, trucks, and industry it may be too late.

I'd grown up in foreign service so the prospect of living overseas wasn't frightening, but I developed a new respect for my mother and other women I have known over the years who coped with international relocation. An amazing amount of stuff collects in a house in twenty years but we gritted our teeth and gradually sorted everything into piles marked "storage," "throw out," "give away," and "take." The "take" pile had to be sorted three ways—hand luggage, air freight, and sea freight. We did well choosing what we couldn't live without for two years but when we had it to do over again we took even less. We put a lot of thought into packing the four suitcases and two pieces of hand luggage we limited ourselves to. We were told to carry everything in our hand luggage we would need to live in a rented house until our air freight arrived. The house would have living and dining room furniture and beds, but we had to provide sheets, pillows, and a minimum of kitchen supplies.

Indiana University deluged us with printed information about the project and Malaysia. We read everything. In late June 1987, we went to Bloomington along with the dozen other families who would be the new faculty in Shah Alam that fall. For three days we listened to people who had worked with the program and Malaysian students who had successfully adjusted to living in the U.S. They did it . . . so could we!

Gradually, one rung at a time we climbed and now we were exactly where we wanted to be: at the end of the board with nothing to do except jump.

---

[3]The Malaysian language. The word "bahasa" means language and is often used alone to refer to the Malaysian language. See glossary.

FIRST IMPRESSIONS

Our sons, Michael and John, doubted our ability to care for ourselves halfway around the world and two days before leaving we had reason to doubt ourselves. After our airfreight was picked up we realized the airline tickets were carefully secured in the strong box inside the trunk. We didn't sleep much that night and in the morning were relieved to learn that the air freight hadn't left Hammond yet. We could have had the tickets reissued but then the Malaysian government would have had good reason to wonder about our competence.

▼

In San Francisco we were bumped up to business class because the airline computer assigned us to economy section seats that didn't exist. Wider seats and more leg room made the long flight much more comfortable.

▼

Our short stopover in Hong Kong was a blur of confused images. Surely so small an island couldn't support such a mass of humanity. The taxi ride from the airport and back, our first experience with left-hand driving, was terrifying, and the sights and smells as we walked along the streets made an indelible impression.

▼

MAS - Malaysian Air Service - was our first contact with a beautiful, gentle people and the last lap of what seemed an endless journey. The relatively short flight to Kuala Lumpur was a pleasure after the twelve-hour stretch across the Pacific. Subang International Airport passport control took only minutes. We claimed our luggage, walked the green line (nothing to declare), and were greeted by the heat and humidity of the tropics. Average daytime temperatures would run 31° C (88° F).

After a few months we adjusted to the heat and humidity, but at first we suffered a great deal of physical discomfort. Our appetites vanished and we lost an amazing amount of weight. The diet of fresh fruit, rice, vegetables, and very little meat kept us from regaining what we had lost, and we avoided sending pictures home. We didn't know it was possible to sweat so much. Our clothes would literally be wringing wet, as if we had been caught in a downpour.

▼

We had no jet lag at all. We weren't sure if this was due to

4

the special diet we followed before we left or because we were keyed up. The diet alternated feast/fast meals for three days before departure, changed sleep habits to fit the new time zone, and suggested drinking lots of non-alcoholic liquid in flight.

Our first days were spent at Shah's Village Motel in the New Town section of Petaling Jaya. The air-conditioned rooms had Malaysian beds, slats with a thin mattress, and we followed the Malaysian custom of not wearing shoes in our rooms.

A survival hint for travelers in Asia: wear slip-on shoes. Tie shoes are a nuisance when you are required to be barefoot or in stocking feet indoors.

The food at the motel was wonderful and the staff were exceptionally nice to us. The new faculty and their families all looked forward to evening gatherings around the pool when we shared the day's adventures. After only a few days in Malaysia we had opened a bank account, rented a house, and bought a car.

On our first walk into New Town we were impressed with the depth of the storm drains and the number of restaurants. The deep drains keep homes and shops from being inundated when it rains. We're talking about serious rain, rain heavier than we had ever seen before. The drains around the house we rented regularly overflowed and flooded the backyard. Malaysia doesn't have violent storms but the wind is often strong. Thunder and lightning were impressive and during one memorable storm, a strong lightning bolt blew out every bulb that was on in the house at the time. The drains are a hazard to life and limb as Richard was to find out. He was lucky he didn't seriously injure himself when he "did a drain," as falling into one is referred to by expats[4].

I remember as a child being told to hold my head high and look straight ahead while walking. This is dangerous advice to follow in Malaysia. In addition to the hazard of storm drains, sidewalk levels change frequently. The change varies anywhere from an inch or two to several steps and the only way to avoid bad falls is to pay careful attention. In Malacca the British decreed stores

---

[4]Short form of "expatriate" used to refer to foreigners living abroad. See glossary.

Richard and the drain he fell into.

had to have a six-foot sidewalk in front. The merchants complied with the order but also built walls perpendicular from each end of the store, forcing pedestrians into the street every ten or twelve feet.

▼

Handicapped people have a difficult time getting around and, in general, buildings are not wheelchair accessible. We did not see many handicapped people but those we did see were not left to struggle by themselves. There were always family, friends, or strangers willing to help.

▼

Dress in KL[5] and PJ[6] (used universally when referring to these cities) was cosmopolitan in contrast to conservative Shah Alam, where the Muslim code of long dresses and head coverings was more evident.

Indian women, often employed as road crews or to clean up parks and buildings, wore saris to work and were a constant reminder we were indeed living in a different culture.

▼

The water in cities is safe to drink and we ate, even from street vendors, without any ill effects.

▼

When waiting for long periods of time many natives assume a squatting position even if a bench or chair is available. When we tried it our hips and knee joints hurt and our circulation shut down after only a few minutes. We decided muscles and joints have to be stretched from childhood for it to become second nature as an adult.

▼

Another reminder of cultural differences came with house hunting. We were discouraged by how dirty the houses were and later learned landlords generally cleaned, painted, and repaired after rather than before a contract was signed. In general, building maintenance was poor with little money or energy spent on upkeep. Walls were poured concrete and brick. Wiring and plumbing were usually in plain sight. One friend rented a house with the upstairs bathroom plumbing visible in the corner of the living room ceiling!

▼

Malaysians do not wait in line. It is not considered bad manners to push and shove.

▼

Perfect strangers stopped what they were doing to show us the way if we were lost or to help out when we had car trouble.

---

[5]Kuala Lumpur, territorial capitol of Malaysia. See glossary.
[6]Petaling Jaya, suburb of Kuala Lumpur. See glossary.

▼

Shaking hands is not done between members of the opposite sex. Instead, the area of the heart is touched with the fingers of the right hand as a greeting. Members of the same sex use both hands in a gentle clasp of greeting in addition to touching the heart.

▼

Our first adventures in eating at a local fish place and a north Indian restaurant told us right away we were going to love the food! Lunch at a food stall, a plate full of noodles, shrimp, fried meats, and vegetables and a bottle of orange soda, cost U.S. 88¢. A carry out drink in a plastic bag with straw and a rubber band about the top to keep it from leaking, worked fine as long as we didn't need to set it down. However, we could hang our drinks on a tree or bush limb, the fence post, a handy nail, or a doorknob.

▼

Sweet corn, imported from Japan, is a popular snack but the kernels are much harder than what we were used to in the mid-west. The Malaysians use corn to make desserts, including ice cream. Ais kecong, made from shaved ice, green noodles, red beans, corn, and sweetened condensed milk is delicious.

▼

The saying "only mad dogs and Englishmen go out in the midday sun" surely originated in the tropics. Mornings and evenings weren't too bad but from 11 a.m. to 3 p.m. is a good time to sit in the shade and sip fresh lime juice.

▼

We quickly learned to speak British English: lift for elevator, petrol for gas, bonnet, windscreen and boot on the car, etc.

▼

Fortunately, cold showers were a refreshing relief from the heat since outside of international class hotels, cold or luke warm water was about all we ever got. Water tanks on the roofs were heated by the sun, and supplementary heaters inside, when they existed, had to be turned on and off manually.

▼

"No problem lah!" and "Never mind!", two phrases we heard a lot during our first two years, reflected the mellowed-out attitude predominating relationships in Malaysia. We had been told we

8

would lose face if we showed anger. We smiled a lot in public and saved our tantrums for when we were alone. It didn't take long for us to adopt a more relaxed way of life and shrug off problems that weren't life threatening. Close to the end of our first two-year stay I did blow my cool. Termites infested the kitchen and after months of telling us we didn't have a problem, the inspector was busily destroying the inside of a kitchen cabinet. Overcome with enthusiasm for the job, he poked a large hole up through the formica counter top! Even though it wasn't my counter top, I threw him out and called the landlady. She arrived the next day with the **President** of the company and they had a royal row. I stayed out of it but she did tell him that I had a temper to be reckoned with and he must fix the counter to suit me.

▼

Sidewalk vendors were everywhere: sidewalk secretaries typed letters or filled out forms for a small fee; shoe repairmen set up shop and repaired our shoes while we waited; vendors spread wallets, watches, and calculators on the sidewalk and squatted beside them.

▼

Arrows painted on ceilings of hotel rooms, indicating the direction to Mecca, were standard.

▼

Stop signs in Malaysia were ignored by drivers. A friend in the program made the mistake of stopping her car at a stop sign. The driver of the bus that hit her car insisted the accident was her fault because she should have known better than to stop. When the police arrived, they agreed!

▼

The daily frustrations are enormous. On the surface, Malaysia is a modern country but in reality nothing works as we expect it to. Our hostess, Roberta Dees, helped us adjust and encouraged us to consider a day successful if we crossed <u>ONE</u> item off our list of things to do! At our orientation meetings we had all laughed at the funny things that had happened to the first groups of faculty. Now, as strange things were happening to us, it was a struggle to maintain a sense of humor.

RETURN ENGAGEMENT: 1991-1993

In February 1991, Richard was asked whether he would like to return to teach in the IU/MUCIA/ITM program in Malaysia. The Gulf War and uncertainty about living in Muslim countries had made recruiting difficult and many applicants had withdrawn. We decided the opportunity was too good to pass up. We did check with the State Department and were re-assured to hear only the recorded warning about drug trafficking. Richard applied, the approval letter arrived in April, and we were in Shah Alam in time to begin the 1991 summer session.

John and Susan Coffey, a young couple in the Purdue Calumet math department, agreed to take care of our house. We closed off one bedroom to use for storage and packed the crawl space full. John, Susan, and their son, Daniel, lived in the house for the two years we were away. Their commitment facilitated our speedy departure and gave us peace of mind while we were overseas.

The week before leaving for Malaysia, we made five trips to O'Hare. Richard's folks came for a short visit and John left for his summer in Florence, Italy. We had sold both our cars so we used John's car the last few days and then left it parked at Michael's apartment. On May 12, Michael took us to the airport. Our plane left O'Hare about twenty minutes late and was about a half hour early in Los Angeles. We stored our luggage at the airport, checked into a motel, took a long walk, and ate supper at a Mexican restaurant.

Security for the trans-Pacific flight was very tight. MAS went through all our luggage and made us transfer our camera to carry-on. They inspected the computer disks by hand. Lunch at the airport - two salads (mostly lettuce) and two large drinks - cost $7.75!!

We were a half hour late leaving LA and never made up the time. It was 2:30 a.m. by the time our plane landed in KL. Howard Pollock was waiting patiently. We spent our first night in a Holiday Inn suite in Shah Alam because they weren't expecting us until afternoon. It was 4:15 before we got to bed but we were up early to meet with Tim Diemer and the Gilletts, who were new to the math department and the program. We were moved to a regular room and discovered we were lucky they had an empty room for us. When the Holiday

Inn in Shah Alam opened just before we left two years ago, we wondered how they would ever get it filled. It was now overflowing with tourists and businessmen, and reservations were difficult to obtain.

In spite of panic about our housing situation, we enjoyed rediscovering our adopted country. There had been changes—not all for the better—but much was familiar and comfortable. We celebrated our thirtieth wedding anniversary with an excellent dinner at Baluchi's, a restaurant in PJ whose name sounded more Italian than North Indian. The number and quality of restaurants in Shah Alam had improved since 1989 and we quickly deserted the overpriced hotel for cheaper and better local eateries. To save money, we took our dirty clothes to the Section 2 shophouse laundry in Shah Alam. One day we left a few dirty clothes in the hotel's plastic laundry bag and the maid picked it up and sent them to the hotel laundry. Having those few clothes washed by the hotel laundry cost more than several weeks worth of wash did at the shophouses. In fact, the laundry in Section 2 charged so much less that we continued to use it even after we moved to PJ. The rest of the time we lived in the hotel we were careful to hide the laundry bag from the maids.

During the nineteen days we spent in the Holiday Inn we looked at every available house in Shah Alam, Subang Jaya, and PJ. We decided we liked a house in PJ occupied by the Olans, who were leaving the program in July, and were negotiating with the landlady when our airfreight arrived on May 24. The Olans let us have it delivered there. We never lived in that house. The landlady backed out on renting it to us.

During the first weeks we spent a lot of time house hunting with Phil and Dooie Gillett. We were also house hunting for Bipin and Vrinda Pai and their three children, who were joining the program in August, and looking for two cars, one for us and one for them. We found a car for ourselves rather quickly. It was a clone of the '80 Datsun we had before but tan instead of grey. We had it "on approval" for a weekend before we told the dealer we would definitely buy it. Then we drove it for about a month without papers and without any money changing hands because the owner was vacationing in Australia. We did eventually find and buy a car for the Pais. We felt as if we were in the real estate and used car business.

The housing situation was difficult. Our housing allowance

11

would only partially cover rents which had skyrocketed in the two years we'd been gone. Landlords had become wary of foreigners who trashed their houses and left them with monstrous phone bills. We found homes only partially furnished, with drapes and fixtures missing. We couldn't blame the landlords; they'd been badly treated and were reacting in the only way they knew. The program had begun to withdraw from the fray and, outside of lists of realtors and homes recently vacated by ex-pats, we were on our own. By the following year there was virtually no support for new faculty in their search for housing, but the allowances did increase right after we signed a rental agreement.

The level of pollution in the Klang Valley was almost unbearable. There were times when the blue mosque in Shah Alam was almost totally obscured by smog, and we wondered whether we were going to survive. In fact, in the spring of 1993 a doctor looking at an x-ray of my lungs asked me whether I was a smoker.

DAILY LIFE: 1987-1989

SHAH ALAM

KL, the original capital of Selangor, became a Federal Territory and capital of Malaysia similar to the District of Columbia. Shah Alam, the new capital of Selangor and a planned community, was still in the process of being developed when we moved there. The Sultan maintains a residence and the state government buildings compete for attention with the mosque. The Sultan's fascination with ships is reflected in the design of the main government building. The town has wide streets, beautifully landscaped parkways, and a city park which is kept immaculate by a mowing crew and numerous women with Indian style brooms who sweep up clippings and fallen leaves. Each tree has its own cycle and leaves fall constantly in the tropics. At home we complain about raking leaves once a year! There it is a year round job.

Shah Alam Mosque: Masjid Sultan Salahuddin Abdul Aziz Shah.

The mosque, the largest in Southeast Asia, dominates Shah Alam. It had just been completed when we moved there in August of 1987 and we were among the last to tour it before the dedication in March of 1988. Masjid Sultan Salahuddin Abdul Aziz Shah

Interior view of the Shah Alam Mosque.

took eight years to construct. The main prayer hall holds 7000 and the women's gallery above accommodates 3000 with room for an additional 5000 faithful on the verandas. After dedication many areas were closed to non-Muslims, and female visitors are now required to wear headcoverings and long black robes.

The dome and the minarets are visible from almost anywhere in town, and after the dedication the muezzin's call woke us every morning at 5 a.m., following the custom in Mecca of summoning the faithful to read the Koran for an hour before the 6 a.m. call to prayer. The blue dome and white marble walls shimmering in sunlight and bathed in floodlights at night resemble a Disneyland fantasy, appearing to float free of the earth like a dream vision that might disappear if touched.

Shah Alam is laid out in sections, each having its own block or two of shophouses where we could buy almost all the necessities of life, have our hair done, order a suit made, have class notes duplicated, leave laundry or dry cleaning, buy bottled gas, have our car or a motorcycle repaired, or enjoy a meal at the corner restaurant. These family-run businesses with living quarters above the store are the economic backbone of Malaysia and all of Asia. Large stores and shopping malls are plentiful in PJ and KL but even in those larger cities, the shophouse is still the center of community life just as the corner store was in the U.S. fifty years ago. The owners of the few small shops we frequented were friendly but communication was a challenge. The tailor shop did beautiful work, and the tailor certainly had never seen legs as long as Richard's. His shirts needed to have one shoulder cut one-half inch narrower than the other but the first one ended up with epaulet decoration because of our inability to communicate.

The Komplex, the main shopping center in Shah Alam, is a collection of small shops and eating places. The two exceptions are the department store and the grocery store which are parts of major chains. For about a year the large grocery store sold pork and bacon, and we appreciated having these forbidden food products available in the grocery store. Muslims are forbidden to eat pork. At the checkout counter clerks would put on protective gloves to handle "unclean" packages, so I usually held them myself to enable the clerk to read the price before I bagged the item. Indians were employed at the meat counter to handle unpackaged goods. Muslims only eat halal[7] meat that has been ritually killed and blessed by the imam[8]. The animal must be fac-

Interior view of the Shah Alam Mosque with Ellen and Maria Yates.

[7]"Halal" means permissible. It applies to all food and is similar to the Jewish term, "kosher." All fruits and vegetables are halal; non-pork meats and meat products are halal only if properly processed.
[8]A Muslim man who exercises spiritual and temporal leadership over a region. See glossary.

15

ing Mecca and specific prayers are said as it is killed. In the spring of 1988 the store discontinued the sale of non-halal food, and the Chinese restaurant on the lake was also prohibited from offering pork dishes.

Government buildings around the lake in Shah Alam.

In order to attract more business, the shops would set up stalls in the central commons area. We marveled at the effort it took to set up these displays each day, and to set up for the day and night markets. Shopkeepers hauled produce or merchandise in a truck and once or twice a day set up displays in a different part of town. These movable markets had everything imaginable for sale and there were always food stalls. We often ate as we shopped.

Shah Alam has a special Saturday morning farmers' market where only locally grown produce is sold. We bought fruit, vegetables, milk, fish, and meat there. Cooked food is also available. Barbequed chicken, quail, or a large assortment of home cooked goodies from the ladies supporting the local mosque provided us with a "take-away" meal.

16

Monument on State House Hill in Shah Alam.

Middle- and upper-class houses in Shah Alam are large, airy, and surrounded by high, ornamental stone walls or iron fences. The smallest we could find had living room, dining room, study, kitchen, bath, storage room, maid's room and bath on the first floor and upstairs were three bedrooms with two baths and a large open area at the top of the stairs that eventually became our work room. Miss Lim, our landlady, entrusted us with nineteen keys, five of which were needed just to open the gate and front door. It was like living in a fortress. Decorative iron grating covered all the windows and doors with additional locks on those protecting the patios and doors.

Meat stall at the farmer's market.

Our house in Shah Alam.

Robberies, infrequent in Shah Alam, were more common in PJ and KL. Crimes of this sort are seldom violent. However, thieves prefer to have someone home who knows where gold and jewelry are hidden. Break-ins are traumatic but the victim is seldom harmed.

We hardly ever closed doors or windows, and in addition to cool breezes and rain, just about everything that walked, crawled, or flew wandered through at one time or another. Ciceks are everywhere. These small, mosquito-eating lizards are welcome indoors in spite of the fact they aren't housebroken and make a very strange chirping sound. They move with lightning speed, and encountering one on the doorknob in the middle of the night can cause near heart failure. The cockroaches are the largest I have ever seen and I expected to come downstairs one morning to find the living room furniture had been removed during the night by a crew of these monsters. We became fanatic about not leaving the slightest bit of food anywhere, which kept their numbers down but never eliminated them.

The Malays own cats, but most cats that wandered into the house weren't interested in making friends. One did bring his dinner, a freshly killed mouse, into the kitchen one evening and acted offended when we took exception to that. The last few weeks of our two-year stay in Malaysia we were adopted by a female cat whom we named Khalwat. In Bahasa that means "close proximity" and since she had attached herself to us we felt it was an apt name.

KL & PJ

We're sure a lot of our friends thought we were going to be living in a grass hut in the jungle. In reality KL and PJ are large metropolitan areas with buildings that could win prizes in international architectural competitions. We were taken to the Embassy in KL the first week to register, and a city tour afterwards provided some idea of the main sights. It took us a month to work up courage to drive in on our own. That was quite an adventure.

Our first try was a trip to Batu Cave, under twenty miles from Shah Alam and only a few miles north of Kuala Lumpur. Since many of the streets have no signs, and the highways are not numbered and have few signs that we couldn't read anyway, we were suddenly in downtown KL. We did NOT want to be there. As navigator I tried frantically to figure out where we were and to translate signs. We carried a dictionary everywhere but had not yet figured out Bahasa, which is usually a root word plus prefix. Not knowing the root word made finding it in the dictionary impossible. We were thwarted by one-way streets going the

Arch across the highway at the Selangor/Federal Territory border.

Downtown KL buildings.

Moorish vs. modern architecture in downtown KL.

Richard's parents in front of the Dayabumi building.

Jaime Mosque in downtown KL.

Selangor Club and cricket field in downtown KL.

The Parliament buildings in KL.

wrong way, and "no right turn" signs where we wanted to turn right! A local joke about the foreigner who followed Jalan Sahala all over KL before discovering the sign indicated "one-way street," was no longer funny. We went through one roundabout (traffic circle) at least six times. Roundabouts work well in small towns with little traffic but are not suitable for large metropolitan areas and by 1989 there were plans to gradually replace the main roundabouts in KL with flyovers (overpasses).

Considerably more than an hour later we had our first sight of a huge limestone mountain. Seeping water has carved holes all through it and the largest, Batu Cave, is a Hindu shrine with 374 steep steps leading to the cave entrance. There are wild monkeys running everywhere and pestering people. These adorable but nasty little beasts snatch packages, purses, or cameras from unwary tourists if they aren't careful.

Inside the cave are more stairs to climb. We decided to skip the museum cave which cost 50 sen[9] (20¢) apiece and later discovered we had missed the best part. These two caves are decorated with paintings and statues depicting the various incarnations of

---

[9]Malaysian word meaning "cent."

24

Staircase leading up to Batu Cave.

the Hindu gods, Shiva and Parvati. The caves never ceased to delight us and we lost count of the number of times during the two years we brought visitors there and climbed the steps with them.

Nearby, in an appallingly dilapidated building, workers produce beautiful batik fabric. Using hot wax the artist draws a design on silk or cotton fabric. Dye is applied to the unwaxed portions and then the piece is dipped in hot water to dissolve the wax. A repeated design can be made using metal stamps.

Genting Highlands is one of the British Hill stations built as an escape from the oppressive heat. The extremely steep road pushed our car to its limit. A new road was being planned by the time we left Malaysia. Genting, above 5500 feet, is cool and often shrouded in clouds and fog. The hotels and casino are deluxe. In all our future trips to the Highlands we had only one day clear enough to see across the valley to Port Klang (Port Swetenham under the British). As far as the eye could see were mountains covered with dense jungle. The old road down the mountain was in danger of being taken over by the jungle when we drove down it the first time. Bamboo trees had sent shoots across the road and were in the process of closing it in.

Several resorts offering golf, swimming, and tennis have been built on the hill and a cablecar from a halfway point on the road provides access to the children's amusement park, resort, and gambling casino at the top. The casino is a problem for the Muslim government which on one hand disapproves of gambling and, on the other, benefits from the profits. Muslims are not allowed to enter the casino. Non-Muslim men are required to wear coat and tie or long sleeved batik shirt.

Our trip back through KL and on home was a rerun of our trip to the caves. We had the same problems, aggravated by the fact that our map wasn't very accurate and night was falling. We circled the infamous roundabout many more times before we finally chose the right exit and miraculously found ourselves on the Federal Highway headed toward Shah Alam.

Apparently none of the maps is very accurate. The government deliberately keeps all maps inaccurate to prevent possible use by enemy invaders. The government can relax. We traveled by car all over Malaysia and never found a map that accurately depicted where we were, where we were going, or where we had been.

By December, when our sons visited, our ability to find our

way had improved. When we made a wrong turn we knew what we had done wrong and how to get ourselves back where we wanted to be. By August 1988 driving in KL was "No Problem Lah!"

AMAHS, GARDENERS, AND SHOPKEEPERS

We'd never had servants but our resolve to do all our own work lasted about a week after we moved into the house. Ironing clothes and mopping floors in the tropics is exhausting. The house had a large yard and we would have had to buy a lot of equipment to do it ourselves. We didn't even have to talk ourselves into hiring both a maid (amah) and a gardener.

It is common to hire the amah who worked for the previous renters. Murugaie (it took me months to learn how to spell her name) started to work about a month after we moved in. Her background was Indian and although she had never been to school, she spoke English, Tamil (the south Indian dialect), Bahasa, and a little Chinese. Her niece, Debbie, was fourteen at the time and also had never been to school. She did not have Murugaie's ability with languages but was learning to be an amah. Most of the first year we enjoyed the luxury of having two amahs for the price of one. Neither Debbie nor Murugaie could read. Written instructions had to be taken home for her husband, Ghopal, to read or to the teachers at the pre-school in back of us. Murugaie recognized the number of the bus she took to work each day, but Debbie couldn't do that.

Murugaie was thirty-four years old in 1987. A sister died in childbirth a week after Murugaie and Ghopal were married and the infant, a daughter, was raised as their own. Their natural child, a fourteen-year-old boy, had a severe heart defect. He was under the regular care of an American doctor and at the time we left, surgery had been discussed many times but never performed. Ghopal's brother had taken the boy's records to India where doctors concurred everything possible was being done.

Murugaie kept a small herd of cows and sold the milk for extra income. Not much fresh milk was available in Malaysia and most cheese was imported and expensive. Powdered milk, available in the stores, was used more—probably because it didn't spoil. The family lived in a kampung (small village) outside of

Murugaie and her family in front of their house.

Shah Alam. The small house, concrete floor and thin plywood walls, was clean and lovingly decorated. It had a living room, a large kitchen, one bedroom, and we think a bathroom although we never had occasion to use it. The family all slept in the one bedroom and often there were other relatives living with them. Murugaie and Ghopal were on a list for government housing but when approval came through, Murugaie refused to move. She said she couldn't imagine everyone having separate bedrooms and the kitchen in the new apartment was too small!

We were honored to be invited twice for Deepavali celebrations (the Hindu festival of lights) and to a farewell party for departing members of the math department who employed Murugaie. Murugaie was an excellent cook and prepared feasts for these occasions. Since she and Ghopal thought all foreigners drank beer, I managed to oblige when we were invited there.

Toward the end of our second year Murugaie and Ghopal were in a motorcycle accident and were unable to work for about a month. His brother and wife took the whole family into their home and cared for them and when Murugaie was able to come back to work, the sister-in-law came along to help. The brother-in-law is in the sheet metal business. When we sold our mattresses we asked him if he would deliver them with his truck. He would have done the job for free if we had let him because he said we were family! We are sure they would have given us bed and board. Hospitality is the way of life in Malaysia.

Ghopal drove a government lorry (truck) so they were fairly prosperous by Malaysian standards. While he was recovering from their motorcycle accident, he helped Murugaie with the final cleaning of our house. In general, Malaysian men are handy about the house and help with chores. Fathers routinely take an active role in caring for all their children.

Murugaie taught us a lot about her religion and culture. When she and Ghopal first wanted to get married her family objected. They made a pilgrimage to Batu Caves during Thaipusam to ask for a blessing on their intentions and that her family would agree to the marriage. They also made a pilgrimage there to ask for healing for their son and were seriously considering having Ghopal go to one of the holy places in India to ask for healing. They used Chinese medicine or went to a bomo (medicine man) for most of their ailments and I am convinced, whatever the reason, the cures worked. Murugaie was in the hospital several times and told me she never slept because she was sure she would die if she went to sleep there.

▼

Getting trees and plants to grow in the tropics is easy. Miss Lim, our landlady, brought us banana and papaya trees and we enjoyed fruit from both trees before the two years were over. Murugaie was extremely upset with us because we harvested the bananas a few at a time and didn't cut down the whole stalk at once. She told us what we were doing would bring bad luck. We also learned the flower had to be cut off before the hand of bananas would ripen. It is thought to be bad luck if the flower is cut by a menstruating woman.

Miss Lim also gave us a bare tree limb to stick in the ground outside the front gate and told us to water it regularly. It quickly sprouted branches and leaves and within two years was over ten feet tall. If we hadn't hired someone to trim the trees and bushes, we soon would have been living in a jungle.

Our adventures with gardeners did not go smoothly. Logan, a friend of Aziz who had helped us find our car, was our first gardener. He was a handsome Indian lad until he smiled, but the high sugar diet and lack of dental care had ruined his teeth. He was a hard worker and knew a lot about the care of shrubs and plants but didn't own a lawnmower. He had to contract that out.

In addition, he lived in a kampung that experienced severe flooding every time it rained, which kept him from coming on the day he was supposed to. We finally had to admit that even though he was a nice boy, he just wasn't able to give our lawn the care it needed.

We moved on to Wilfred. He lasted about a year. He worked with a crew of two or three young Indians who did not speak English. They had all the necessary equipment but the little hand mower was a lethal weapon in their hands. Each time they mowed we would go around the yard to see what damage they had done to new plants we were trying to get started. At least they were fairly reliable until April of our last year when they vanished into thin air! We even tracked down Wilfred's house and were told by neighbors he had left town because of a family emergency.

So for the last four months Moron mowed our lawn. The name is pronounced just the way it looks and we learned to say it with a straight face. He also was Indian and he and his wife were expecting their first child. He had worked for several others in the program and we wish we had discovered him sooner. By the time we left we found him several other new jobs.

▼

I fought a losing battle with the garbage collectors. They came three times a week but each time would only pick up one bag. After the grass was cut we would have several bags that would be ignored until I asked the driver to let me throw them on the truck! The Indian workers would help but the Malay crew just stood and watched and finally the driver told me he wouldn't take our yard debris anymore. We gave up and started a compost heap. We never did figure out how to get them to take large tree branches. Dumping them in the storm drains worked because eventually the town crew would come clean those out, but we felt guilty about doing that. Recently someone suggested we should have paid the driver a small sum each week. At the time we never thought of doing that.

▼

Postal service was erratic; we decided overseas mail came in batches. We had trouble convincing our postman not to stick the mail in the gate where it would get wet. Quite a bit of mail simply never made it to us, either because it was lost or delivered to the wrong address.

▼

The shopkeepers and repairmen in Shah Alam were wonderful to us but no help at all in our efforts to learn Bahasa. We would try out our Bahasa on them and they would speak English back to us. We bought mostly local products and they were always helpful when we couldn't find something. The repairmen who came to the house often didn't charge if the problem was simple to fix.

The native Malays are beautiful people—very small and delicate looking—so it was difficult to treat them as adults. The workman who looked fifteen was probably closer to thirty and had a wife and three children. We decided the signals indicating age to us are missing in Asians.

They had similar problems deciding how old we were. It wasn't unusual to be approached by a stranger who wanted to practice his English. Along with all the other questions, he would almost always ask our ages. We would answer and then explain that in our country it wasn't considered polite to ask someone's age! "How old are you?" and "How much did it cost?" were two questions we never got used to being asked but both seemed a standard part of any conversation. When asked how much things cost we usually would just say we didn't remember or quote a ridiculously low figure and let the person asking wonder how we could possibly have made such a good bargain.

Bargaining also took some adjustment. Most shopkeepers expected us to bargain and at the very least to ask if there was a discount. Getting a good bargain added to the fun but we always wondered if we could have done better.

HOUSEKEEPING AND COOKING

Except when Murugaie was ill, I did no housekeeping. The floors were impossible to keep clean in between her twice weekly ministrations, but it was easier to scrub our feet with a nail brush than to do the mopping ourselves. Of course we wiped up spills and became fanatic about the odd crumb or bit of food that might be left about. We certainly didn't want to encourage the roaches.

We did our own laundry, although the machine was closer to a toy than a real appliance. It would hold one sheet, a pillowcase and some underwear as a load so it is easy to understand why many of the expats simply took their dirty clothes to the local laundry. At the end of the cycle we had to untie the clothes. I have never before had a machine that tied things in knots as this one did.

There were a few clotheslines in the amah's room when we moved in and Richard added several more, allowing us to hang all our clothes inside. We never left clothes hanging outdoors when we were going to be away since there was always such a high possibility of rain. However, our neighbors just left the clothes out in the rain. We guess they figured a little more water wouldn't hurt and they would dry eventually. We had forgotten how much longer it takes to hang clothes on a line than to throw them in a dryer.

We told a Malaysian friend that if we lived in her country permanently there were two things we would have in the house. The first was a dishwasher and the second a dryer. She puzzled over that for a few minutes and then said, "But you would have a live-in amah to do those things." We suppose she is right. Actually, there is a third convenience we would have and that is an automatic gate opener. Of course if we had one of those we would have to find a way of getting around the fact the electricity goes off a lot.

Our kitchen had a small refrigerator and an oven/range combination that ran on bottled gas. Early on we tried to convince the bottled gas supplier to leave us an extra tank to have on hand, but never made ourselves understood. They were good about replacing the tank within a half hour or less when it ran out and it never caused any major problem. We cooked hardly at all the first year, as we were too busy trying out every new restaurant.

By the second year, when eating out every night had lost its charm, we bought a wok and learned to stir fry. That is a fast way to fix an easy meal. You don't need a recipe—just chop up an assortment of veggies and a little meat and add things to the wok starting with whatever takes longest to cook. Adding soy sauce, oyster sauce and water keeps the mixture from burning. We never had the same combination twice and the results were delicious.

To avoid the problem of keeping bugs out of uncooked rice at home, we bought cooked rice from the food service at school. A friend had an Indian amah who would bring a home-cooked meal to our house for RM7 (US$2.80). Of course, Indian food was her specialty but she also cooked Chinese, Malay, and western. Everything she provided was excellent. Once, after she had left the meal, we opened the bag to find a whole coconut. The top had been cut off and resealed with a flour paste. Inside was a marvelous concoction of chicken and vegetables in coconut-flavored sauce. We never did figure out how it was made. Her western dinners were good but not like anything we had ever eaten before and her enchiladas had a certain Indian flavor. She bought the largest jars of cayenne pepper we had ever seen and her meals were always spicy.

The management of the food service at school changed three times in two years. The last franchise offered such a large variety of dishes that students and faculty often ate their main meal of the day at noon. We could get a large plate of rice with meat and vegetables and a cola to drink for under US 50¢. Fresh fruits and juices were always available for similar low prices.

BATHROOMS

Orientation material assured us houses available for rent would have western toilets, but we should be prepared to use the squat toilet more common in Asia. I'd encountered my first "Turkish toilet" in France about thirty-five years ago. The typical Malaysian bathroom has a sink, a squat toilet, and in one corner a waist-high, 18-inch-square enclosure. This is filled with water, and a small plastic pan with a straight handle is used to ladle the water over your body. In kampungs where bathing is done outdoors at the village well, a woman can wash herself and her sarong and never expose any part of her body. She slips a dry sarong over her head and removes the wet one with a grace born of long practice. The dipper method of bathing is effective and we used it especially when water pressure was almost non-existent.

We took a shower curtain with us and installed a tension rod to hold it. In hindsight we probably would have been better off without the curtain since it was a good place for mildew to grow. Only westerners keep strange things like shower curtains, towels and toilet paper in a bathroom. Cleaning a Malaysian bathroom is a child's dream come true. The walls and floor are scrubbed down with a mixture of cleaner and disinfectant and the contents of buckets of water hurled around the room with abandon. Bathroom floors have a drain and are several inches below that of the adjoining room. Considering the humidity, the walls and floor dry with surprising speed.

The left hand is considered unclean because it and water are used for cleansing after using the bathroom. In areas where water is scarce, dirt or sand substitute so it is even more important that the left hand not be used for eating or passing food.

We threatened to write a book entitled "Bathrooms and Toilets in Southeast Asia" but would probably never find a publisher. Anyone who is squeamish, overly modest, or requires frequent rest stops is in trouble. Many articles and editorials in the newspapers suggested the need to improve sanitation, and fines are now imposed on hotels or restaurants that fail to comply with minimum standards. Travel outside large cities demands either extreme bladder control or a willingness to use available facilities no matter how primitive or unsanitary. A woman traveling in Asia is wise not to wear slacks and to carry a shoulder bag since there is seldom a clean place available to set a purse down while using the bathroom.

HOUSE HUNTING: 1991-1993

FRUSTRATION

We spent most of the 1991 summer session living in the Shah Alam Condos. Tim Diemer, the assistant provost, wanted to hold on to one of the terrace houses for faculty arriving in the fall, so we agreed to live there and let Bud Dixon use the upstairs. The condos were built when we were in Malaysia before but had remained unoccupied because of the economic slump. Since they were new, they were relatively clean and well maintained. By the time we left Malaysia in May of 1993, their condition had deteriorated.

The condos were quieter than we expected. We heard music occasionally and were near enough to the clubhouse to be aware of cooking noise and smells during the daytime. We heard no noise from the pool. There was a lot of street traffic during the daytime but at night we turned on the air-conditioner. Having to air-condition at night was a big disadvantage since there was enough of a breeze that sleeping with the windows open would have been comfortable, but there were no grilles on the windows and doors so we were reluctant to leave them open at night. The guardhouse and fence around the area wouldn't have stopped a persistent prowler. There were no ceiling fans, and the one standing fan was not a reasonable substitute. In reality we were probably a lot safer in Malaysia with an open house than behind dead-bolted doors in Munster, Indiana.

A living/dining room, entry, kitchen, one bedroom and bathroom, and two patios made up the main floor. The only clothes closet in the whole condo was in the first floor bedroom and there was a large storage closet under the stairs. When Bud moved in, he used one of the bedrooms and the bath upstairs. He bought a standing clothesline and set it in the second upstairs bedroom to use as a clothes rack.

Despite the lack of furniture, we managed to find a place for everything. It seemed odd to have the linens and towels in the kitchen cupboards and financial and computer stuff in the nightstand which held the computer in the living room! I covered a large packing box with a lightweight blanket to serve as a mini-dresser.

The bathrooms had no medicine cabinets, toothbrush holders, or shelves. We could put things on the window ledge or the back of the toilet but anything set at the end of the tub got wet. We bought a free-standing rack to augment the single, short towel bar.

The compact kitchen barely held the normal amount of dishes, pots, and pans, etc. However, it was clean and the only bugs were ants and the occasional fly.

We bought a standing clothesline and a laundry basket. Only one washing machine in the condo laundry room was available for community use. Signs on two other machines in the room identified them as belonging to individual families. The communal machine was a newer model of the same brand and worked better than what we had in Miss Lim's house.

The condo supplied one sheet, one pillow and pillowcase, and one comforter for each bed. We were responsible for washing them. The sheet wasn't big enough to stay tucked so we used one of our sheets on the bottom with theirs as a top sheet.

The clubhouse area had indoor squash and badminton courts, an outdoor pool and tennis courts and a mini-market. The mini-market also had a small selection of crafts. The wet market in Section 6, open every morning, and night markets on Tuesday and Friday provided us with fruit, vegetables, and fish.

We requested a telephone. The clerk spent about fifteen minutes entering information into the computer and then told us there was no line available for the terrace house! We told her there had been a phone up until two days before. We were told to check back the following Monday. The Gilletts moved into a house and were told the trunk line wouldn't be installed until December. That turned out not to be true. Neither of us waited long for a phone. We have no idea why we got the initial negative response and then such fast service.

One experience we missed was that of living with Malaysians, since most of the condo renters were expats.

▼

Mike and Terri Olan were leaving the program in August. Their landlady, Dr. Tai, said she would rent the house to us for RM1800 a month. It was a larger house than we needed but it appealed to us. A few days before we were to sign an agreement, she showed up with a MAS pilot and his family in tow. They had offered RM2500 a month rent! We met with her soon after that and offered RM1800 cash (one month's advance rent) if she would sign the rental agreement. She didn't take the money or sign the agreement but said she would let us know. She said she was thinking about living in the house herself! We knew we had been beaten. We experienced a feeling of satisfaction when the pilot found another house his family liked better.

Another house we looked at was in Shah Alam. It was owned by a Malay who was being posted to East Malaysia. The rent was RM1500 a month, and the house was completely furnished. There was also a swimming pool; the first private one we had seen in Malaysia. The decor was Malaysian-rococo, with red satin, fringed curtains, overstuffed red velour furniture, multi-colored artificial arrangements, bright colored fans and wall decorations, cast-plaster ceilings, and crystal chandeliers! It had to be seen to be believed. One of the bedrooms was painted a vivid blue. The interior was filthy and would be particularly difficult to clean because the family planned to leave a lot of their personal possessions. It was also built into a hillside so that several of the rooms had windows on only one side. It would probably have had no breeze and been hot.

During the same period Herb Davis, the new provost, and his wife were also house-hunting. They decided to take the Olan house and Dr. Tai had agreed to do everything they wanted. Just before they were to sign the papers she called to tell them she had rented it to someone else! The more we learned about her the more thankful we were that she backed out on us. The Davis' eventually rented an elegant, western-looking house near us. The owner left all the furnishings, some of which were antiques, plus **THREE** functioning washing machines, a dryer, a dishwasher, **THREE** TV's, a complete stereo system and a VCR!!! Their rent was RM3,700 (US$1350) a month. They talked the owner down from RM5,000. They were higher on the hill than we were and, since the house lacked a storage tank, they were without water much of the time.

37

▼

The Pais rented a house that came on the market after they arrived. The decor was unusual, concrete block and wood, and the walls leaked during the rainy season. They continued to have mosquito problems in spite of following all the precautions suggested by old-timers. One afternoon, Vrinda was lying on the couch watching a bird outside one of the high windows in the vaulted ceiling. All of a sudden the bird was inside the house! It turned out there was no glass in that window. They called the owner's representative and he said the former tenant had complained about mosquitoes but they had never figured out where they were coming in so the window must have been missing for a long time. They had a lot fewer mosquitoes in the house after they replaced the window.

SUCCESS AT LAST!

On June 14, we looked at a semi-detached (duplex) house in PJ. We liked it and rented it even though the roof obviously leaked badly. The first floor had an L-shaped living/dining room, kitchen, air-conditioned bedroom, and bath with shower (no hot water). The upstairs had an air-conditioned, two-room master bedroom suite with private tub/shower bath and a large, covered balcony (on the east so it was shaded from mid-morning on), a large top-of-the-stairs area with ceiling fan that made a good computer room, another bedroom, and another bath with shower. Both of the upstairs baths had hot water. Outdoors at the back was a paved, roofed laundry area and there was a carport for the car. For RM1500 a month the landlady, Puan Faridah, agreed to have a new roof put on, paint inside and out, clean, and have it ready for us to move in July 15. She provided twin beds for the master bedroom and an automatic washing machine. She was surprised that our amah wasn't going to do all our laundry and even more surprised to learn we weren't going to have a daily amah.

The house was filthy when we took possession. The painters, in addition to leaving everything paint-splattered, had tracked in a lot of dirt and used the downstairs as an ashtray. They even left muddy shoe prints on the toilet seat! Bud Dixon

Our house in PJ.

helped and the three of us spent two long, tiring days scrubbing and cleaning. We thought it looked good but when
Murugaie came she said she thought the house needed cleaning! The bottoms of our feet were black so we knew she was
right. Murugaie spent the first weeks on her hands and knees
scrubbing layers of dirt off the terrazzo floors. Because of the
industrial and automobile pollution, the house turned out to be
very hard to keep clean. Every time she came, Puan Faridah
commented on how clean we kept the house. Before we
moved out she told us she wanted us to leave it as clean as it
was when we moved in! Murugaie said she thought it would
be impossible for us to get it as dirty as it was the first time she
came to clean.

We did a lot to make that house livable. The mosquitoes
ate us alive the first few nights. Although Malaysians do not
screen any windows, we installed our own home-made screens
as quickly as possible. Richard removed the kitchen door
which hindered opening the refrigerator door and painted a
table for us to use in the kitchen. He also installed numerous

towel bars in the bathrooms and a new shower head in the upstairs bathroom we intended to use. We wanted one that would be mounted on the wall rather than hand-held. Using a hand drill through brick walls covered with stucco was a difficult project. He used a hammer to drive it in.

The refrigerator drained water onto the floor because the drain inside the back of the box inside was not connected to the tube leading to the water collection box. We had to unload the refrigerator and tip it to be able to re-connect the tube. We are lucky we didn't end up with the refrigerator on top of us!

Richard cleaned the clogged drains in front of the house. The city was supposed to keep them clean but Emily, our neighbor, said she called to complain a year ago. The city cleaned them then but hadn't been back.

Termites had invaded the vanity in the upstairs bathroom. The several months it took to convince the inspector that we had a problem allowed more damage and what the termites hadn't destroyed, the inspector finished off by poking around with his screwdriver. The cabinet under the bathroom sink had to be torn out and when we left Malaysia in May 1993, it had not been replaced. Puan Faridah did contract with a regular service to spray the house. In spite of our protests, they left puddles of bug killer on the floors every time they sprayed.

The house had several problems that were never fixed while we lived there. The kitchen sink was rusted and leaked into the cabinet below. It was held in place by the pipe underneath and we expected it to fall through any day. The terrazzo floors needed professional polishing, and even the new roof leaked enough that a ceiling panel in one of the upstairs bedrooms fell. Faridah had the panel replaced but we never convinced any workman to look at the roof.

When it came time to renew our lease for the second year Puan Faridah's brother sent us a special delivery letter telling us she was raising our rent! Our contract specifically said she couldn't do that. We pointed that out and never heard another word about it.

NEIGHBORS

Emily Tan, our neighbor who lived in the semi-detached unit to the east of us, became a good friend. Her house was the mirror image of ours. However, a kitchen, dining room, bathroom, and store room had replaced our covered porch and the kitchen was converted into a sitting room for TV viewing. The lowered ceiling in the living area was covered with wood, one living room wall was wood paneled, and another was covered with marble. Parquet on the stairs covered the original ceramic tile. During the spring of 1992 we kept about seventy-five of her orchid plants in our yard while Emily had the front of her house remodeled. About the same time Bob and Tina Hvitfeldt gave us a lot of their orchids when they left Malaysia, so we lived in a fantastic flower display for several months.

Emily's daughter, Lisa, worked for American Express and Lisa's husband, Hamid, worked for Arthur Anderson, a management consultant firm. Hamid was Malay but we saw no sign that he was a practicing Muslim and a lot of Emily's family were Christian. Hamid's mother wore a tudung so his parents had adopted some of the more conservative Muslim practices. Lisa and Hamid lived outside of St Louis for six years while they went to school and had known one another since they were children.

One of the first things Emily's workmen did was take out the fence and hedge between our two yards (much to Puan Faridah's distress) so Emily used our clothesline and could take care of her orchids. We enjoyed having her orchids but the mess from the renovation was incredible. Puan Faridah was unhappy about the hedge. The hedge hadn't been much to look at and probably harbored mosquitoes so we thought the plastered brick wall was an improvement since Emily had it painted on both sides. She made sure we knew how much it cost but we've forgotten.

▼

On March 3, 1992, we came home to discover the other half of our semi-detached was being remodeled! We were surrounded by debris, noise, and confusion. Workmen tore down about 1/3 of the house that was attached to ours, and demolished the wall that separated the two yards at the back.

The neighbors, Dato Haji Bin Haji Ahmad and Datin Nik Noraini Yahya, who lived in the other half of our semi-detached, had been to California, Canada, and Australia so they were used to western ways. Most of our neighbors thought

41

we were English or Australian. In general, Malaysians cannot distinguish accents. Nik Noraini spoke excellent English but her husband only spoke Bahasa. They decided to spend RM100,000 to remodel because both she and her husband had family living nearby and the children were happy with the school. A daughter was married in July so the remodeling was finished by then.

In order to have access to shared walls, some of the workmen had to be in our yard. One of the workmen asked where we were from. He was from Bangladesh and thought Malaysia was very hot. I told him we were from Chicago. He had friends going to school in Canada, and that exchange of information exhausted our ability to communicate.

When the workmen replaced the wall dividing the property at the back, they left a mess on our side and it took months of haggling to get them to plaster the wall. During the rainy season we had a stream of water running across the back porch. As far as we know, they never corrected that problem. They finally came back to plaster and did an excellent job. Unfortunately, it rained and ruined some of their plaster before it dried so the final job had a patched look.

The construction next door caused electrical problems: the circuit breaker in our half of the house kept flipping off. We had the electrician come several times but he couldn't find anything wrong. We decided that the vibration from the pounding next door kept tripping it.

Datin Nik Noriaini Yahya gave me a grand tour of her house after the remodeling was finished. The furnishings were Malaysian-rococo but the new kitchen and the tile floors in the newly redone main rooms, stairs, and balconies were beautiful. The family had eight children! One was away at boarding school but with the three servants there were twelve people living in that house.

▼

The neighbors across the street, Ida and Sharif, had lived in England for six years. She was Malacca Chinese and he was Malay. They were definitely liberal Muslims; they celebrated all the holidays. Sharif occasionally accepted a beer at parties and served beer at their own parties. They had two boys, one ten and the other three. During Ramadan the ten-year-old fasted a half day. After he turns twelve, he will fast all day. All Muslim children continue to attend school during Ramadan.

Ida's family was a real United Nations. By marriage they included Canadian, Japanese, Iban, Malay, Chinese/Nyonya[10], Philippine, and Singaporean. We noticed a new amah a few months after we moved in. Ida said the former amah had started dating an Indonesian boy and the family insisted they marry. Ida said if she had known soon enough she would have tried to help the girl get out of the match. We were included in their Hari Raya celebrations with their non-Muslim friends. In spite of the hours stated on the invitation, the first guests were at least a half hour late arriving and stayed long after the party was supposed to have ended.

▼

Cats were everywhere and tended to be skittish around humans. Periodically, a cat would come into the house, and in the spring of 1992 we developed a "cat under the stairs" problem. We listened to pitiful meowing for a long time before we realized it was coming from the cupboard under the stairs. We opened the door and the mother cat went in but didn't bring the kitten out so there was nothing for us to do but unload the whole closet. We deposited the kitten on the bank at the back of the house and mama cat came and took it away. Then we scrubbed the floor, sorted the junk and put back what we thought needed to be saved. We had to block the space under the door with wood to convince mama cat that our closet wasn't a good place to have her next litter.

---

[10]A subculture in and around Malacca, formed by Malaysian men married to Chinese women. See glossary.

43

JOYS AND FRUSTRATIONS

RE-LEARNING TO DRIVE

At the orientation session in Bloomington we listened to horror stories about driving in Malaysia. We were confident we wouldn't have any problem because we had driven in Chicago, Italy, and Mexico. What could be worse?

Malaysia is most definitely worse! In 1987 only one highway connected Kuala Lumpur with Port Klang on the coast. As Subang Jaya and Shah Alam, the two cities in between, grew so did the traffic and the traffic jams. By the middle of our second year there was no time that wasn't rush hour. Add to this the fact that the Malaysians, the most gentle people in the world, turn into maniacs behind the wheel of a car or on a motorcycle, and chaos reigns. During the two years there was an effort to build more pedestrian crossings, but people would still make mad dashes across the highway, endangering their lives and those of drivers who might try to avoid hitting them.

Malaysia has some excellent roads. The equivalent of an interstate highway extends south from Kuala Lumpur toward Singapore, with plans to build north to Thailand, and an absolutely beautiful stretch of four-lane, limited access road between Ipoh and Kuala Kangsar is expected eventually to connect with Butterworth. Other roads between most cities and towns are dreadful: narrow and overcrowded with the added hazard of bicycle, motorcycle, pedestrian, and animal traffic.

Malaysian driving habits reflect their philosophy of "Insh'Allah" (Allah wills) and a belief in a pre-ordained time of death. Their macho behavior is often reckless. It is well known the Sultan of Johore shot a man who had the effrontery to pass him on the highway. The Sultan was found guilty but pardoned himself! Ordinary Malaysians don't like being passed on the highway either but everyone agreed the Sultan's behavior was extreme. Malaysian drivers are generally skillful but take terrible chances. There are thousands of motorcycles on the roads and entire families, up to five or six people, pile onto them. The vendors have all their wares and portable stalls heaped on the back of a motorcycle and our gardener carried a full-sized lawnmower and all his other equipment on the back of one. The younger drivers

45

especially love to weave in and out of traffic and often there is only a hair's breadth separating them from disaster.

The Federal Highway is hard to describe. When we first arrived, there were often livestock on the road but as the year progressed, that occurred less and less. In addition to cars, trucks, and motorcycles, there were all sorts of heavy equipment moving at a very slow pace from one job to another. The stretch of highway between Subang and Klang was only four lane and we experienced some impressive traffic jams.

The lane markings might as well not have been there since traffic tended to pack itself as tightly as possible. Once we were on our way to Templar Park at Chinese New Year on a two-lane road which was quickly turned into four lanes by those in a hurry. If passing on the correct side was blocked, the driver would use the shoulder. Being passed on a curve was routine and it was not unusual for the passing car to be passed by another car at the same time so we would be driving three abreast down a two-lane highway.

▼

No one ever waits his turn and this is true in all aspects of Malaysian life. Waiting in a queue simply is not done and we never saw anyone get upset at having his place taken in line by someone who didn't belong there. On campus we made a great effort to help the students understand that breaking the queue was not acceptable in the U.S., but we suspected they did not really understand what we were talking about.

▼

There is excellent public transportation in the big cities and we could easily have gotten along without owning a car. The project provided van service to and from campus and many of our people used it or the bus system regularly. There are train or bus connections all over Malaysia and we took the train to Singapore once and from Butterworth to KL once. Both rides were tolerable but not great. The roadbed is maintained reasonably well but long sections are single track. We spent a lot of our time on sidings waiting for the train going the other direction to pass by.

We never took a bus for a long trip but had heard that frightening people to death seemed to be a game the bus drivers enjoyed playing. On our way to Kuantan we saw a bus round a corner on two wheels and were sure it was going to land in front or on top of us. The bus drivers generally drive faster and take

46

more chances than anyone else. Come to think of it, I recall a wild bus ride between Providence, Rhode Island, and Hartford, Connecticut . . . is it possible there is a world-wide training school for bus drivers?

▼

In spite of being in a constant state of panic, we drove all over Malaysia. Richard adapted to driving on the left better than I did and found the feeling of combat we experienced, even on local trips, stimulating.

Our Datsun 200L had once been a pretty nice car but our letters home failed to convey the feeling of frustration we experienced with all the regular breakdowns. However, we never were stranded far from help or in a dangerous situation, and repairs were cheap. In fact, we could not have afforded to own such a car in the U.S. Our mechanic often would spend an entire afternoon sorting out some problem and the bill for parts and labor would be less than US$5.

Malaysians take good care of their cars and their own skills or those of a mechanic keep them running almost indefinitely. In two years we only saw two abandoned cars along the Federal Highway. Even those were put to good use. Over a period of a week or ten days each car disappeared one piece at a time. We figured some enterprising soul was building himself a new machine!

1991-1993: PROGRESS EQUALS MORE HIGHWAYS–MORE TRAFFIC MORE MAYHEM

By the time we left Malaysia in 1989, traffic jams were a fact of life on the Federal Highway. By May of 1991, construction to widen the Federal Highway had begun and traffic was worse than ever. The PLUS road, connecting Klang with the North South Highway, was finished. However, it was a toll road and had no exit at Shah Alam so it wasn't of much use to us. Locals objected to paying the toll on the PLUS road, but as soon as the Federal Highway construction was finished, it also would be toll. The highway construction combined with the numerous golf courses being built in Selangor, made drastic changes in the configuration of the landscape. Large hills were completely leveled and wide patches of jungle disappeared. The Japanese could play golf in Malaysia for less (including airfare) than they could in Japan. As the jungle was cut down, rains washed away the topsoil and highways were frequently flooded. The engineers in charge of the highway construction managed to keep traffic moving better than we had expected. The highway was supposed to be completed by July 1993.

Malaysian driving habits had not changed. Authorities were beginning to realize that slaughter on the highways had become a national disgrace. An effort to enforce existing laws fell far short of solving the problem. Individual Malaysian drivers simply were not convinced that laws should apply to them. Essentially they are skillful drivers, otherwise the death toll on the highways would be outrageous. However, they take unreasonable chances and even short trips become excercises in terror.

▼

Because we chose to own a car, we relied on the Malaysian Automobile Association to transfer the title and do all the other paperwork. A few days after submitting our application, MAA called to say they couldn't process the forms to change ownership on the car! It turned out the car was owned for a short time by a man named Charlie Chan but the papers were never properly stamped. Richard had to make a trip to the Division of Motor Vehicles. He spent most of an afternoon being shuttled from one person to another. No one ever admitted that the papers hadn't been done properly but finally someone agreed to authorize the needed document that allowed us to buy the car. All the DMV files were in green folders piled from floor to ceiling; no wonder they had trouble keeping track of things.

The Datsun gave us only minor problems. An electrical malfunction ran down the battery and the mechanic fixed that for free. The idler arm and the bushings had to be replaced. The cost was RM30 (US$11). After two tries at fixing the air-conditioner compressor, the mechanic found a used compressor, took it and ours apart and meshed the good parts. One part was bad in both so he did replace that. The whole job cost US$91.

We found a 1979 Datsun with automatic transmission for

48

the Pais. Getting money wired from the U.S. was a hassle for Bipin and a worry for us since the U.S. bank told Bipin that such transfers often went wrong and were not guaranteed. We stored the car with Diemers and then in our yard and enjoyed the brief luxury of being a two-car family.

Our old grey Datsun had been purchased by another faculty member. He was in an accident and in trying to make an insurance claim discovered that Aziz, the agent who handled the sale, not only hadn't paid the insurance, he never turned the money over to the previous owner. The car was repossessed. Two other couples in the program who bought cars from Aziz, either directly or indirectly, had to hire lawyers in order to get title to their cars. Aziz was a wheeler/dealer when we originally knew him but in two years of selling cars, he had adopted some highly questionable practices.

At the beginning of our second year we bought a used Proton Saga from Howard Pollock, who was leaving the program. The Proton Saga is the Malaysian national car built in cooperation with the Mitsubishi Company. It had some fancy gadgets including a remote door lock and an alarm system. The instruction book was missing so we learned by trial and error. If we used the remote to lock the car, we had to use it to open it. Otherwise we would set off the alarm and the delayed activator sounded like a bomb ticking.

We sold the Datsun to David Fox, an ESL[11] faculty member who taught in another program in 1987. He and his wife had lived in the house we rented in PJ, and he told us they had trouble getting the deposit back from Puan Faridah. Because of his experience, we withheld the amount of our deposit (two month's rent) at the end and came out even. He and his family were pleased with the car.

A few days before we sold the Datsun, we took the Proton to the station to have routine work done and planned to drive the Datsun to school instead. About a block from the station the Datsun coughed and stalled. Richard pushed it to the roadside and went back to get the mechanic. The mechanic worked for quite some time and finally said he didn't think gas was coming through the line. He was smoking while he worked so the lack of gas probably explained why there hadn't been an explosion! Anyway, three employees

[11]English as a Second Language. See glossary.

49

from the station pushed the car backwards down the street while Richard waved oncoming traffic aside. The fuel pump had gone bad so David got a car with a brand new fuel pump.

A few weeks before leaving Malaysia, we put an ad in the local paper and were deluged with calls from people wanting to buy the Proton. We made a date to show it but before we could leave the house we had several more calls. One woman seemed particularly interested so we agreed to meet her in front of the mosque near the Jaya supermarket because she didn't know PJ well and was afraid she couldn't find our house. We only waited for her a few minutes, and she hardly looked at the car before offering us earnest money, part cash and part check. Her company was buying the car for her. She seemed very concerned that we not sell the car to anyone else. She had put earnest money on a car the previous week and it had been sold out from under her. The man claimed her husband (she is single) had called to cancel the deal. At least he refunded her money. She agreed to let us keep the car until after Richard's last final. When it came time to turn over the car we met in front of Victoria Station, a restaurant in KL near where she lived. All the papers were in order and she had a cashier's check for us in U.S. dollars. It was pouring so she took us back to her house and served us Sarsi (a Malaysian drink similar to root beer) while we waited for a cab.

▼

One of Richard's students asked for a make-up because she had to take her drivers' test on the day of the exam. He thought that was a pretty novel excuse for missing a test and wondered if she just wanted extra time to study. The second time a student used the same excuse, Richard probed further and discovered that driver training is done by private driving schools which then set up test dates without consulting the student. If the student misses the date, he or she has to repeat part of the course to get a place in line again.

BANKING AND BILL PAYING: 1987-1989

Banking in Malaysia is not easy. The Hong Kong Bank where we did business was one of the best but in the summer of 1989 was just beginning to computerize. Drive-up windows were unheard of and inside the bank lines were long. A draft presented for withdrawal had to be approved by several people, and even after approval was given we sat and waited for our money. Banks often opened several minutes past the scheduled time or, if they were prompt, the tellers wouldn't be ready for business. Records were kept by hand and checked several times. However, strikes were civilized. Business would progress as usual but the tellers would wear small signs on their lapels listing grievances. Picketing was done at break time and during lunch hour!

Our account was a savings account since almost no one would accept a check; we paid all local bills in cash in person. Gradually we learned what times the lines might be short but we always carried something to read and never went to pay a bill when we didn't have lots of time to spare. At least we could pay the electric, water, and phone bills together at any of their offices or at the post office. The phone and utility companies also kept all their records by hand and when there was a dispute they would laboriously search through ledgers to discover the problem. If our two years in Asia taught us anything it was patience.

Before returning to the U.S. we spent part of a day closing our account and converting our money into traveler's checks. We also wanted a small supply of German marks and U.S. dollars. The Hong Kong Bank had dollars but didn't have marks so we went down the street to a local bank. They had marks so we filled out all the required forms. The teller took our ringgits[12] and gave us a receipt. We sat down to wait and watched the clerk make his way through the chain of command for the required signatures. Soon he came back to ask if we could return later that afternoon? The only manager with a key to the vault had gone to lunch! Since it was inconvenient for us to return we asked him to destroy the forms we had so carefully filled out and we simply waited until another day to get our German marks.

BANKING UPDATE

We opened a checking account at the Malaysian Bank in Shah Alam and were pleasantly surprised at how quickly and efficiently they handled everything. Richard's local paycheck was deposited there and we kept enough in the account to pay rent and some other bills by check. Eventually, we each

---

[12]Malaysian word meaning "dollar." See glossary.

had an ATM card but my first card was sent to the wrong address and showed up after it had been canceled by the bank because we reported it missing. Ismail, the bank officer, was most apologetic about the inconvenience and the time it took to get me a valid card.

We kept our Hong Kong Bank savings account because it drew interest and accepted U.S. deposits more readily. The Hong Kong Bank's attitude toward expatriate accounts changed during our second year and the bank was much less cooperative.

In general, lines at the banks were still long and, in spite of newly installed computers, everything was also recorded by hand. Checks were regarded with suspicion. A check issued on an account in the Maybank in Shah Alam could not be cashed at the Maybank in PJ or KL. An application for traveler's checks took several hours to process.

SQUARE DANCING: 1987-1989

Richard and I both learned to square dance as children, and twenty years ago in Kansas we belonged to a group. Before going to Malaysia we heard about the Faculty Squares from our friend, Roberta Dees, who was a member, and we were pleased to be invited to join in October of our first year. The group was directed by Tina and Bob Hvitfeldt, ESL faculty members with the program. In Kansas we always had air-conditioned rooms to dance in so were dubious about square dancing in the tropics. The Faculty Squares included several Malaysians and the interesting thing was that they did not sweat much. We danced barefooted and their feet didn't get dirty either. We figured not sweating had to do with the fact they had grown up in the tropics but we never did figure out why their feet stayed clean. In contrast, we sweat buckets and our feet were filthy by the end of the evening. Dancing with the group turned out to be a fantastic experience. Os Pombos, a local country/western band, provided live music when we performed in the KL area, raising money for various charities or entertaining at Malaysian/American functions. In Butterworth and Ipoh we were accompanied by The Wheelers. In recognition of the number of non-faculty members who had joined the group by 1988, we changed the name to Klang Valley Country Dancers.

The band in Butterworth, The Wheelers, paid for our airline

52

tickets to Penang and our train tickets back to KL. The Sapphire Club, where we were to perform, had only been open about three months. There was a neon sign but otherwise from the outside it looked like all the other shop houses in Malaysia. The stairway and the entire room upstairs were painted blue, and carpeting on the floor and walls behind the band helped mute the sound. Several sheets of plywood nailed over the carpeting worked well for us to dance on even though it was oblong instead of square.

Tickets were completely sold out for both nights and people who didn't have reservations were turned away. Pre-performance publicity in the paper had changed our name to "Louisiana Country Dancers." We suppose in all our telephone negotiations "Louisiana" sounded like "Indiana." We square danced and rested alternately from 10 p.m. until after 1:30 a.m., and did a lot of ballroom dancing in between. We had prepared three square dances to do with the band, and Tina and Bob, the group leaders, did three clogging routines. That worked out about right for the first night. For the second performance we added a round dance we had made up and one of the couples did a polka. All the dances went well and we repeated some of them when the audience demanded more.

The Metro Hotel, where we spent the night, was Chinese and that set the tone. The beds were made with one sheet covered with a light spread which served as top sheet and/or blanket. One small, paper-thin towel was provided per room and there was no hot water. We kept telling ourselves cold showers were refreshing. The rooms were air-conditioned and after the first night of being cold and getting up to turn it off periodically, Richard opened the unit and turned down the thermostat. There was no control knob.

We took pictures of the junk piled along the stairs going up to the hotel and of the "view" out the front door, complete with garbage dump. The inside of the hotel was clean and the owners and maids were lovely to us. Sunday morning before we left, we gave the staff a basket of food for Chinese New Year. We hope they shared it with the long-suffering night watchman and the night clerk we had to wake up to let us in each morning!

Since Penang Island was only a short ferry ride away, we decided to do some sightseeing on Saturday. After a breakfast of shrimp/pork noodle soup and tea with sugar and sweetened condensed milk, we took the ferry. The Island can also be reached by driving across the longest suspension bridge in Southeast Asia.

Richard and Maria dancing between squares.

We visited the China Handicraft shop and saw some exquisite things. We considered buying a 100-year-old piece of needlepoint but it wasn't the right size and shape for us to use at home.

The taxi driver we hired for the afternoon took us to the Buddhist Snake Temple which has sedated vipers crawling around, some with their fangs removed allowing us to handle them if we wanted to, then to the Temple of the Golden Buddhas which was large and ornate with several large gold (or gold covered) Buddhas, and finally to the cable railroad for a ride to the top of Penang Hill (about 2300 feet). It was actually cool up there.

Welcome to the square dancers in Ipoh.

We ate ice cream, missed the first train back, and were very late getting to the Sapphire Club for practice. When we got off the ferry in Butterworth none of the taxi drivers knew where the Sapphire Club was. We finally found a young man who knew who the "Wheelers" were and that pinpointed the club.

The second evening we were an even bigger success, we say modestly. The enthusiastic audience kept demanding more and we danced until almost 3 a.m. The owner showed up about 2:15 to see some of our routines. We asked if there was a legal closing time for bars. He said, "Oh yes. We are required to close at midnight, but you can't make any money that way!"

The musicians, of Portuguese background from Malacca, did not read music. Their music and songs, learned from tapes, imitated Nashville country/western music and sounded like the real thing. The drummer called one of the square dances and sounded as if he came from Texas. The club owners and the two or three other investors seemed pleased with the way things had gone. We all had fun and appreciated the delicious Chinese meals provided as part of the weekend.

Before taking the train from Butterworth to KL, we made sure we had a take-away lunch of Kentucky Fried Chicken, fruit and cookies to enjoy during the the six-hour ride. The bus ride from the KL station to PJ was part of the adventure. We each had a suitcase and a carry-on bag, so fitting our large-sized bodies plus luggage on a minibus was a challenge. We could understand enough to know our fellow riders thought we were crazy and foreigners ought to have enough money to pay cab fare!

▼

Our second out-of-town "gig" was in Ipoh to dance with the Wheelers while they were performing at the Cowboy's Saloon. That weekend national horse races were being run, making hotel rooms hard to find, but the band finally found space for us in a Japanese hotel. The rooms had been closed off for a long time. We begged towels and soap and wished we could open the windows! The pillows must have been made of concrete. Our dancing was well received and we didn't spend much time in the hotel room. "No problem lah!"

▼

Country/western music is extremely popular in Malaysia. The Longhorn Saloon, in PJ where the Os Pombos Band played, was full to overflowing every night. A bar in Malaysia is closer to an English or Australian pub than to a bar as we know it. Food is served and families are welcome and encouraged. We never saw anyone even slightly drunk.

Because of the Muslim influence, alcohol is expensive. Besides economics, there are religious prohibitions for Muslims and Indians. The Chinese drink a lot of brandy and scotch but otherwise not much hard liquor is sold or drunk. The main alcoholic beverage is beer. The Anchor Brewery is in KL and there is a Guinness brewery in PJ. From movies and TV Asians have the impression that all foreigners drink a lot of alcohol. We drank tea or fresh lime juice because the occasional beer only made the heat seem worse.

EATING OUT

An entire book could be written about the delights of eating out in Malaysia. In four years we never had a bad meal and we ate everywhere, including the fanciest hotel dining room and the corner food stalls. We didn't eat in fancy hotels often, mainly because the cost was higher and often the food was toned down to meet western taste buds. The PJ Hilton did have an excellent high tea and we went there frequently, mainly because they offered a salad bar.

We both missed tossed salads and baked potatoes. Salad ingredients were available in the stores but we never came up with what we considered an authentic mixture. Potatoes were readily available but we never found Idaho bakers. In addition, oven meals weren't high on our list of things we wanted to do.

There are four kinds of restaurants: four-walled, usually fancy and air-conditioned; three-walled, front open to the street; two-walled, located on a corner, open to the street on two sides, often with tables out on the sidewalk and perhaps independent food stalls operating around the edges; and no-walled, movable feasts provided by roving street vendors.

Service in Chinese restaurants is fantastic. Hot tea comes right away and our glass or cup was always kept full. If we asked for a glass of water it would be hot, presumably to let us know it had been boiled. The waiter or waitress would bring a bowl of ice for making iced tea or iced water. I suspect expats were the only ones who asked for ice, which probably was made from unboiled water! A dish of peanuts was served whether we ordered them or not, and either a hot or cold towel was provided both before and after the meal. A small charge was added to the bill for these items. Tipping is not considered proper.

We had several favorite places. One three-walled restaurant near the airport served giant Sri Lankan crabs. The first time we ate there we ordered two crabs plus fried rice and a dish of mixed veggies. When the crabs came they were the size of extra large dinner plates and the amount of crab in each claw was what one would expect from a good sized Maine lobster. It took us three hours but we managed to consume it all. In the future we were careful to order only one crab to share.

The Hakka restaurant in downtown KL was special. The Hakka are a nomadic people and their food is totally different from anything Chinese we had eaten before. We were first taken there by a Canadian friend, Mary Garlicki, and she ordered the meal. One dish called Hakka pork turned out to be sow belly with a black bean sauce. It sounds awful but tasted delicious and did not give us indigestion. They served a crab and onion tempura that melted in our mouths, and chive flowers became one of our favorite vegetables.

We'd never eaten Indian food before moving to Malaysia and again, were introduced to it by a friend, Emmy Wohlenberg. We fell in love. It was spicy/hot but when well done, each dish had a distinctly different flavor. The tandoori ovens made of brick and cow dung cook delicious meat and bread in extremely high heat.

We frequented several banana leaf restaurants where we ate the meal, served on a banana leaf, with our fingers. It always amazed us the natives were so neat and we were so messy. They would form a ball of rice, meat, vegetables, and curry and pop it into their mouths. We would attempt the same thing and end up covered in curry sauce to our elbows.

The first week in Malaysia we ordered chili prawns. They were served unpeeled, in a spicy chili sauce. Other diners were eating the shells, probably a good source of calcium in a country where milk is not a big item on the menu. We decided we weren't ready for munching on prawn shells. When we tried to peel them we were soon a mess and obviously a source of entertainment for everyone around us. The waiter finally took pity and brought us a roll of toilet paper to clean up with. Later we learned napkins were often not available in restaurants but there was always a sink in one corner. Private homes often have a sink in one corner of the dining room.

We were adventurous when it came to food and tried everything, but decided what we ate for breakfast was a cultural constant not to be tampered with. Everywhere we went we ate the local breakfast but at home in Shah Alam we stuck to tea and toast or cereal with an occasional sweet roll or egg for variety. Boring but comforting.

Back in Munster I borrowed recipe books (*The Cooking of India*, Santha Rama Ran, Time Life Books and *The Complete Asian Cookbook*, Charmaine Solomon, McGraw Hill), and we managed to produce an Indian meal without benefit of a tandoori oven. We cooked the chicken on our Weber grill. The bread, baked in a standard oven, was the least authentic part of the meal. It really should be cooked in the tandoori oven where it hangs from the side and the weight of the dough stretches the bread into a thin, teardrop shape. We used a Malaysian rather than Indian recipe for rice and I never did find a recipe for palak paneer (spinach with cheese) so I made up my own based on what I learned from the cookbook. I have made raita many times and it is a wonderful dressing for pita bread sandwiches.

TANDOORI CHICKEN

16 pieces chicken: boned and skinned
1 cup plain yogurt
1/2 cup olive oil
1/4 cup lemon juice
1 piece fresh ginger, 2 to 3 inches, peeled & cut into chunks
6 cloves garlic, peeled & coarsely chopped
1-2 teaspoons salt
1 1/2 teaspoons ground coriander
1 teaspoon orange food coloring (1/2 tsp each red & yellow)
1/2-2 teaspoons each: ground cumin, freshly ground black pepper
1/2 teaspoon ground cardamom
1/4-1 teaspoon cayenne
1/4-1/2 teaspoon ground cloves garnish
1 medium onion, sliced paper thin in rings, held in ice water
2 lemons or limes cut in wedges

With sharp knife score each piece of chicken in three places.
Marinate chicken 6 hours or overnight, turn once to make sure all sides are coated.
Remove chicken from refrigerator 1 hour before cooking.
Place on charcoal grill, skin side down, and cook for 15-25 minutes.
Turn several times while cooking and baste with Safflower oil after final turning.
Serve on warm platter with drained onion rings on top and lemon or lime wedges around.

COCONUT RICE (NASI LEMAK)

2 cups long grain rice
2 cups water
2 cups coconut milk (one can of coconut milk is approx. 2 cups)
2 teaspoons salt, if desired
Mix all ingredients and stir once or twice.

Bring mixture to a boil, cover tightly and simmer 15 minutes.
Do not lift lid.
Remove from heat and let stand 10 minutes before serving.
Makes 8 cups cooked rice.

59

INDIAN BREAD (NAAN)

4 cups flour
1 tablespoon sugar
1 tablespoon double acting baking powder
1/4 teaspoon baking soda
1/2 teaspoon salt
2 eggs
1 cup lukewarm milk

Combine flour, sugar, baking powder, baking soda, & salt in food processor until well mixed. Add eggs. Mix. With processor running add milk in slow, thin stream until well combined. Gather dough in ball on a smooth slick surface. Knead about 10 minutes or until it is a soft sticky ball. Place in bowl, cover and let rise for about 3 hours. Preheat oven and 2 ungreased baking sheets to 450 degrees. Divide the dough into 6 equal portions. Flatten and form each portion into a tear-drop shaped leaf 6 inches long and 3 1/2 inches wide and 3/8 inch thick. (Do not let thickness exceed 3/8". If necessary make longer or wider.)
Bake for 6 minutes or until firm to touch.
Broil for 1 minute to brown. Serve warm.

CUCUMBER-TOMATO RAITA

1 medium cucumber
1 tablespoon finely chopped onion
1 tablespoon salt
1 small tomato sliced into 1/4 inch cubes
1 cup plain yogurt
1 teaspoon ground coriander
1 teaspoon cumin toasted in ungreased skillet over low heat for 30 sec.

Peel cucumber and remove seeds. Cut into 1/8 inch slices and then into 1/2 inch pieces. Combine cucumber, onions and salt in a bowl. Mix and let stand 5 minutes. Squeeze cucumbers gently to remove excess liquid and drain. Add tomato and coriander and mix gently. Combine yogurt and cumin and pour over vegetables, coating them evenly. Taste for seasoning. Cover tightly and refrigerate for at least one hour.

PALAK PANEER

l lb frozen, chopped spinach
1 medium onion (chopped)
1 tablespoon oil
1/2 teaspoon mustard seed
1/2 teaspoon chili powder
1 1/2 teaspoon salt
1 teaspoon ginger
1/2 teaspoon garam masala (see below)
8 ounces soft cheese cubes (muenster)
lemon juice to taste

Cook spinach half the time directed on the package. Drain well. Combine all ingredients, including spinach, in food processor. Puree. Put in casserole with cubes of soft cheese and heat about 1/2 hour if spinach is still warm or 1 hour if casserole has been stored in the refrigerator.

GARAM MASALA

4 tablespoons coriander
2 tablespoons cumin
1 tablespoon peppercorns
2 teaspoons cardamom
1 teaspoon cinnamon
1 teaspoon whole cloves
1 nutmeg

Grind and roast spices in ungreased iron skillet for two minutes. If substituting ground spices when the recipe calls for whole use the following amounts: 1/2 teaspoon pepper, 1/8 teaspoon cloves and 1/4 teaspoon nutmeg.

TABLE MANNERS AND ETIQUETTE

We were given a long list of do's and don'ts before we moved to Malaysia and basically they turned out to be good guidelines for living comfortably in a different society. However, Malaysians and Asians in general were tolerant of our peculiar ways and not at all offended by our occasional lapses.

I am left handed but have always used a fork with my right hand. Because of the fine muscle control needed for chopsticks, I use those left-handed and except for an occasional fencing match with whoever was seated on my left, I was ignored. When eating with our fingers I was careful to use my right hand but waiters would often bring each of us a spoon and a fork to use. Malaysians use the fork as a pusher and the spoon to eat with and we quickly adopted their way. As part of the table setting a knife is rare since for most Asian cuisine, meats and vegetables are cut into bite-sized pieces before cooking. The cleaver is used with abandon and slivers of bone, even in soup, are a problem. Most of the time we had no idea what part of the critter we were eating. Chicken was the primary meat, with mutton and seafood close seconds. However, the Malay word for mutton and goat is the same so we presume we ate a lot of goat. Local beef was poor, but good beef was imported from Australia, New Zealand, and the U.S.

We enjoyed a wonderful variety of seafood and learned to steam fish in our wok. We could buy a medium sized red snapper at the market for 50¢! We ate fish at every opportunity because we knew fresh fish would not be available or inexpensive when we returned to Munster.

Because much of the food had bones in it, the proper thing to do was spit the bones out on the table beside our plates. After a meal the piles of debris would often be wiped off onto the floor. In spite of the fact floors in restaurants were mopped once or twice a day, they were never really clean. Dishes were washed at the curbside in large plastic dish pans filled with cold water and soap. Our Chinese landlady assured us hot water was not necessary as long as soap was used!

At a Chinese meal, dishes are not passed unless the meal is served at a very large table without a lazy Susan in the center. We used our chopsticks to transfer food from the serving plate to our plate. Reaching across the table is not considered impolite. In deference to western manners we were often provided with serving spoons.

It is considered impolite to tip. In hotels and larger restaurants there is a surcharge on the bill but in the smaller places we simply left the few coins that were returned as change after we paid our bill. Remembering to leave a tip was one of the many readjustments we had to make traveling home through Europe and returning to the U.S.

UPDATES: 1991-1993

EATING OUT

When Richard's PUC[13] students asked him why he wanted to go back to Malaysia he said, "**TO EAT!**" We cooked at home once or twice a week but local food was so delicious and such a bargain that we ate out frequently. As long as we ate Asian food we could eat as much as we liked without gaining weight. The students on campus were addicted to American fast food and their diets contained more meat, so they were generally heavier than the students of two years ago.

The following paragraphs are meant to give the reader more samples of the joys of eating in Malaysia.

The Hakka restaurant was still the best place to eat in KL. When we parked our car the attendant greeted us as if we had only been gone two weeks instead of two years. The crab tempura and kai choi fa (chive flower buds) were heavenly.

Ingredients for tossed salads were more readily available.

The most unusual Easter brunch we ever had was the Chinese Bak Kuh Teh (pork and rice brunch) at Fairy Tom's. The pork and chicken were marinated in a special spiced broth and cooked for a long time.

One of the new taste treats we experienced was "pea sprouts." The entire young pea plant, stem and all, is stir fried with garlic and a little oil.

▼

Satay, small pieces of meat on a bamboo skewer cooked over a charcoal fire, can be chicken, beef or pork (for the Chinese). It is served with a spicy peanut sauce, sliced cucumbers and raw onion.

---

[13]Purdue University Calumet. See glossary.

Emily, our neighbor, cooked vegetables and meat to deliver to private homes; sort of a Malaysian meals-on-wheels. The clients provided their own rice. For a few months she had two of the biggest chickens we had ever seen. We named them Maude and Harriet because we thought anything that large ought to have a name. They were funny to watch because they were so large and overweight they had trouble walking. My father said some Asian breeds of chicken are quite large. Maude and Harriet were eventually served to hungry customers in clay pot or curry chicken.

One Saturday, Emily spent most of the day sitting crossed legged on the floor of her front porch, cooking what looked like small pancakes on a grill. The "pancakes" were a delicious, crisp, lacy cookie. She shared some with us and filled tins to give as Chinese New Year gifts.

Huge tiger prawns were available at the wet market. We fried them with garlic and broccoli for a hot evening meal. We saved a few of the cooked prawns to combine with canned dace with black bean sauce as a dressing for a tossed salad.

▼

Sambal sauce, made from belacan (rotten fish paste), was toasted before it could be used. Emily made huge batches and the smell was awful. It didn't taste as bad as it smelled but we never developed a liking for it. When Emily's son-in-law, Hamid, brought home a trunkload of fruit from her brother's farm, including durians, rambutans, longans, and mangosteens, the smell of durian permeated the neighborhood. He said he was going to have to buy some charcoal to put in his trunk to get rid of the smell. Emily gave us a durian and we were surprised to find the taste rather mild but the rotten meat smell and the aftertaste stayed with us for days. I considered borrowing some charcoal to fumigate our refrigerator!

▼

A nearby restaurant served sting-ray. The place was one in a collection of food stalls. We would order sting-ray and noodles in black sauce. We almost always took some sting-ray home to have cold for lunch the next day The ambiance was classic Malaysian—blazing fires, sizzling food, and dishes washed in cold soapy water in plastic pans at curbside.

▼

The cost of fruits and vegetables had gone up. Pineapples were US32¢ peeled!

▼

On November 27, 1992, a large number of the faculty turned out for the Thanksgiving potluck. Except for turkey and cranberry sauce, the meal bore only a passing resemblance to traditional fare and we had to tolerate hordes of mosquitoes as uninvited guests! The host's house was totally screened but, because of the large crowd, the tables were set up outside. At least we had a clear night and the catering service that provided tables, chairs, and table service also did the cleanup so we had the advantage of real plates and cutlery without having to wash dishes!

▼

Emily shared curry fried chicken and some kai lan (a green vegetable) in ginger sauce with us. We liked it so much we ordered it the next time we went to Red Tablecloths, a two walled Chinese restaurant near us. The waitress was dubious and had obviously never heard of putting ginger sauce on kai lan. The cook tried but the results were not even close to what Emily had served us.

▼

Fresh meats, fruits, and vegetables were available at "wet" and "dry" markets. We struggled to clarify the terms. Fruit, eggs, and items such as dry onions and garlic were "dry," whereas fish and vegetables were "wet." That didn't clear up the puzzle as to why limes were considered "wet" but oranges were "dry."

REPAIRS

Repairs still were generally cheap and repairmen came promptly when called. Often there was no charge for fixing a simple problem and no extra charge for multiple visits. When we moved into the condo, the drains in both bathrooms were stopped up. The plumber came, unclogged them, and left the pile of gunk on the floor! The stopper in the sink still leaked so he came back, at our request. He said he couldn't do anything about the stopper, but Richard decided the problem was the seal and fixed it with epoxy.

When we moved into the house in PJ, the doorbell and one outlet didn't work. An electrician from the local shophouses came and charged RM21 (US$8). Only US$2 was for labor. He had arrived one day just as we were leaving so we asked that he come back the following day. We wouldn't be able to do that in Indiana without paying two service calls. The doorbell needed a new transformer but the main problem was the nest of ants that filled the box and disrupted the circuit.

Murugaie told us she had broken the "ironing board." We couldn't imagine how she had done that. It turned out she had dropped the iron and broken part of the handle. Richard managed to glue it back together. He put a new cord on the iron when we were here before so for the rest of our stay in Malaysia she considered him a genius. She brought a radio that didn't work, that her son had bought in the night market and since Richard had repaired the irons, she was certain he could fix anything. He took the radio apart and all the wiring seemed sound so the problem must have been in the speakers or one of the chips. Since that wasn't anything he could fix, we encouraged her to try to exchange it and to make sure the new one worked.

One afternoon I was working on the computer when the screen contracted drastically a couple of times and then smoke began pouring out of the monitor!! The directions for the FM tuner Richard built years ago from a kit said, "If it smokes when plugged in, **UNPLUG IT!**", so that's what I did. Then I called the repairman. By the time he arrived the upstairs only smelled faintly of an electrical fire. He took the monitor apart and we could see a blackened streak along the inner left side of the case but no sign of anything having melted. The fuse hadn't blown, probably because they put in a bigger one than they should have when they fixed it before. A new monitor was delivered that afternoon.

▼

The shower head in the upstairs bathroom developed a leak, and the plumber managed to file down a washer so it would fit. The faucet no longer leaked but it restricted the flow of water so much that there was almost no pressure. Richard re-did the job with a better washer he made from a piece of plastic.

▼

We needed a new condenser for the car air-conditioning. It cost over US$100 but it worked a lot better than the old one did.

▼

We had a new zipper put in Michael's old hooded jacket that Richard wore in Tibet. The cobbler did such a good job we decided it was a good idea to have the zipper replaced in the old coat of John's that I was using. The cobbler was puzzled because the coats were identical and he wondered what had happened to the new zipper he'd just put in! The zipper and labor cost US$8. The cobbler also put new insoles in my hiking boots and repaired my leather purse. He charged US$12.

▼

Some repairs carried a built-in amusement factor. A motorcyclist ran into Karen Easterday's car. The repair shop said the car would be ready on Saturday but that if she picked it up Saturday she would have to bring it back for polishing. She said she would rather have the job complete before she picked up the car. How long would that take? They told her to check back on Saturday because it might be ready! We weren't surprised when it wasn't.

MAIL SERVICE

Our American Express change of address form was

returned with a note that addresses of more than four lines weren't acceptable!!! The computer would accept the name line, two information lines and the five-digit zip code. This company is supposed to be world-wide. Fitting our address into those guidelines was impossible. There was also a twenty character limit for each line. We finally settled on 8 Jln. 22/38 Petaling for the first line and Jaya, Slngr, Malaysia for the second. They also wouldn't accept ', /, and a fairly long assortment of other symbols. We left in the / since there was just no other way to write it. The post office used those numbers rather than the street name so if those were missing the street name was useless.

▼

Mail service was erratic, with long periods of no mail followed by a deluge. When we used the campus address, our letters often arrived with the stamps pulled off. We were convinced mail was held in the U.S. or in Malaysia until there was a batch to be delivered. Also, more mail was lost during 1991-1993 than during 1987-1989.

▼

Anything too large to fit in the box (it was a VERY small box) was stuck in the gate or thrown on the driveway. Packages subject to customs inspection had to be picked up at the main post office. Sue Gustat mailed the bedspread I forgot to pack and added a couple of tubes of toothpaste. The package took about six weeks and arrived in good condition just as we were about to run out of Crest gel. For some unknown reason, gels are not popular in Malaysia.

▼

Postal rates were still reasonable, although they were raised in April 1992. Locally, an unsealed card cost US5¢, a sealed letter US8¢, and an aerogram US16¢ (raised to US20¢). Overseas letters (two sheets of computer paper) cost US44¢.

There was always a slow-down in mail service due to Ramadan and the approach of Hari Raya. As part of the celebration everyone sent Hari Raya cards. It was also traditional for postal employees to take vacations at this time so the post office was not only overwhelmed, it was short-handed. Privatization, which took place in 1992, helped. A second daily delivery was added whenever mail volume began to pile up.

▼

On July 24, 1992, we received a notice in the mail that we had a package at the main post office in KL. We had no idea what it could be but added that to our list of things to do on the following Thursday. Wednesday we had a letter from Hazel and Dick Banlow, friends of Richard's folks, saying that Dick was going to the post office the next day (July 14) to mail us a video tape of Richard's father's funeral. For the notice to have been delivered to us on Tuesday the package had to have arrived in KL by Monday morning at the latest. That was a record. A friend in the program had just received a video that had been three months in transit! Hers was delivered to the house but it had been opened so she knew it had been inspected and viewed by the censorship board.

We redeemed our tape with minimal hassle. We had to present ourselves at seven counters (eight if you count going back to retrieve the copy of Richard's passport we had to leave at the second counter), sign two registers, and wait while the tape was viewed. The whole process took under a half hour and everyone was polite. At the next to the last counter the attendant asked about Richard's height. We had a discussion about comparative height of our offspring. This man was about 5' so at 6'4" Richard must have looked like a giant.

Having redeemed the tape, we faced the challenge of finding a VCR to view it. Since the TV system is completely different (perhaps the same as Europe) an American tape won't play at all on a Malaysian VCR. We should have asked the people at the post office if we could sit and watch it there! They have VCRs that will handle all systems. We finally remembered there was a convertible VCR at the campus and were allowed to view it there.

▼

The Hvitfeldts, who moved from Malaysia to Singapore in 1992, had a gas grill that needed a tube welded on it. A similar part had been welded to their old grill when they lived in Malaysia. The shop they went to in Singapore refused to do the job, so they brought the grill back to Malaysia when they came to visit. It turned out they needed to have brought the regulator (the part that would ultimately connect to the tube) so they mailed it to the shop when they got home. The repairman at the shop called the day before we left for Dubai to tell us he didn't want to take the time to go to the post office to pick up the part! I agreed to have him mail us the card and said we would go as soon as we returned from our trip. By the time we returned from Dubai about three weeks had passed since the card had been delivered to the shop and we thought the part might have been sent back to Singapore. The first clerk at the post office asked Richard if he was Mr Chan!! When he said he was picking the package up for Mr. Chan, she told us we needed a letter from him authorizing us to pick up the package! We had visions of the difficulties involved in getting a letter and ultimately coming back to discover they had already returned the package because our time had run out. She finally agreed to let us tell our story to the clerk at the next station. The second clerk never batted an eye when Richard handed him an ITM ID card. He wrote down Mr. Chan's name and beside it Richard's name with all the ID numbers. From there on it was smooth sailing and we were through the process and back to the car in under half an hour. We understand why they won't let just anyone pick up a package for someone else without authorization but we are glad they waived the rules in this instance. We delivered the regulator to the shop and assumed this would be the end of our involvement since the shop was supposed to mail the completed grill to the Hvitfeldts in Singapore. WRONG AGAIN! Several weeks later we came home to find the grill sitting on our dining room table. Fortunately, Murugaie had been at the house to accept delivery. Otherwise, it would probably have been tossed over the fence. It took a while, but we finally found someone going to Singapore by car who would deliver the grill.

Bob Pour arranged with Texas Instruments to borrow twenty of their high-powered graphing calculators for use in our classes. Bob also volunteered to give a seminar at the International School on the use of this particular calculator. In return, TI donated two of them for our program to keep. Bob told TI to ship the calculators to ITM labeled "Educational Materials-Duty Free — Attention: Dr. Robert Pour." TI ignored his request and addressed the package to him. The carrying case (shipped separately) came through customs without any problem. The calculators were held for weeks in customs pending payment of duty. They were there so long they began accumulating a daily storage fee on top of the duty. The PPP[14] Bursar tried to explain the situation but accomplished nothing. Meanwhile, the cables and other apparatus, (also shipped separately) to be used to hook these calculators to TV monitors, arrived in customs. A high duty began to accumulate on those. None of this was any surprise to those of us who have worked within this system. The calculators finally made it through customs (duty free) in time to be useful for the last part of the semester and for the summer session.

PASSPORTS

During our second stay in Malaysia, immigration and PPP were in possession of our passports more than we were. The first visas and work permit covered only three months! Even the Malaysian representative from campus told the immigration people he thought this was stupid. They told him that was their decision and we were going to have to live with it. ITM paid a fee every time a passport was processed so the money was just being passed from one government agency to another. Each time they returned our passports just barely in time for us to leave the country. When Richard's mother died our passports were in immigration and we spent the morning at the office retrieving them. They went back to immigration as soon as we returned to Malaysia and were held for another two months. When our passports were returned in October 1992, they had work permit and visa good until the end of July! That meant, (barring loss or theft) except for turning Richard's in for tax purposes right before we left, we were finished with immigration. When Suhuddin, the man in PPP who is responsible, took them for the tax check, he had the work permit changed to May. Malaysia wouldn't let Richard leave the country until his work permit was officially canceled.

▼

Some of the problems with immigration could have been

---

[14]Abbreviation for the Malaysian name for "Center for Preparatory Studies" which was the Malaysian administrative equivalent to our Indiana University administration. See glossary.

avoided. Bipin Pai had told Bloomington that his wife, Vrinda, had an Indian passport. Bloomington had assured them, "No Problem." As hosts, we met their plane and, after a two hour wait, Bipin came outside the arrival hall followed by a customs official. Bipin and the girls would be allowed into Malaysia but Vrinda needed a visa. At one point we thought Vrinda was going to have to go to India to apply for a visa to enter Malaysia! They spent the night on benches in the arrival hall at the airport. Vrinda said the only good thing was that they got lots of attention. By morning they were ready to get on the next plane to the U.S. and forget about teaching in Malaysia. The ITM authorities who were working on the problem showed up about noon with lots of forms to be filled out. By mid-afternoon Vrinda had a 3-day permit to be in the country and, in fact, was in better shape than the rest of us since her passport was given special attention.

Vrinda's problems weren't over. As a green card holder, she was required to apply for a re-entry permit before she left the United States. They intended to stay in Malaysia for two years and applications for the permit needed to be at least a year prior to re-entry. Shirley Summers, who is Malaysian, applied for a similar permit about the same time. Hers arrived in August 1991, about a month after the application date. Vrinda's canceled check came back but the permit didn't arrive. They wrote the immigration department in Indianapolis every other month for almost a year asking for a replacement permit or at least an explanation of what was going on and what they should do. There was no response! In desperation Vrinda contacted the U.S. Embassy in KL and was told there wasn't anything they could do. She wrote the congressman from Indiana. We FAXed all the details to Malaysia House in Bloomington. We wrote to our friends, Fred and Evelyn Corban, in Indianapolis, who finally solved the puzzle of why Vrinda hadn't heard from immigration. The office in Indianapolis said the permit had been mailed and had not been returned. Therefore, they considered the case closed.

Fred also suggested the card might have been delivered to Munster. The card was there! It had arrived in August 1991, and the renters had just stuck it in a drawer without opening it or calling Premier Properties. The envelope was stamped, "Do Not Forward," as is the often the case with tax refunds and other official documents.

During the 1993 spring semester, immigration imposed a retroactive, higher rate for work permits. When we drove to Singapore, we were concerned that our fees hadn't been paid. People who tried to leave the country by plane had to pay the fee before getting an exit stamp. But at Singapore they didn't seem to care at all. They knew we couldn't do much except turn around and drive back. As of March 19, 1993, PPP didn't have enough money to pay for the faculty who wanted to go on spring break so MUCIA paid the fees and then was reimbursed. The fact that PPP wasn't ready on time with the fees meant that they were one day late being turned into immigration. Pearl had to go to the bank to get drafts in the exact amount for each passport because that is the only way immigration would accept the fees. Since most faculty wanted to travel at spring break, many of us wanted our passports at the same time. Immigration said they couldn't process seven passports in one day. Dave and Stephanie Dobson were leaving for Nepal on Saturday. Dave went to immigration Wednesday with his tickets and a letter written in Bahasa asking that they give him his passport. They said to come back Thursday or Friday. He said he had classes and needed to get this taken care of NOW. They kept him waiting for several hours and sent him to many different windows but he finally left in possession of his passport.

FESTIVALS: 1987-1989

The cultural mix in Malaysia means everyone celebrates secular and religious holidays throughout the year. Shopping days prior to Hari Raya are equivalent to the day after Thanksgiving madness that grips everyone in the U.S. The first year we made the mistake of planning errands the weekend before Hari Raya and spent hours just stuck in traffic trying to get into KL.

During the fasting month of Ramadan, a Muslim cannot consume food or water in the daytime. However, as soon as the sun sets the feasting begins. The time is set locally by the imam and in Shah Alam a cannon is fired at the exact moment as a signal people can eat and drink. Religious services at the mosque are broadcast over loudspeakers starting about 9:30 p.m. and lasting until well after midnight. We were pretty crabby by the end of the month from lack of sleep. Fireworks are also part of the nighttime festivities. At the end of Ramadan, Hari Raya cards are exchanged.

▼

Chinese New Year lasts several weeks and since a large percentage of businesses are Chinese owned, comes closest of any holiday to closing the country down. Our neighborhood was predominantly Chinese and again fireworks set off to frighten away bad spirits were an important part of the celebration. The government fought a losing battle to have them banned.

Lion dances were everywhere. The strenuous dance requires acrobatic skills and months of labor to make the huge lion head and body. A troupe usually has twelve members who exchange a piece of lettuce, symbolic of money, and an orange, symbolic of prosperity, for an ang poh, a red envelope full of money given them by the homeowner or proprietor of the store. A lion dance at a place of business or a home insures prosperity for the coming year. A thorough housecleaning must be done and businessmen accomplish this by offering everything in their stores at discount prices. A feast is held New Year's eve but no cooking is done New Year's day since using a knife or breaking a plate would be bad luck.

▼

Watching the Hindu celebration of Thaipusam was an amazing experience for us. The faithful construct kavadis, huge metal cages weighing up to 32 kilos, and carry them on their shoulders up the 374 steps to Batu Cave. The Federal Highway was almost deserted at 5 a.m. so we were as close as we could get to Batu Cave by car shortly after 5:30. We walked about one kilometer to the entrance. The area inside the gate was packed with people. Barefoot pilgrims danced and whirled for miles while carrying their kavadis. They also had steel skewers sticking through their cheeks, tongues, and lips, and limes hung from barbs stuck into their bodies. They moved and danced in a trance while family members and friends followed with offerings of food and flowers and a chair or stool for the man carrying the cage to rest on once in awhile. They had to get themselves and all that contraption up the very steep staircase without falling over. Once inside the cave they danced and gyrated in front of the altar. Then the spears and barbs were removed and lime juice squeezed on the wounds to prevent infection.

We sat down on the floor of the cave and ate our breakfast —sweet roll, tangerine, and juice which we had carried in a knapsack—and then gradually worked our way back down the steps and out to the road. With so many people and more dancers to watch, our progress was fairly slow. We walked along the road to the river where the processions were being organized.

We were impressed with how orderly the crowd was. Two spectators who fainted were carried down the steps as the crowd parted to make room. Security guards were visible but we never felt any danger of the mob losing control. The faithful are there to do penance for past sins, to petition the gods for health and favors, and to give thanks for past blessings. Murugaie told us houses must be cleaned thoroughly and special food cooked to be shared with family and friends.

▼

Christmas was celebrated with enthusiasm. The stores started playing Christmas carols the day after Thanksgiving and all the same sorts of things we would expect to find in the U.S. were available. Big hotels had displays of snowmen and Santa Claus complete with sleigh, reindeer, and artificial snow hanging from the palm trees and other tropical plants. Inside an air-conditioned hotel we felt as if it really was winter. The TV had special Christmas shows and Os Pombos, the band that played for us when we square danced, was asked to appear on a local Christmas program. The producer told the men they would have to cut their hair and couldn't wear blue jeans. The girl singer was told to wear a skirt and it could not be made from denim fabric. Songs chosen could not mention Jesus, Christmas, Santa Claus, or snow. They sang "Amazing Grace."

RELIGION

1987-1989

Religion was a topic we were told not to discuss, and it is against the law in Malaysia to question Islam, the state religion. In fact, we learned very little about Islam simply because no one was willing to talk with us about it. If we were interested in embracing Islam then we could attend classes, but unlike Christianity, there was little proselytizing. Toward the end of our stay we bought a few books in English and they were informative. Islam, a philosophy as well as a religion, dictates every aspect of daily life.

A Muslim man is exhorted by his religion to work only as much as is required to provide basic necessities for himself and his family. He is to spend the rest of his time praying. A Muslim woman is encouraged to pray but not to attend mosque regularly and when she does attend, is relegated to the women's balcony or gallery. Some of our students told us their modest dress and head covering protected them from sexual advances. When we pressed the point, asking if their fathers, brothers, or teachers had ever made improper advances they were shocked. The seed of fear has been planted and many have an extremely low opinion of men which is not at all borne out by their real experiences.

The Syarikat, the Islamic Court, is making efforts to put all Malaysians under its rule. That would mean Muslims and non-Muslims could be tried and sentenced by the court. Caning is still used as punishment and some of the radicals want to see the return of an "eye for an eye" type of justice. They want to cut off the hands of thieves and stone adulterers.

The marriage laws follow the old ways with parents making the arrangements. In some cases the man or the woman has the right of refusal. Young people who have been educated overseas are less willing to marry someone chosen by their parents. Under Islamic law unmarried men and women cannot be alone together so dating, as we know it, does not exist. We were told that unmarried men and women don't touch but we did not think this was followed as strictly as we were led to believe. As in everything religious, there are no doubt degrees of conformity. In our travels we noticed a much more relaxed attitude in different states, especially Malacca and East Malaysia.

The Raja Muda of Selangor chose a bride from the United States and, according to the Muslim custom, the marriage ceremony was performed with the bride and groom in separate rooms. Before the marriage she was circumcised and given ritual gifts. She embraced Islam but because she is a foreigner, she will be prohibited from attending any official functions.

One newspaper story we followed involved a German man and a Muslim woman. After giving their illegitimate baby to a Muslim foster family, the woman followed her lover to Germany where they married. It was illegal in Malaysia for a Muslim to marry a non-Muslim. She returned to claim custody of the child. The court, unable to decide, gave the child to the sultan who ruled in favor of the natural mother. Mother and child returned to Germany. The Syarikat then tried to extradite the mother to be tried for zina, sexual intercourse outside of marriage. The German government refused, saying that wasn't a crime in Germany. The Syarikat then threatened to put the woman's father in jail for not having his daughter under control!

Unmarried Muslim couples are subject to jail or fine if caught in a closed room together without a chaperone.

Male students on campus dress in jeans and a t-shirt. They have to keep their hair short and the shirt has to have a collar, but otherwise their dress is similar to that of U.S. students. The girls wear a wide variety of costumes. The first year we were there, several even wore western dress but the Islamic student organization soon stepped in with a dress code and short skirts disappeared. The number of girls without the tudung head covering had decreased by the second year also. We were told once a girl accepts the tudung she wears it for life, much like a nun.

Even more extreme are the girls who wear a dark habit, long veil, and gloves. While on campus they are not allowed to wear the cloth that covers the lower part of the face. These girls have a knit cap over their hair and pin the tudung to that and have a baju kurang under the dark habit. They must have been very warm and uncomfortable in that climate. Baju kurang translated means "prison shirt." The dress is a long skirt with a long-sleeved 3/4 length tunic. The black, grey, or brown chardor-like covering worn over the baju kurang is looked on by the older generation as a form of rebellion much as we viewed our hippies of the 60's. The extreme modesty of radical believers carries over into all parts of their lives and often the only medical treatment a woman has is medicine prescribed by a doctor who "sees" her through a male intermediary (either husband or father).

The Islamic Student Association controlled most of the campus extracurricular activities, making it difficult to win approval for particular functions. In spite of the restrictions students and faculty found opportunities for fun, recreation, and learning outside the classroom.

Islamic dietary laws parallel those of the Old Testament with pork and shellfish strictly forbidden, although Malaysian Muslims eat shrimp and other shellfish. When we invited Muslims to join us for meals, we were careful to provide halal food and paper plates. All the U.S. fast food chains in Malaysia serve halal food. The bookroom helpers always wanted to go to Kentucky Fried Chicken or MacDonald's after working at distribution.

In the U.S., kosher food is an acceptable substitute for halal but in Malaysia there is a great deal of animosity toward Jews and a general concern among students that Jewish professors would not be fair in grading Muslim students. The students expressed surprise when Richard assured them this would not be the case and a person's religion was of no importance in the classroom situation.

Making a Haj, a pilgrimage to Mecca, is a meaningful part of a Muslim man's life. The government maintains Terminal II at the airport for that specific purpose. Planes operate out of it only one month of the year and non-Muslims are prohibited from entering. A complex of buildings in PJ is used by pilgrims preparing for their Haj.

Before making a Haj, a Muslim man must be sure his family will be provided for in case he dies on the trip. In one family we were aquainted with, the father was concerned that he had no sons to care for his wife and daughters in the event of his death. His older daughter, a successful business woman who had been to school overseas, refused his suggestion that she marry a man of his choosing. The second daughter, Fatimah, was starting a clothing business but gave in to her father's wish. The young man, who is now her husband, was a friend but they had not previously considered marriage.

Not all the students on our campus were Muslim. Being bumiputra was one of the entrance requirements but in East Malaysia many bumiputra are also Christian. We asked the Christian students if they felt uncomfortable or pressured in their relationships with Muslim students but they assured us they didn't have a problem. At speech nights on campus we were impressed by how outspoken the students were and, as with any group, there was always a mixture of attitudes and ideas.

The Malaysians of Chinese ancestry practice an assortment of religions. Our Chinese neighbors owned dogs which were allowed to bark and howl at will, evidently believing their ancestors might have been reincarnated as dogs and thus to reprimand would be wrong. The Chinese have a great reverence for family, which includes dead ancestors. Many Chinese who convert to Christianity still follow the custom of bringing food offerings to the departed. Religious customs get rather mixed together and it is almost impossible for converts to discard the old ways.

Miss Lim, our landlady, had become a Roman Catholic. Her brother chose to live the life of a vagrant in spite of family efforts to help, and when he died a Christian neighbor told Miss Lim that it would be wrong to pray for his soul because he had been heathen. We encouraged her to ask her priest to say masses for her brother and then kept our fingers crossed the priest would agree. Prayers could do no harm and would most certainly make the family feel better. Even as a good Christian she told us she hoped he would have an easier life in his next reincarnation.

Local bridal salons use Caucasian dummies to model the gowns displayed in their windows. Christian converts almost always wear traditional western rather than Asian wedding dress.

Malaysians from India are predominantly Hindu who worship one god with many manifestations. Their temples are extremely ornate and worshipers regularly bring food and flower offerings. Animal sacrifice is practiced but on the other hand, Hindus have a great reverence for living things. Wearing anything made of leather is forbidden in Hindu temples. Buddha started life as a Hindu and many of the Hindu teachings about life have found their way into Buddhism and Christianity.

We attended the Anglican church in Malaysia. St. Paul's in PJ was a very large Indian congregation and basically had the same sort of church organization we were used to but with services in Tamil as well as English. Sermons were VERY long. The walls of the church opened and with ceiling fans it was reasonably comfortable. The cathedral in KL was a typical English country church and even with windows open and fans on, it was pretty uncomfortable. English services were held in the air-conditioned chapel.

Most of the time we went to St. Barnabas church in Klang, also an Indian congregation, led by a charismatic priest named "Jumbo." The congregation supported a daycare center and a residence for high school students as well as a drug-rehabilitation unit. We never did figure out what had gone wrong but a supply priest always celebrated mass and sometime during our second year "Jumbo" and his family were moved out of the rectory and a young priest took over. The new young man's speech impediment that was worse when he was excited made his sermons almost impossible to understand. Under his guidance the church was cleaned up and painted, the organ repaired, and a new roof installed. The interior ceiling had to be replaced to rid the church of an attic garden sprouted from seeds dropped by birds. Birds routinely flew in and out of church during mass.

One Sunday during the renovation period we could smell hot wiring. Pretty soon one of the fan switches in the hall burst into flames. The fire was quickly put out and since all the wiring was outside the walls and visible, we were sure it wouldn't start again without our knowing about it. Only a few minutes before the fire started the priest had reported the cost of an electrical inspection which had been done the previous week. We hoped the vestry asked for a refund.

We used the English hymnal which had the words printed but no music. Most of the time if we knew the words the tune would be unfamiliar and if the tune was familiar, we didn't know the words. Singing was further complicated by the person next to or behind us singing in Tamil. Until the organ was repaired the accompaniment was played on a harmonium.

The priest, layreaders, and acolytes generally were in their stocking feet and many parishioners went barefoot to the altar rail to receive communion. We were often distracted from our prayers by the exquisite saris the women wore.

At Christmas the congregation was allowed to go caroling, but a permit had to be applied for several months in advance, and the list of names turned in with the application could not be added to at a later date.

Money given to a church or temple is not tax deductible under Malaysian law and permits for new churches or temples are difficult to get. Donations to the mosque are tax deductible and new mosques are paid for with tax money taken from the general populace.

RELIGION UPDATE

Public displays of affection between unmarried Muslim

couples is still a punishable offense. Affection in public between married Muslim couples and between parents and children is discouraged. However, students on campus talked openly about private relationships and sexual matters. Some of the female students assured us that wearing the tudung didn't mean they only had "pure" thoughts.

▼

During the time we were having so much trouble getting the neighbors to plaster the dividing wall at the back of the duplex, Puan Faridah asked if she could bring an imam to the house to say peacemaking prayers. We were certainly not going to object to anything that would facilitate getting the repairs done.

▼

The speech department coordinator's wedding was organized by his Chinese landlady. The invitations, red with gold Chinese characters, opened left to right rather than the way we were used to. Joe and Marie's parents weren't able to come so the landlady's husband gave the bride away. The church was air-conditioned and it was a cool day so the bride wasn't too uncomfortable in her beaded satin wedding gown. She wore a traditional red with white embroidered Chinese wedding dress for the first part of the reception and then changed into a baju kurang. She wanted an Indian wedding sari as a third outfit but couldn't find one. All of these gowns were rented.

▼

The imam sighted the stars to determine when the religious observances would begin. Most other Muslim countries depend on scientists. The uncertainty played havoc with the semester schedules.

▼

Murugaie and Ghopal's 1991 Deepavali celebration was curtailed because of the sudden death of Ghopal's brother. Going to temple, a big part of the Deepavali celebration, was prohibited for the year following a death in the family. They performed a special purification ceremony on the anniversary of the brother's death in time for them to celebrate Deepavali the following year. Ghopal, a vegetarian, didn't object to Murugaie and the children eating meat but he said he didn't like the smell. Murugaie was an excellent cook and spent days preparing a traditional Indian meal for us to enjoy. Beer was always served because they were convinced all westerners drank beer.

▼

Just before Chinese New Year Puan Faridah came to the house. Using a small trowel she buried a small slip of paper under the rambutan tree in the front yard and sprinkled some sort of powder over it. She said this was a prayer to protect the house from being robbed over the Chinese New Year! We decided this was similar to lighting a candle in church.

▼

On July 3, 1992, we were invited next door to celebrate a wedding. We were only invited for the dinner. I asked the bride's mother to clarify the invitation and she said the ceremony preceding the dinner was only for Muslims. The dinner started promptly at 9:15. That was unusual for Malaysia. We had adjusted to people being anywhere from a half hour to several hours late arriving at functions. The guests who came to this party ate, paid their respects to the couple and their parents and left. We were in bed before 10:30! The bride's uncle sat at our table. He said the couple weren't having the usual "bersanding" (blessing of the marriage by family and friends) for religious reasons. The 22-year-old bride and groom recently graduated from law school.

▼

Sarah Archer, a friend who worked in Bangladesh, came to Malaysia on business. She was accompanied by Aktar, a colleague. As part of our sightseeing tour, we took them to the Shah Alam Mosque. Aktar, a practicing Muslim, was pleased to be at the mosque for the late afternoon prayer. At the mosque we encountered a young guide, who tried to encourage us to convert to Islam (our first experience with Islamic proselytizing.) When Sarah assured him we were "people of the Book", he said Muslims revered Jesus as a prophet and holy man. When Sarah asked if she could take pictures of the prayer hall he told her to go ahead and didn't stop her when she walked inside. Aktar said exclusion of Christians and women from mosque prayer halls is not written in the Koran, and he believed all faiths should be welcomed in the sacred parts of Mecca! When they were in the Philippines Sarah went to a Roman church because there wasn't an Anglican one. Aktar wanted to go but wasn't ready in time and it was so crowded she couldn't save him a seat. He sat in a different area and when time for communion came, he went to the rail and received along with the rest of the congregation. It's probably a good thing the priest didn't know, but we think God must have smiled. Aktar said his evening prayers at our house before we went to dinner. He must have washed thoroughly because he managed to get the bathroom fairly wet performing his ablutions.

Ramadan, the fasting month for Muslims, meant no food service and empty drink machines on campus. Muslim-owned restaurants near the campus were closed from sunrise to sunset but in PJ and KL the larger ones stayed open to serve non-Muslim clientele. There were ads in the paper about how to avoid gaining weight during Ramadan. Eating or drinking in the daytime was forbidden, but high calorie foods were part of the ritual feasting after dark and into the early hours of the morning. It seemed like a strange approach to fasting. Hari Raya marked the end of Ramadan. The official moon sightings weren't done until the night before. Students who had long distances to travel had problems because PPP purchased discount tickets in advance that could not be changed. Often students would miss several days of class on either end of the vacation.

CULTURE SHOCK: 1991-1993

Cultural differences made life in Malaysia an adventure for us. Many of the day to day realities quickly became "old hat" and comfortable, some never ceased to amaze, others provoked laughter or tears, and a few were downright annoying. The following collection of paragraphs, which vary considerably in length and have no relationship to one another, are intended to offer the reader a slice of Malaysian life and customs. In spite of the many trials and tribulations we encountered, we developed an affection for Malaysia and the good memories predominate; the rough spots have softened.

Puan Faridah, our landlady, was a liberated Malaysian lady. She had two brothers and two sisters and all of them had university degrees. She was educated in England and was married to an Englishman (he died the first year we were there). She wore western style clothes and taught library science at one of the national universities south of KL.

The local lumber yard cut pieces of wood for Richard to use in putting screen on the kitchen window. He went to the trouble to figure lengths in meters only to find out lumber measurements were in feet. Tailors also worked in inches and feet. It was puzzling since in all other areas Malaysians used the metric system.

One Saturday morning when we had the front gate open, the mosquito inspector wandered into our yard. He took a sample of the water standing in the dish under a big flower pot and told us it was full of aedes larvae. The dish had been dry the day before but no amount of arguing would convince him. We ended up having to pay the RM50 fine (about US$20). Aedes mosquitoes carry dengue fever that is sometime fatal to Asians. The medical officer at Subang told us it was only fatal in cases where medical treatment was delayed.

Sidewalk vendors, once a fascinating part of city life, are

fast becoming a hazard. It is no longer safe for pedestrians to be crowded off the sidewalk into the streets.

▼

Mahathir, the prime minister, is exhorting Muslims to have large families. By the year 2020 he envisions a population of 80 million, although the present population is only about 17 million.

▼

According to Buddhist teachings there are five major areas of sin. They are wine, women, meat, fish, and sexual congress. The U.S. certainly has a sexual congress!

▼

We celebrated Chinese New Year with our next door neighbors. Emily served soup, rice, and eight or ten other dishes. There were enough guests for several sittings, and a friend had told us we should leave the table as soon as we were finished eating to make room for other guests. We were served soft drinks before dinner and offered either soft drinks or beer with dinner. For dessert, Emily served the wafer-thin, folded cookies called "love letters." After dinner a group played cards until the wee hours of the morning.

▼

In 1988, Murugaie and Ghopal put a down payment on a link-house in a government housing project. Because they were Indian, they had to pay considerably more than if they had been bumiputra. The standard house had an 8 x 15 living room, three small bedrooms, a bath and an efficiency size kitchen. Even though these houses were made from concrete and brick and are sturdier than the house they lived in, Murugaie was not satisfied with it. She and Ghopal spent three years making improvements. They enlarged the kitchen, probably quadrupling the original space, tiled the walls and floor, and added a double sink. The bathroom was completely tiled, had a western toilet and a Malaysian style shower sprayed the entire room. The floors throughout the house were marble. They extended the roof to cover the front patio and tiled the patio floor. Her brother installed an iron gate and grill along the front. Like their house in the kampung, it was by far the nicest and most cared for looking house on the block. Their neighbors were predominantly Malay but there was at least one other Indian family on the block.

We were invited to the blessing of their new home. Until it was blessed, they couldn't move any furniture into the house. When we arrived we were greeted by one of the family holding a silver tray. She first sprinkled water on both of us. The tray had a small dish of yellow liquid and another of red powder. We dipped a finger in each and anointed our foreheads. They had chairs on the patio and served us fruit drinks while we waited for the ceremony to begin. Inside the house we sat on new mats spread on the floor. The doors of the house were anointed with the yellow liquid and red powder. An altar had been built towards one end and to the side of the living room. It was decorated with fruits and flowers and a picture of the gods Siva and Ganesh. On either side were burning oil lamps. The priest built a fire (a shield of bricks protected the floor), and in it he burned grains of rice, flower petals, herbs, ghee, wood, and assorted other things we couldn't identify. As the flames increased, we wondered how many new homes burn down before the families even move in! Early in the ceremony he used twisted vines to make rings for Murugaie and Ghopal. He put an ornate necklace of flowers around their necks. Many aspects of the ceremony made us think the relationship was similar to a marriage between the homeowners and the home.

Just about the time we began to think we would be asphyxiated, the ceremony moved outside. The priest anointed the house again and quartered a melon as an offering to Ganesh, who is the manifestation of God in the form of an elephant that is the patron of all Hindu homes. They started a fire on the patio and boiled milk in an earthen pot. What boiled over the top was caught in a bucket and served to us later as part of the ritual meal. Rice and spices were added to the rest and that also was served to us later. While the milk was cooking we talked with the priest. He explained the ceremony was to cleanse all the evil spirits from the house. The fruits and flowers represented the bounty of the earth and the fire takes their essence to God. The offering was one of thanksgiving and request for health and prosperity.

The priest was born to the priesthood by virtue of his caste. His son, who served as acolyte, will follow his father's footsteps and be sent to India to study when he comes of age. In addition to serving a temple in Klang, this priest worked in the government immigration office.

While the milk was cooking we were entertained with classical Indian dances performed by a four-year-old who was just learning and a ten year old who was accomplished. We were again served juice. When the milk and rice mixture finished cooking, we all moved back indoors for more prayers and bell ringing. Murugaie and Ghopal paid homage to Ghopal's mother and three other elderly relatives, each of whom sprinkled rice on their heads. A meal was served on banana leaves. All of us were still sitting inside on the floor. The meal included the rice, an Indian donut, pieces of sweet cake, dal curry on fine rice noodles, a glass of fruit juice, and a glass of milk. The milk had a slightly burned taste and didn't really taste like milk at all. Murugaie told us it was very important that we drink the milk. After the meal was over we were invited to tour the house and then went back to the patio to watch two more dances. Ghopal went off to the temple to pray and since the ceremony was obviously over, we made our goodbyes and left. Even though there was no furniture, ritual required the family to sleep in the house that night to protect it from evil spirits.

▼

Before we made any purchase overseas we asked ourselves, "Do we want to dust it?" We decided the orang asli carving of the "Harimau" was beautiful enough to be worth the effort! We waited three months for ours to be finished. The carver put his name on the bottom along with the title "grandparents foretelling trapping harimau." That was the translation from looking up words in the dictionary. The story behind the carving was that if a man can get a ball in the mouth of the tiger he is safe from attack. The harimau (tiger) has a ball in his mouth that rolls around freely but cannot be removed. In his paws he holds a length of chain. All this was carved from one large chunk of hard wood (neri batu). We took pictures of the carvers working on harimaus in various stages of completion. The carvings became so popular that a commercial tourist hotel was to be built on Carey Island soon. The price of the carvings had already doubled and will probably continue to increase with demand. The tribe was having to search further and further for neri batu.

▼

The quality of life in Malaysia had deteriorated in the two years we were away. From May to November of 1991, the air was so polluted we could hardly see or breathe. The government blamed volcanic eruptions, forest fires in East Malaysia and Indonesia, and the drought before admitting the smog was caused by vehicular and industrial pollution. Malacca suffered severe water shortages and the river was too low to allow sightseeing boats. There were water and electrical shortages all over the Klang Valley. After the BIG BLACKOUT of 1992, when we were without electricity about eight hours and parts of the country were without service for several days, Tenaga Electric admitted that Malaysia's electrical needs had gone beyond the supply.

▼

An ironing board was called an "ironing table."

▼

The Davis' landlord left a piano in the house. They called a tuner who took the insides to the shop to tune them! We'd never heard of that. Pianos are so sensitive to being moved we wondered whether that would work.

▼

Murugaie routinely got up at 3 a.m. to milk her cows and do her own laundry and housework. She cleaned two expat houses every day except Saturday when she worked only in the morning. She had Sunday off only because no one wanted her to come on Sunday. We couldn't imagine when she slept.

▼

One Sunday, two well dressed Malaysian Chinese came to the door. They were Jehovah's Witnesses distributing pamphlets about AIDS. When I told them I wasn't interested they went away. Malaysia is very strict about missionaries but as long as they stay away from Muslims they are free to try to convert people or to distribute public service literature.

▼

The gardener noticed an extra refrigerator out on the

91

back porch and asked if I wanted to sell it. I agreed to call Puan Faridah and she said she'd take US$40 for it. He came back the next day with another man who helped load it into a van. As far as we know it is still working.

▼

"Carcosa," the former British High Commissioner's residence, was elegant and well-maintained. It operated as both a restaurant and hotel and THE Queen stayed there when she visited Malaysia. The prices were outrageous, but that was to be expected in exchange for ambiance. For High Tea we were served finger sandwiches, scones, miniature quiche, chocolate eclairs and fruit tarts along with a choice of tea or

Carver holding our harimau.

coffee. We had hoped for a grand tour of the premises but that wasn't offered so we had to be content with what must have been the main reception room and the spectacular entrance hall and staircase. The main reception room opened onto a wide covered porch. The British did live well.

▼

Hamid used a chain saw to remove two of the three cedar stumps in their yard. He was working in shorts with only thongs on his feet! We could also tell by the smell that he was overheating the saw and he finally gave up and worked at the last stump with an ax. The following morning it was still standing and was eventually incorporated into the landscaping.

▼

"Emily of Emerald Hill" was a one-woman show and the actress was a master at switching back and forth between cultured British English and theChinese/Nyonya/English mixed language used in Malaysia and Singapore. The Chinese actress from Singapore sang a Negro lullaby and a flawless rendition of "My Old Kentucky Home."

▼

Snaps are called "press buttons."

▼

We watched one of our resident ciceks (lizards) shed its skin. For a while he was out in the middle of the room so we had to be very careful not to step on him. In the morning, the empty skin was gone. We assume he either ate it or it blew away.

▼

After showing our Tibet slides at a friend's house, they said their amah had strange dreams that night. The amah explained that since we had arrived at the house after dark we should have washed our feet before coming inside. By neglecting to do this we brought bad spirits in. These were the friends who lived across the street from the man who set their palm trees on fire because he didn't like how they looked! The neighbor, who was a member of the Malaysian Mafia and **VERY** rich and powerful, was also trying to force the landlord to sell the property to him. His house looked more like a hotel than a private home and he was in the process of building a parking lot and garage next door to the house he wanted to buy.

▼

We went to the tailor to order a couple of man-tailored short sleeved shirts for me. The tailor paid no attention at all to what I said but asked Richard what I wanted. When Richard repeated what I said, the tailor wrote it down! The finished shirts were beautiful.

▼

Murugaie and Ghopal paid US$60 a month for Panir Selvin to go to the Indian school in KL and about US$5 for supplies. He took six subjects. The school day was from 8 a.m. to 4:30 p.m. and, since the school was located on the far side of KL, he had a long bus ride.

▼

One of our good hand towels went missing at the laundry but as soon as I walked in the next week, the girl went and got it. She didn't even have to ask, so they must have identified me with a particular batch of laundry.

▼

On October 16, 1992, the control tower at Subang airport burned. The airport closed for several hours and reopened on a limited basis using a combination of Malaysian Air Force and Singapore radar to monitor the flights. It was the second major fire in six months and arson was suspected. The first was caused by careless smoking. A few days later, our flight to Dubai was delayed for several hours by a bomb scare.

▼

A day that began with a dead rat at the front door couldn't do anything but improve! One of our resident cats must have gotten overeager in his feeding frenzy and choked on his meal. At least we knew the cats were useful for something.

▼

Lisa had her third child in early December 1992. Hamid called his three girls, "Charlie's angels." Standard maternity leave was thirty days and during that time the new mother wasn't supposed to leave the house. Lisa went back to her job at American Express soon after the first of the year. One of the two amahs was the primary care giver for the two older children and they hired another amah to care for the new baby. The oldest was nearly four and went to day-care each weekday morning. A relative also came to help with the baby because during her confinement a new mother could only have a limited contact with water. We were invited to a combined birthday party for Apiya (4) and Aliya (2) and the one-month or first moon celebration for Anisya. The birthday party for the two older girls started about 5 p.m. We were invited for dinner at 7:30 after all the families with small children had left but we had a ringside seat of the earlier festivities from the balcony. The later party was a lot more subdued. We took pictures of the girls with their birthday cakes. Apiya had asked for a cake with a house on it. The house was made of gingerbread and the cake was chocolate. Aliya wanted a caterpillar on her cake! She and John, our son, would get along well. Emily's brother, Peter, was a chef at the Ming Court Hotel in KL and the cakes were made there.

The traditional Penang meal for the first moon of a girl baby was sticky rice with chicken curry, orange colored dumplings with ground pea filling, hard boiled eggs dyed red, and curry laksa (a curry-type chicken noodle soup). Lisa and the baby were now officially finished with their one month confinement. Anisya already held her head up and was very alert. Lisa attributed this to all the Chinese herbal potions Emily made her drink during her pregnancy. Lisa was still on a restricted diet heavy on herbs and potions and was forbidden to eat beef for another month. The restriction against excessive contact with water meant Lisa could only bathe once a week for the first three weeks after the birth. She was allowed to use a damp cloth for "touch-ups"! In a cool climate that routine might be tolerable but in the tropics, where it was common to take several showers a day, we think it would seem like cruel and unusual punishment. Lisa agreed that she was pretty miserable. The baby wore a binding cloth tied around her tummy to protect and help heal the umbilical cord. One month after the birth Lisa was as slim and trim as before her pregnancy. A masseuse came daily and the treatment included tight tummy wraps and hot stones!

A chicken took up residence in the backyard. She really lived at the house above us and was probably destined to become nasi ayam (chicken rice). The cats gave her a wide berth.

Beth Pour started out one morning to take her new baby to a well baby clinic in KL. The car broke down on the Federal Highway. A man stopped to help, called AAM (he had a car phone), stayed with her until they came to repair the car, had her sit (and nurse) in his car with the air-conditioning on while he stood in the hot sun and waited, and then followed her home to make sure she arrived safely. They were not any the worse for their experience. There are advantages to living in a society that feels protective towards women.

We went to a belated Deepavali celebration at Murugaie's old house in the kampung. As usual, it was a feast. She invited all the expats she worked for. She served ten different dishes and they were all delicious. We managed to get Ghopal to sit down at the table with us but Murugaie and the other relatives waited on us. We hoped they ate the leftovers since there was way more food than we could possibly eat. Murugaie and Ghopal were temporarily back in the kampung because they and their neighbors were fighting the government for a fair price for the house and the land. The kampung sat as an island in the midst of highway and industrial development. If the neighborhood had been bumiputra they would get RM25,000 for their property, but because the settlement was mostly Indian with a few Chinese the government was offering RM6,000! They probably won't get the RM25,000 but by sticking together they could surely improve their lot. We admired their fortitude. There was little chance that the government would confiscate the land. That isn't the Malaysian way. Ghopal said he expected to have a satisfactory settlement by the first of the year and then they can move back to their new home.

We were surprised at how much the area around the Kampung had been developed. The Japanese companies insisted on good roads and Shah Alam had expanded to connect with Subang Jaya. Soon, PJ, Subang Jaya, and Shah Alam will be one big urban sprawl.

▼

Taj Tandoor, one of our favorite restaurants, was across the street from a large mosque in PJ. At prayer time the street turned into a parking lot. Worshipers parked their cars three and four abreast, making the street impassable until after services were over. The police ignored the problem. Illegal parking was rampant. Parking garages were available but were ignored in favor of illegal spots closer to shops. By 1993, police had begun to use the boot combined with substantial fines.

▼

It took a while to figure out why local newspapers printed

"MUSIA" instead of MUCIA. In bahasa the "C" was pronounced "CH", whereas the "C" in MUCIA was heard as an "S." Verbal interviews made the name sound like MUSIA, but it is really spelled MUCIA.

▼

The windshield on Dave Dobson's car imploded while the car was parked at school. There was no sign of any problem other than heat build up inside the car. It sure made a mess.

▼

In order to give his brother, Robert, his power of attorney, Richard had to go to the American Embassy to have the papers notarized. He called ahead to check on times and procedures but after he got there they told him he needed two witnesses. The official wouldn't allow the secretaries to serve as witnesses. Richard finally found two young Chinese men in the library. The guards had to be talked into letting Richard go from the visa section to the library section without going to the gate for another pass and then they didn't want the Chinese men to pass through the other direction. The gate had their driver's licenses so they had trouble coming up with ID that included pictures. The three of them waited over thirty minutes while the officials got their act together and there was a US$11 fee for the "service"!

▼

Puan Faridah got her name in the papers. A high rise condo was being built next to the condo she lived in and she and her neighbors were complaining about the noise and the mess. We could sympathize. There was a lot of publicity in the local papers about problems with high rise buildings. Neighbors would band together to complain the new buildings were spoiling their "feng shui" (the Chinese science for locating structures through divination.) The Chinese, especially, are very particular about where their buildings are and the direction they face. The city had restrictions on high rise construction but didn't pay much attention unless there were complaints. The Jaya shopping center near us was built four stories higher than allowed and they were not required to tear them down. They paid a RM2000 fine which was about US$500.

▼

When we went to Singapore, Emily asked us to buy her a portable phone. The original price of the brand she wanted was S$195. It was on sale for S$150 which is S$30 less than her friend paid for hers! That was a real coup.

▼

In mid-February wheelchair-bound people going around the world made their way between KL and Klang. Traffic on the Federal Highway was tied up for miles. There was a large truck with blinking lights and signs protecting them from being run over by impatient motorists!

▼

At Math Day one of the students taught Richard how to play congkak. It is a fairly simple game for two people. The shop in the Central Market where I bought the game was out

Richard playing congkak with a student.

of marbles which are needed for the game. They directed me to a Chinese candy shop across the street that sold marbles! I didn't even try to find out why a candy shop carries marbles for congkak games.

▼

A few weeks before we left Malaysia two of Emily's amahs climbed over the fence and ran away. They didn't steal anything, but she had bought them new clothes and gold necklaces for Hari Raya and they took those. She worked them pretty hard but they probably had a better place to live and better food than they would have in Indonesia. The one girl who was left had been with them two years and wanted to come back for another two after taking a month's leave. Before she could take leave, Emily had to find additional help because she couldn't run her food service and take care of three small children by herself.

▼

The L100 course on campus taught composition to our students. The topics given the students were contemporary as the following quote, voted by the faculty to be the "gem of the term," will show. "IUD's cause virginal discharge. Women will suffer from virginia and menstrual loss."

We couldn't do any better in Bahasa but it does seem that there was a great deal lost in the communication process.

▼

Another tidbit from the L100D class: "For those who get a more linear teacher, a grade point average of 2.5 will be easy." We assume the student meant "lenient." English is a hard language to learn. It's amazing that students eventually progress to the point of being able to cope with lectures and taking notes. Spoken words are so easily misunderstood.

▼

We drove around Section 7 in Shah Alam looking at the enormous mansions that were being built there. We were also looking for a particular "No Trespassing" sign that was in front of one of the more fortified residences. It said, "Trespassers will be shot. Survivors will be shot again!" No doubt that kept almost everyone from climbing the fence. We enjoyed looking at the homes and the view from the top of the hill. We took a picture of one large, beautiful mansion that had its laundry draped on the fence surrounding it.

▼

We ate lunch at a Chinese restaurant near one of the stamp shops. The service and ambiance were above average. We had salt baked prawns and a "borecli" with crab sauce dish that turned out to be broccoli. Their spelling makes almost as much sense as "brockley" which is what the chlorophyll lab where Richard worked one summer came up with. We had trouble with that vegetable in Malaysia. Once we ordered broccoli and were served Bok Choy! Obviously there was a communication problem.

▼

At a Math Club meeting to elect officers, one girl said she had never been a treasurer but she had lots of experience! Maybe she should run for Congress?

HEALTH CARE

1987-1989

Subang Clinic, in Subang Jaya between KL and Shah Alam, is a modern hospital. Doctors and nurses speak English and took excellent care of us. Bills for two minor surgeries, routine office visits, and shots were astonishingly low. We never had major surgery but know from the experience of others that the doctors are competent and the results have been praised by U.S. physicians who examined the patients after their return.

Malaysian doctors do not carry malpractice insurance because there is not much danger of being sued. The hospital is clean but there is a more relaxed attitude toward maintaining a totally sterile atmosphere. Sheets in the emergency room aren't changed after each patient and a communal cup is used to hold water for washing down pills. The staff who observed Richard's surgery did not wear either gown or mask.

Prescription drugs are dispensed by hospitals as well as pharmacies, and a number of drugs available on request have to be signed for. Aspirin, a controlled substance, can be bought only in small quantities and is expensive. It never occurred to us to ask if it could be obtained with a prescription.

HEALTH CARE UPDATE

Subang Clinic continues to provide excellent, affordable health care. The Chief Medical Officer advised us to be vaccinated against hepatitis. The cost for the series was substantially less than it would have been at the Munster Clinic. The technician did use a new needle for each of us but we had visions of little girls out back of the hospital washing the needles in plastic tubs of soapy water. We know that didn't happen, but it would make a good LAT cartoon. (LAT is an extremely popular Malaysian political cartoonist who has become a folk hero.)

▼

Bob Hvitfeldt had back surgery at Assunta Hospital. His doctor ordered an NRI instead of a myelogram and the pictures of his backbone were much better than either myelogram or X-ray could have produced. The doctor saved the minute pieces of disc and the calcification around a nerve. Bob's bill for the surgery and hospital stay came to a grand total of US$2,000. That included the NRI test that is so expensive in the states. We were impressed with Assunta Hospital. In 1987, when we were first considering moving to Malaysia, Richard talked with a friend of the Corbans who had lived in Malaysia about ten years ago, and said at that time Assunta was the best hospital in PJ.

▼

After a trip into the orang asli settlement near Jeruntut, Richard developed a slight rash on his arms. In spite of medication, it spread and developed into a major problem. The dermatologist thought it was "contact dermatitis." The rash turned into large blisters which burst and rubbed raw. It seemed as if he was going to lose all his skin. Dr. Yap recommended that Richard see Dr. Adam, a specialist at Universiti Hospital, for a biopsy to confirm the diagnosis of "Pemphigus." Both doctors thought Richard was allergic to himself!! Antibodies from his over-active immune system were attacking his skin. Joan Shull had a similar rash. We were relieved that it did not follow the same pattern.

Universiti Malaya Hospital was the local teaching hospital. Dr. Yap advised us to get there early because even though we had a 10:00 appointment, patients were taken on a first-come first-served basis. We were in a line to pre-register, then another line to register, than another to pay the bill, then another to wait for the doctor and finally a line to get the prescription. All the records are kept by hand and we sat on hard wooden benches to wait for the doctor. We got to the hospital about 8:30 and were back home by 10:30 so for all that waiting we didn't do too badly. The total cost was about US$15 including the pills. The biopsy a few days later would have cost about US$18, but after that first visit we learned we could get free services as government servants. So the rest of our visits and prescriptions cost us nothing.

The biopsy was scheduled in the "minor operations theater." It was difficult to understand what the nurse meant by "minops theater."

The hospital had molded plastic chairs in the waiting room, and the hard wooden benches in the clinics were extremely uncomfortable. We noticed a gurney that looked as if it had been built of used plumbing parts. We couldn't expect luxury in a hospital that dispensed free medical care to government servants. For patients who had to pay, prescriptions were either US$2 or US$4. The building could have used a thorough cleaning.

The biopsy showed that Richard did not have pemphigus. Instead, the diagnosis was sub corneal pustular dermatosis. In twenty years Richard's was only the second case Dr. Adams had seen. In fact, he said the disease was more common in the western hemisphere but not common even there.

Larry Reister mentioned he also broke out with a rash on his arms and ankles every time he visited the orang asli settlement. We wondered if the first rash Richard had was actually an allergic reaction made worse by the drugs. We have read about trees in the jungle that caused some people to break out just walking by them.

▼

Murugaie and Ghopal's son, Panir Selvan, had been scheduled for heart surgery several times between 1987 and 1989. When we returned to Malaysia, the surgery was still pending. After an angiogram showed not one but two holes in Panir Selvan's heart, the doctor advised them to wait another six months, until June 26, 1992 and, in the meantime, build Panir up with vitamin injections.

On the scheduled day his surgery was canceled AGAIN. This time the hospital didn't have a bed available for an Indian! The surgery was rescheduled for October.

Murugaie and Ghopal went to the Subang Clinic to ask how much it would cost to have heart surgery done there. They were told RM35,000 (about US$14,000). The US$4,000 they had saved would have covered the surgery if it had been done by the American doctor at Universiti Hospital. Ghopal's two brothers promised to provide another RM4000.

Murugaie and Ghopal took Panir to a newly opened heart clinic in KL. The doctor used a micro-surgical procedure through a vein in Panir's groin and didn't open his chest. They put a plug in the larger hole and said they could go back later to close the smaller one. There was an immediate improvement in his appetite and his mental alertness. His skin was a healthier color and his face didn't look as pinched. Panir was only in the hospital one day and the cost of the whole procedure was approximately US$200.

Bud Dixon was treated by the ultrasonic machine that destroys kidney stones. The procedure cost US$800. The same procedure at Munster Community Hospital would cost US$5000. Hillary Clinton should come to Malaysia for ideas on how to rework our medical care system, although the simplistic answer is that getting a medical degree shouldn't automatically make one entitled to become a millionaire.

The Malaysian dentist we went to found no problems and told both of us our teeth were in excellent shape and that if we continued to take good care of them we shouldn't have to go to a dentist! He'll never make a living that way and, considering our history of dental problems, we're sure he was wrong. It is common in Asia to have lost a lot of teeth before the age of fifty. We do think the diet was different enough that we didn't get the tartar build-up we had in the states. When we were in Malaysia before we went two years without seeing a dentist and our U.S. dentist thought we were in fine shape. Richard had two upper wisdom teeth pulled in the spring of 1992, and he survived! The teeth were huge. The only hitch was that a piece of one root broke off and had to be dug out but, as the dentist predicted, it was all over in fifteen minutes. The cost of the extraction was US$28! We don't think an American dentist would let a patient sit in his chair for that price.

POLITICS

1987-1989

At our orientation we were told not to discuss politics and of course complied with this request in public. Within our own circle of friends we discussed politics a lot. The Internal Security Act allowed the government to jail and hold without trial anyone overheard saying anything considered a threat or damaging to the state. As of January 1990, sixty-five people were held under the ISA.

The 17 million people in Malaysia, 55 percent Malay, 30 percent Chinese, 10 percent Indian and 5 percent other nationalities, lived together in harmony. Politically, cooperation was more difficult to achieve. The government, dominated by bumiputra, severely restricted activities of opposition political parties and there were several minor "emergencies" during our two years. Government controlled newspaper publication, and delivery was often held up while an issue was checked for anti-government articles. TIME magazine had a standard clause that extended subscriptions by the number of issues confiscated by the government. Nudity and sexual innuendo were considered offensive but depictions of violence or violent death were acceptable. We were told our mail might be censored but we never had any indication that it was. A lot of mail simply wasn't delivered.

In the fall of 1989 the Communist guerrillas surrendered after forty-one years of conflict. Prior to that when we traveled in Malaysia we never made a major trip anywhere without being stopped or slowed down by roadblocks. Usually we were just waved on through since our skin color meant we were not guerrillas.

In Malaysia hanging is accepted punishment for possession or use of drugs for any nationality, and anyone caught with a gun or a bullet is jailed. There were armed guards at all the banks and at a lot of the jewelry stores and in the event of a robbery, guards shot first and asked questions later.

POLITICAL UPDATE

Some of the sultans lived extravagant lives. Their moral and religious wrong-doing was tolerated because royalty was

105

considered above the law. The underhanded dealings became blatant enough to cause Umno, one of the political parties, to propose a code of ethics for Malay rulers.

The Sultan of Kelantan's passion was importing foreign cars, and his downfall was a Lamborghini Diablo. The import duties on that particular car were about RM2.1 million or US$840,000. Customs impounded the car because the Sultan had already exceeded the number of duty free cars he was allowed to import. The Sultan, with his armed bodyguards, took the car from the customs shed. He said it was his right as a sultan to import as many duty free cars as he wanted to. He also said he only had to abide by the laws set forth in the Quran and was above civil law. Customs billed him RM15,000 to cover storage fees accumulated in a fortnight. Investigation showed the sultan had undervalued several of the cars he had imported in the past.

The Sultan of Selangor's first wife died following a long illness. The Sultan's second, much younger wife and an eighteen year old consort were acceptable under Muslim law, but before her death, the Sultana was outspoken in her disapproval of the whole arrangement. The Sultan spent a lot of time in England in order to be away from people who might disapprove of his non-Muslim behavior. He didn't fast during Ramadan and he drank alcohol. His son was married to an American and was reported to be a swinger, so the facade of Shah Alam being a Muslim community may crumble when the son becomes Sultan.

U.S. news and even international problems were overshadowed by the antics of the Sultan of Johore. He beat up a soccer coach! The Sultan of Johore had a history of violent behavior and his son, who was on a soccer team, carried on the tradition.

The trouble started when the son was suspended from the team for attacking an opposing team member. The Sultan retaliated by pulling the state's winning soccer team from an important match. This riled the people. The Sultan tried to force the coach to reinstate his son. When the coach refused, the Sultan (or his palace guards) beat him so badly he required medical attention. The coach went public and the people and the government stood behind him. The moral of the story is "Never mess with a winning soccer team!"

Parliament quickly voted to take away the Sultan's immunity even though the Council of Rulers opposed the bill. The other sultans didn't really approve of violent behavior but losing immunity meant investigation into financial dealings. We thought this would be a long drawn out affair but parliament didn't let public opinion cool off. By the time we left Malaysia, the sultans had lost a lot of their privileges. The government took away support for all but one residence, and had cut back on additional perks such as free storage of private planes at airports and police escorts for trips to town. This could not have happened five years ago when it was an act of sedition to question the rights of the sultans.

CAMPUS

1987-1989

The physical facilities on campus when we arrived could only be described as minimal. The campus had been built as a high school. Long masonry buildings were divided into cubicles for faculty, and the administration occupied a rabbit warren of rooms within rooms we later learned had been designed as living quarters for the high school faculty. A fence with a gate and guardhouse surrounded all the buildings. Students lived in hostels, apartment-like dormitories, also surrounded by a fence and guardhouse. The guards at the campus would send the students back to the hostels if they were not dressed properly or, in the case of the boys, needed a haircut. Guards also felt free to stop and search faculty cars.

Classrooms were cooled by fans, and in a bad rainstorm, water would come through the CLOSED, louvered windows in torrents. Noise from outdoors and the fans made it hard to teach a large class. The coolest temperature in two years was 73 degrees and that day the students were all complaining about the cold. The boys wore corduroys and lined jackets and the girls had on heavy sweaters. Students often dressed in warm clothing when the temperature dropped below 80 degrees.

Students on our campus were hardworking and polite but Malaysian schools follow the British system which stresses memorization, so courses that required reasoning skills were difficult for them. Teaching was a challenge not only because the students' reasoning and language skills needed improving, but many of the illustrations used in teaching mathematics meant nothing to them. Word problems often had to be explained. Poker hands, familiar to U.S. students, were a mystery and Richard had to devise other examples for teaching probability. We also had to be careful to explain the meaning of slang expressions and some of our quaint and curious customs. Richard made the mistake of mentioning "Groundhog Day" in class and never did manage to get the point across. When we thought about it, we decided that Groundhog Day doesn't make a whole lot of sense.

Books were loaned to the students, and after volunteering in the bookroom the first year, I took over as textbook coordinator after Emmy Wohlenberg left. The job was fascinating and frustrating. You would think having books available for the beginning of each semester would be easy. It wasn't and we Xeroxed a lot.

I learned a lot about the textbook business. Textbooks are expensive and after giving them to the students the first two years, Emmy convinced the Malaysians that loaning textbooks would work. She devised a system of numbering all the books and a computer program to keep track of which student had the book and how many semesters it had been used. The textbooks were chosen in Bloomington but as often as possible we tried to buy the Southeast Asian student edition. This would usually be paperback and much cheaper than a hardcover book. However, paperbacks have a shorter lifespan and are more vulnerable to the stresses caused by humidity. After three semesters' use we sold the books to the students at a discount. That policy not only helped the students but allowed us to purchase new books.

Loaning books to the students worked well and saved the program thousands of dollars. A system of fines and withholding

Administration building: F-Block.

registrations cut our book loss to under twenty-five books per semester, not a bad percentage with about seven thousand books in circulation. In 1989 the administration at ITM was considering providing each student with a selected set of books and loaning

110

him the rest. This would involve a different computer program than we had been using. The bookroom now has not only a computer but a telephone!

Because of our need to get maximum use from the books we bought, we saw a lot of Othmann, the bookbinder. For RM6, which is about US$2.40, he would restore even the most battered book to better-than-new condition. Never satisfied with just using glue, he painstakingly sewed the pages back together and if the cover was mutilated beyond repair, would create a new one. Sometimes one of the assortment of relatives who worked for him would drive him to campus in a minivan. More often he showed up alone on his motorbike and would load several dilapidated cardboard boxes full of books on the back. Every time I watched him start off toward Subang I had the nightmare vision of our textbooks strewn down the middle of the Federal Highway. Allah must have smiled on us because he and the books always made it safely.

Ann Dixon was my volunteer assistant and took over for me when we left. Richard and her husband, Bud, put in many hours helping us and we would not have survived without them. We also had help from several faculty wives and high school students for book intakes.

The frustration of working was compounded by the fact that Malaysians wanted everyone to be content and since saying "no" might cause unhappiness, it was a word never used. The code was: "yes, we could do that" meant "no" and would be followed in subsequent weeks by various elaborate but face saving excuses; "yes, we will do that next Monday" meant what you wanted would be done eventually, and "yes, Asman will do that now" meant your request would be taken care of as soon as possible.

Marilyn Moore said that teaching in Shah Alam was like working in an educational MASH unit and she was right. Ann Holden was the only expat secretary on campus. She worked for the provost, Roy Jumper, but always tried to be helpful to faculty. A few manual typewriters and computers were available for faculty use. There was also a Xerox machine and the lines of faculty were long, especially at exam time. We aren't complaining. The experience taught us learning doesn't depend on physical facilities or supplies available, but on interested teachers and enthusiastic students. We are proud of what we accomplished in Malaysia and of the students who represent the program at universities all over the U.S.

By 1991 the IU/MUCIA/ITM program was the only U.S. program in Malaysia. When we left in 1989, plans were on the drawing board for a multi-story, air-conditioned office building for faculty on the Shah Alam campus; when we left in 1993, the plans were still on the drawing board.

Attempts to follow an IU class schedule never succeeded. The problems involved in fitting a 15-week semester in and around deadlines in Bloomington, Indiana, and moveable feasts in Malaysia whose times are determined at the last minute by astrological readings, defy description. To avoid conflict with Hari Raya festivities the 1990 spring semester vacation had to be set for April 25, leaving only a week of classes before final exams. We had no quarrel with taking Malaysian holidays off, even when it meant making time up on a Saturday. After all, we were living in Malaysia and when in the U.S. the students would have to adjust to our holidays. We cheerfully exchanged greetings and were pleased when the students would wish us "Happy Christmas."

Classes were not scheduled during Friday afternoon prayer times and there were always students who wanted to be excused for daily prayers. The Malaysian staff had all the local government and religious holidays off and that meant days lost in terms of getting things accomplished. Exams were produced on "Big Bertha," a heavy duty Xerox machine, lovingly tended by Siti who, it turned out, had the only set of keys to the room inhabited by "Big Bertha."

One particular staff vacation day several faculty members were clustered outside the door wondering what to do about the exams that were locked inside. I pointed out the door hinges were on the outside and suggested someone handy with a screwdriver could easily remove the door. Everyone looked at me in horror. Such an obvious "American" solution to the problem wasn't even to be considered. As I recall, everybody involved postponed their exam one day. After all, our motto for survival was "never mind."

Siti was a delight to work with. She had learned that we like to tease and she gave back as much teasing as she endured. As "book lady" the Xerox jobs I asked for always needed to be ready yesterday, and she never let me down. She was patient with my problems in producing a workable master copy and in dealing with the temperamental Xerox machine used by faculty.

I would not have survived without the support of Kamariah—a wisp of a girl with haunting dark eyes and a beautiful smile. Of all the Malaysians I worked with, she was the one who had some real understanding of the basic differences between Asians and westerners and an appreciation of our need to accomplish specific goals within a limited time frame. Kamariah went to bat for me so many times I lost track but somehow, even if she couldn't solve a problem, she always managed to help me see it from an Asian perspective and would often show me the way around the roadblock.

▼

Scheduling exams for large groups never did work out too well on campus. The campus facilities were shared by a Texas program similar to ours. The first year, finals were all set up but through some glitch it turned out exams for students from both Texas and Indiana were scheduled in the same room at the same time. That was certainly a wild day but we eventually got everything all sorted out and all unoccupied faculty and administrators on campus were pressed into proctoring classrooms full of students.

Many of the regular tests were given at night in large lecture halls reserved ahead through PPP. PPP was the Center for Preparatory Studies and the Malaysian administrative unit sharing responsibility for the MUCIA program. A professor and students would arrive to find the room empty but locked, and someone would have to find a security guard with keys. One particularly frustrating evening Richard waited with his class while the guard went home and put on his uniform! At least it wasn't cold.

▼

Our effort to learn Bahasa Melayu gave us some insight into what it was like to attend a university in Malaysia. The main ITM campus, located atop one of the higher hills in Shah Alam, offered free classes to expats. Roberta Dees and I set out on foot one day to register and discovered that particular hill was higher than it looked. The elevators in the thirteen-story main building were out of order, which we later learned wasn't unusual, so in addition to the hill, we had eight flights of stairs to climb. By the time we found the language office we looked as if we had been standing out in the rain.

Our class, taught by three volunteer teachers, met three mornings a week. Lessons were not coordinated, with the result that we were given an average of fifty new words to learn at each

113

session. We were soon overwhelmed and can honestly say the experience was demoralizing.

Besides us, there was one other student in the class: Franck Ybert who was in Malaysia serving out his military obligation to the French government. Our friendship with Franck, which developed during the hours waiting for teachers who never came, was the one positive result of our efforts to learn Bahasa.

We did learn enough Bahasa during the two years to make ourselves understood for minimal communication. One problem with learning the language was that the Malaysians always wanted to practice English and would answer in English when we tried a Bahasa sentence.

Bahasa is a simple language but totally different from any we had tried to learn before. Past or future tenses are indicated by use of qualifying words. There is also no plural — instead, the word is repeated. Several English words have a Malaysian derivation. For example, orangutan is a combination of orang which means man and hutan which means jungle. The literal translation of orangutan is jungle man.

CAMPUS UPDATE

In May of 1991 the atmosphere on campus was strained. The Malaysian faculty and staff were still gracious and smiling but there was an undercurrent of resentment. This resentment was apparent off-campus too. Malaysia was a country in a hurry to progress. International investment had been encouraged. Experts from all over the world had been invited to help expand the infrastructure. MAS Airlines was kept flying by Australian pilots and British mechanics (who were asked to stay out of sight whenever dignitaries visited the hangers). In Shah Alam, Southeast Asia's largest stadium was being built by the Yugoslavians. The Japanese, the Chinese, and the Koreans had set up cooperative business ventures. Foreign tourists were everywhere. The 1990 Visit Malaysia Year had shown Malaysians they could charge top dollar for hotels and food. Prices for goods and services had doubled or tripled. Malaysians had begun to taste what they perceived of as the good life. They also thought they were losing control of their own country and losing jobs to foreigners. The Malaysian administration and faculty thought they could educate students without help from Americans and they wanted us gone as soon as possible. PPP had appointed "shadow coordinators" who met secretly to plan an agenda for the campus. Student services published an unauthorized handbook with ITM courses. Most significantly, PPP fired all the expat ESL faculty and began to hire Malaysians to teach English.

Herb Davis, who replaced Roy Jumper as Provost in 1991, initiated a self-study with Richard as associate provost in charge. The finished report provided an in-depth look at the strengths and weaknesses of the program. The success of our students at U.S. institutions was proof that, in spite of problems, the program could be counted as a success. However, the second two years in Malaysia was highly stressful for expat and local faculty. There was fault on both sides. The Provost and many of the expat faculty were unwilling to adapt to the local culture and the Malaysians retaliated by putting roadblocks in front of faculty and student projects.

The Provost hired me to work on campus publications and publicity. The first summer, I revised the Student Handbook with the help of Sidique, one of the advisors in Student Services. After it was printed, Sidique began working on an update but left for graduate school in the UK before the project was completed. His replacement produced the unauthorized version that was released in December 1991.

I made copies of all the preliminary NCA documents and all the final copies of the appendix. Commercial copying was expensive and was used only for the main body of the document. PPP allowed me to use the Xerox machine that had replaced "Big Bertha." It was a wonderful machine. Shortly after "Big Bertha" was replaced our bursar, Judy, was talking to Nasri, who was in charge in that office. He had thought "Bertha" was the name of an expat staff member who happened to be "big"! Judy explained that Americans often have names for machines and cars, etc. "Big Bertha" fit the old machine because she was much like a lumbering elephant. The new machine was sleek and very fast. Our resident poet, Kathleen Mullen, suggested "Tonya" as a pun on the fact that we depend on a ready supply of toner to make good copies. Advisors from Indianapolis had stressed that the self-study should call attention to problem areas "in the strongest possible terms." The three English Area faculty who proofread it had high praise for the layout and content. The narrative (97

115

pages with 308 pages of appendices), painted a picture of a strong program that had some problems that were in the process of being corrected and a few problems that we would have to live with because they were an outgrowth of cultural differences.

Richard headed the committee in charge of the 1991 summer recognition ceremony, and was grand marshall for all the awards ceremonies held while we were in Malaysia. I arranged to have photographs taken and made posters for awards ceremonies and other special events. The education editor of the *New Straits Times* wanted to do an article about our program but PPP prohibited publicity until a new program director arrived in 1993. Then stories about "MUSIA" began to appear.

Recognition ceremonies were always stressful. The Malaysians never did anything until the last minute. The provost's secretary often was typing the last words of the script only minutes before the start of the procession. By some miracle, it always went smoothly.

Physical facilities had improved in two years but new faculty were usually shocked at the condition of classrooms. The students worked hard and the ones who contacted us after transferring to the U.S. were amazed at the facilities available to them at American universities. In Shah Alam, the electricity was off frequently. The campus had copiers and computer labs but the machines were poorly maintained. By the second year the library did have a state of the art CD-ROM that would have been the envy of any major U.S. institution. For some reason the library was given unlimited funds.

I provided copy and photographs for an issue of *The Mucia Newsletter*. I also edited a newsletter called *Faculty Update* that was published twice a semester. Once a semester I wrote and edited *Spotlight*, a publication that focused on special campus research projects or programs. Richard designed the masthead for the first *Spotlight*. Tim Diemer did layout for subsequent issues and after he left, Rozhan, from the computer lab, was a collaborator in the project. I also edited and formatted a collection of faculty research papers that was published in 1992.

The *Spotlight* on the Internship Program was posted at the American Embassy! As a result, the Embassy applied for two of our student interns. Copies of the *Spotlight* along with a cover letter were mailed to over 200 companies in Malaysia and there was an overwhelming response.

One of the program's weaknesses was the faculty and staff turnover. Just when people were getting used to the job, they'd leave. Professors coming for one semester or a year hardly had time to adjust to the climate or the culture before they were making return travel plans. A secretary or book-

Richard and student at Recognition ceremonies.

keeper needed at least a semester to learn all the nuances of dealing with the PPP/ITM/Malaysian system. The Malaysian assistants to the provost, in charge of passports, visas, housing and car reimbursements, etc., were hardly given time to learn faculty names before being replaced.

One of the things the NCA report brought out was that Malaysia had made great leaps forward in terms of technology but had skipped intermediate steps in achieving progress. On

117

Richard and student at Recognition ceremonies.

campus we had all sorts of fancy gadgets but had trouble keeping them serviced. We also lacked a reasonable phone system, adequate typewriters and computers for faculty, simple audio-visual equipment, and an up-to-date card catalog in the library. Several coordinators mentioned that the library didn't have a copy of *Books in Print* but the library said they had a copy. Investigation revealed that the copy wasn't listed in the card catalog and most probably was not where it should have been on the shelves even if it had been listed.

The student body had changed in two years. More of our

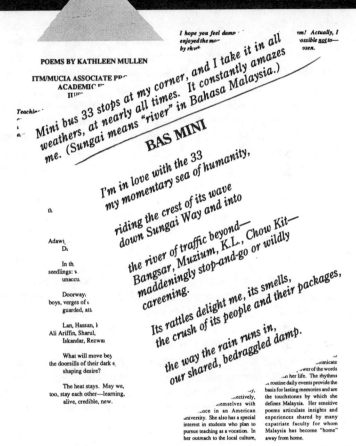

Spotlight

ITM/MUCIA - Indiana University Cooperative Program
No 3 March 1992

I hope you feel damp
enjoyed the mo
by rh...

rm! Actually, I
ossible not to—
osen.

POEMS BY KATHLEEN MULLEN

ITM/MUCIA ASSOCIATE PP...
ACADEMIC F...
IU/...

Teachin...

Mini bus 33 stops at my corner, and I take it in all weathers, at nearly all times. It constantly amazes me. (Sungai means "river" in Bahasa Malaysia.)

BAS MINI

I'm in love with the 33
my momentary sea of humanity,

riding the crest of its wave
down Sungai Way and into

the river of traffic beyond—
Bangsar, Muzium, K.L., Chow Kit—
maddeningly stop-and-go or wildly
careening.

Its rattles delight me, its smells,
the crush of its people and their packages,

the way the rain runs in,
our shared, bedraggled damp.

th

Adawi
D.

In th.
seedlings: ...
unaccu.

Doorway.
boys, verges of ...
guarded, att.

Lan, Hassan, ...
Ali Ariffin, Sharul,
Iskandar, Rezwa...

What will move be...
the doorsills of their dark ...
shaping desire?

The heat stays. May we,
too, stay each other—learning,
alive, credible, new.

...ectively,
...emselves with
...nce in an American
university. She also has a special
interest in students who plan to
pursue teaching as a vocation. In
her outreach to the local culture,

...unicate
...wer of the words
...n her life. The rhythms
...t routine daily events provide the
basis for lasting memories and are
the touchstones by which she
defines Malaysia. Her sensitive
poems articulate insights and
experiences shared by many
expatriate faculty for whom
Malaysia has become "home"
away from home.

students came from affluent or influential backgrounds. The program was no longer limited to disadvantaged students. When the son of the Deputy Minister from Penang received a certificate from our program, the presence of his family at the ceremony caused a stir. One of the PPP platform committee insisted he could no longer sit on the platform because that would put him above the Deputy Minister. Soft arm chairs were set in the front row of the auditorium and a special refreshment tent was set up outside to accommodate the dignitaries.

During the 1991 Christmas break PPP started a major remodelling job of the wing in F-Block that housed the Xerox machines and faculty computers. The people who had offices there were unceremoniously displaced. They returned to find all their belongings moved, and filing cabinets dumped over. What hadn't been moved was covered with plaster dust and debris! The remodelling was supposed to have been finished by January 6, as a pleasant surprise for the expat faculty. Instead, PPP sued the contractor because the job was so badly botched.

The "GRADE SCANDAL OF 1992" had long-term repercussions and severely damaged the program. Some grades were changed between the time they were turned in to the registrar in Shah Alam and their transmission to Bloomington. Unfortunately, the registrar was Malaysian. Whether she or one of her associates changed the grades was not the primary concern. The grades had lain, untended, in a folder on a desk in student services. Anyone could have tampered with the grade sheets. Ultimately, the registrar was held responsible and fired. MUCIA used this as leverage in bargaining for a new contract. A new registrar and a new head of student services, BOTH Americans, were hired without going through proper approval procedures. The hard-nosed stance back-fired. Relations between PPP and IU/MUCIA/ITM deteriorated. Time and energy were squandered in unproductive maneuvering and one-upmanship. Faculty morale plummeted.

Ultimately, sixteen grade tamperings for eleven students were confirmed! Three unauthorized grade changes occurred in the previous semester. Several universities refused to accept chemistry credits on ITM transcripts. MUCIA demanded that chemistry be returned to the IU transcript, but that did not happen.

There was enough blame for the grade mess to be shared by PPP, ITM, IU, and MUCIA. Primarily, the responsibility for the integrity of the transcripts rested with the Malaysian registrar, but the ultimate responsibility was with the registrar in Indianapolis.

▼

Speech Night 1991 was quite a show. The two students who won first and second place did very well. We also heard the worst speech we've ever sat through at one of these evenings. The young man's topic was "Beware of Rape" and he must have gotten his facts from a scandal sheet. He said, "In the U.S. a woman is raped every six minutes. That's ten times each hour or 240 rapes per day. So when you girls are in the U.S. remember that if you happen to be the only woman raped that day, you get it 240 times." We had been trying not to laugh at his speech, but when he came out with that we couldn't stop ourselves.

The entertainment while the judges deliberated was provided by a three piece band. Two of the band members were faculty and the group performed regularly in one of the local pubs. There was a drummer and the other two played electric guitars. The rock music wasn't what we would have chosen but the students loved it. The first thing one of the faculty performers did was take off his shirt!! We suspect the only reason the band was allowed to perform was that no one asked permission.

Speech Night 1992 was also memorable. The winner spoke excellent English and we suspect she had learned it before entering our program. The entertainment was extremely American and inappropriate for a Muslim student group. It started with a group doing the traditional Malaysian Candle Dance. The second solo performer brought down the house with his rendition of what must have been one of the Malaysian Top Ten popular songs. The third group did a modern dance that could have appeared on MTV at home. It was extremely seductive and sensual.

In 1994 HEP[15] declared that entertainment would no longer be allowed at Speech Nights!

In the summer of 1992 work on improvements to the physical plant was begun. A large, carpeted, air-conditioned lecture hall was added, new tile floor was installed in F-Block and, over the next ten-month period, buildings on the entire campus were painted. The large trees on campus were trimmed drastically and looked better once they grew back. Generally, the landscaping on the grounds was refurbished and improved.

---

[15]Office of Student Affairs. See glossary.

▼

The faculty routinely met with students about to leave for the U.S. The sessions were enlightening for both faculty and students. At the 1993 orientation, one boy asked if he should buy a gun when he got to the U.S.! We hope we discouraged him.

▼

In the spring of 1993, PPP announced an intake of mostly economics and business majors. The students were assigned ITM student numbers. By fall of 1993 PPP was openly admitting to having appointed "shadow coordinators" and their desire to take over the program.

▼

Exams for large classes were scheduled in the Dewan Besar (Great Hall). In the spring of 1993, the chemistry faculty arrived at 7:30 for an 8 a.m. exam. There were no chairs in the room. A little before 8:00 the PPP person in charge of scheduling rooms arrived and Ellen (the provost's secretary) learned that the Dewan Besar was being cleaned and the floors polished for Recognition Day and would not be available all week! This had happened before and by noon Ben, the registrar, had everything rescheduled for the rest of the week.

▼

Acquisition and distribution of textbooks continued to be a problem. Textbooks, still loaned to the students, often did not arrive in time for the beginning of the semester. When textbooks were available, a few students would get one from the bookstore and make copies for the rest of the class. Students and parents complained about not being given the cash book allowance that was part of their contract. In the fall of 1993, PPP started giving students a book allowance. With PPP's support, faculty outlawed Xerox copies, and purchasing a textbook became a requirement for each student.

▼

Bud Dixon's father had been a locksmith and, after reading an article in the January 30, 1993, *New Straits Times* about tools used for housebreaking, he bought some as a gag gift for his father's birthday. When the lock on Bud's office jammed he wished he'd kept the tools for himself. Richard was involved in the efforts to get the door open. They ended up using ordinary scissors to pry the door open after removing a strip of molding. The cleaning ladies watched the whole operation and thought it was pretty funny.

▼

In the spring of 1993, Richard was asked to teach a WordPerfect Seminar for faculty and staff. Several other faculty and I helped. It was supposed to be an experienced class but there were people who didn't know much about computers. Kim assured us ours went more smoothly than the previous one but we felt sorry for the people who could have moved through the entire lesson in one session. In addition to having novices in the class, we also had problems with some of the machines.

▼

The painters finally made it to Richard's office about the middle of February. We did all we could to protect things we cared about because we had seen the disaster they had made in other offices. In spite of all our precautions, they made a terrible mess. If we stood far enough back and squinted, the new paint was an improvement but the floor, desk, and chairs were paint-splattered. They used red trim on the exteriors of the classroom buildings but for some reason chose aqua for F-Block. Yuk!! The bathroom on our floor was an unspeakable mess. They poured paint down the sink drain and clogged it, and the toilet seat was bumpy with large globs of dried paint.

"Rank Hath Its Privileges!" To prepare for painting the administrative offices, workmen brought in yards of plastic drop cloths and didn't make the mess they made elsewhere on campus. The bathroom was even pristine. PPP did complain about the paint spots on the new tile in F-Block and workmen spent hours scraping dried paint.

▼

Math Day was a success. The students had arranged for a room full of computers programmed with games to play. There were also standard board games available. Walt Sadler gave a talk and after lunch there was a treasure hunt. Richard's team won second place and each of the winning team members was given a plaque. Richard supplied some of the questions for the problem solving contest. The few students who tried, spent most of the day working problems. Richard sat on the floor to play congkak, one of the local games, and the next day his hips were so sore he could hardly move. His ankles were sore, too, since the treasure hunt involved a lot of running around looking for clues. He was on a team with two girls in their first semester of the academic program. He was sure they were surprised he could keep up with them.

TRAVEL IN MALAYSIA

Car travel was a good way for us to really see the country, but for the ordinary tourist, left hand driving and time limitations make package tours much more reasonable. The tour books put out for the 1990 "Visit Malaysia Year" listed a variety of affordable tours, and reading through it made us want to return. We'd like to tell you about some of the places we visited.

MALACCA

The first 75-80 miles south from KL was four-lane highway as good as any interstate in the U.S. except for animals on the road, people walking across it, and very slow trucks going up some of the hills. The last 15-20 miles of local two-lane highway was crowded with pedestrians, livestock, bicycles, motorcycles, and everything else you can imagine. After looking at two Chinese Hotels, we checked into the Merlin. Later we learned that Chinese-run hotels were usually clean and we could have been comfortable in one. Evening is a good time to climb the hill in the center of town. The night air is cool and the view of town and harbor haunting in the moonlight. The town has grown around Christ Church, a museum which is a reproduction of the sultan's palace, the historical ruins of St. Paul's Church, the Dutch Stadthuys[16], and the city gate.

In Malacca we had our first experience with trishaws, three-wheeled cabs with either a bicycle or motorcycle in front, which replaced the rickshaw in most of Asia. We didn't ride in these often because we felt vulnerable to larger vehicles and sorry for how hard the driver had to work in the heat. By western standards we are tall and slender but our combined weight was two or three times that of a Malaysian man.

While we were eating lunch at the Shah's Beach Resort we were approached by a television crew videotaping a promotional ad. We agreed to be in it. They rehearsed us and after three takes, were satisfied. In exchange for our efforts we were given T-shirts, post cards, and a sketch of Malacca.

Malacca Woodworks and Malacca Handicrafts sell rosewood

---

[16]Dutch word meaning "statehouse." See glossary.

Riverfront in Malacca.

furniture and would make furniture from our own design. Stores selling furniture and antiques all along Jalan Hang Jebat are almost museums, and we spent hours admiring the wares and bargaining.

Portuguese Square, surrounded by an assortment of restaurants, was the venue for ethnic dance programs every Saturday night.

We attended Christ Church—the oldest Anglican church in Malaysia. It was built in the early 1600s as a Roman Catholic (Portuguese) church, became Protestant when the Dutch took over, and then Anglican under the British. The red exterior matched other buildings around the historic square and the interior was almost puritan in severity. Each ceiling beam was made from an entire tree. The service was LONG.

A north/south coast road, all two-lane with heavy traffic, was a slower route between Shah Alam and Malacca. The scenery included oil palm, coconut, and rubber plantations, with occasional glimpses of sea shore. Port Dickson, a resort town, and Morib, a little further north with a poorly maintained public beach, provided rest stops along the way.

We made many trips to Malacca and came to know it almost as well as Shah Alam. Declared the Historical Capital of Malaysia in 1989, it was undergoing a major facelift: a sound and light show was a big attraction, Christ Church had been renovated and the

Typical entrance to Malaccan house.

Stadthuys was being worked on, and there were plans to restore St. Paul's Church. We developed a tour for family and friends who visited us, making sure to include the river trip and a stop at the park with reproductions of typical Malaysian houses from each state.

TAMAN NEGARA

To protect the environment, Taman Negara, the national park in the center of the country, restricts the number of visitors. Located deep in the jungle, the park is accessible only by boat. We treasure the experience but this was definitely not a relaxing, luxurious four days. In 1989 the park was privatized which resulted in improved cabins and food. It is still not a trip to be undertaken by anyone who lacks a spirit of adventure.

Aziz took us to the Taman Negara office in KL so that he could have the use of our car while we were gone. We assembled with six other hardy souls. After a long wait Richard and I and two girls were sent on our way in an air-conditioned taxi. I don't know anywhere else we would take a 135-mile trip in a taxi, but that isn't unusual in Malaysia. We paid US$5.60 per person and definitely had the better ride. The other four made the journey in a run-down van. The two girls were English and had flown from

London the day before. Going directly into the jungle was brave or foolish, depending on your point of view.

We ate lunch at the Kuala Tembeling boat-landing canteen and the boat left promptly at 2 p.m. as scheduled. It was about five feet wide, 50 to 60 feet long, and had a sheet-metal awning running the full length. There were thirteen passengers and a crew of two. In addition to our luggage it carried a load of supplies for the restaurants. It was low in the water—6 to 8 inches to spare—and we sat on the bottom with our legs straight out in front of us—not too comfortable a position for a three hour trip—but at least it was cool once we were moving.

Heavy jungle lined the river all the way with occasional villages or individual houses along the banks. The vegetation was absorbing, but we saw no wildlife to speak of. We arrived sooner than expected because the river was full (and muddy) from rains upstream. When the water level is low there are problems with sandbars and shallows.

With simple cots, mosquito nets over the beds, a shower with no shower head, etc., our "chalet" was several notches below summer camp. We asked about moving to one of the new cottages we thought looked better, and the second day we changed to a nicer looking cabin with real beds, a tile bath with shower that worked, more space and a quieter ceiling fan. On the other hand, it was not really above summer camp standards. There was only one sheet on each bed, no hot water, some of the floor boards sagged so much we were afraid to step on them, and the layer of dirt on the mosquito net was thick enough to prevent air circulation. However, we did fine under them and needed the blanket that was provided. It was cool at night and was still pleasantly cool at mid-morning.

We ate dinner in the lesser of the two restaurants. When our first and second selections from the menu were unavailable we asked the waiter what they had, which was very little, and chose from that. It wasn't gourmet but was perfectly acceptable.

A grocery store housed in a small, ramshackle building near the cabins stocked minimal provisions for hiking and a limited supply of soft drinks. A very tame deer stood watch at the doorway and allowed us to pet him. We also saw a beautiful pair of black and white birds. A family of tapirs wandered behind our cabin one night. There were a lot of different birds singing every morning—it must be a bird watcher's paradise.

We went for a 15-minute hike to a sandy beach on the riverside where people swim. We looped back a different way that was supposed to take thirty minutes, but altogether we took over two hours. We forded two streams and there were very steep climbs up and down the hills.

The jungle is incredible. The lushness and density of the vegetation is beyond description, and we felt shut in even on a well cleared trail.

Bukit Terisek was supposed to be a 45-minute climb but took us two and a half hours round trip. It was a steep, rocky trail and the jungle is hot, humid, and airless. We sweat unbelievably. On the way up we saw a monitor lizard about three feet long near the path. He was just walking along, searching the ground with his tongue, and seemed completely unconcerned about our being near. At the top from the first view point we looked east across the Tembeling River to the hills on the other side. From the second view point we could see Gunung Tahan, the highest mountain (7175 feet) in peninsular Malaysia, in addition to several other tall mountains, a large limestone monolith, and a panorama of the Tahan-Tembeling valley between the two rivers.

The trails were well-maintained and basically rubbish-free. Even though there seemed to be a lot of people around, we didn't meet many on the trails. We had the feeling of being in the wilderness alone. The mountains in the park were low by Rocky Mountain standards, but the heat would make climbing any higher ones an ordeal.

The park can be explored on foot or by boat. We spent two days on combined boat/hiking tours. On the first half-hour boat trip we saw a very large monitor lizard and several beautiful kingfishers. We were puzzled by a loud sound like a fire siren or air raid alarm that would go on for a long time and then suddenly stop. Our guide said it was cicadas. If so, the sound seemed much louder than we were used to, perhaps because of the quiet of the jungle far from the noises of civilization.

After docking we hiked another half hour upriver to cascades where we stayed for about two and a half hours, climbing on the rocks and dangling our feet in the water. We spent a lot of time sitting and looking at the cascades. It was beautiful and peaceful. In that setting the lunch of cold fried rice with a fried egg, also cold, and a slice of cucumber on top was a feast.

We enjoyed watching the guides play on the rocks and in the water. We guessed their ages to be about nineteen but Malays generally look young to us. They were agile on the rocks, and at home in the water. The current was strong but didn't bother them a bit. There was enough detergent foam at the quiet parts of the pool for them to wash their hair; it was sad to see the polluted water. Inhabitants used the river as a wash basin: we saw one woman brushing her teeth, lots of families bathing, and some shampooing. We assumed the river was also their toilet.

On the trip downstream the guides turned the engine off, allowing us to watch the birds and butterflies and listen to the sounds of the jungle as the boat drifted along.

A second boat ride to Kuala Trengganu also took about half an hour. We went up seven rapids and got splashed quite a bit. There we went hiking for an hour to another hide[17]. (The day before we had walked to a hide about five minutes from our cabin.) There were several hides throughout the park but animals usually only visit the salt licks around them at night. We had been fortunate to see a giant monitor lizard and a family of tapirs. This hide was considerably larger and had six bunks and a bathroom for people to stay overnight. After inspecting the condition of the bunks and the pillows, we knew our decision not to stay overnight had been wise.

While we were hiking our guides had gone fishing. They caught two fish, one 12-15 inches long and the other 20 inches or so. Our guidebook said carp and catfish were plentiful in these waters, and these looked like carp.

The ride back splashed us even more than going up but was fun. Steering the boats up and down the river and through the rapids was second nature to the guides. They knew where all the rocks and fallen trees were. Passengers sometimes had to get out and wade for a while when the river was low. We doubted any of these young men knew how to drive a car, but they certainly knew how to handle a boat.

Leeches, a problem for most hikers in the park, did not bother us much. The first day we each had one on the outside of our shoes. Altogether we had a total of five attach themselves to our shoes or socks but none managed to connect with skin. A leech is difficult to remove and its bite leaves a circular sore about an eighth of an inch in diameter, which bleeds for a long time.

Our clothes and sneakers suffered a great deal with all the

[17]A small, enclosed shelter often built on stilts, offering shelter to humans wishing to observe animals in their native habitat. Some have primitive bed and toilet facilities. See glossary.

hiking and mud. It rained every day—either late afternoon or at night—and the trails never really dried in between.

The park has two restaurants. The one we ate in the first night offered a standard limited menu of three Malaysian noodle dishes, fried rice, chop suey, and noodle soup for lunch and dinner. American and Continental breakfasts were available in addition to some Malaysian dishes such as fish curry. The second restaurant was more elegant and catered to tour groups, offering a similar breakfast with a set Malaysian lunch and dinner each day. The one dinner we ate there included curried chicken, omelet, sardines, French fries, mixed vegetables with chicken livers, and rice with fruit for dessert and tea or coffee to drink. It was delicious but since the meal wasn't served until 7:30 p.m. it was too much to eat and digest before going to bed. We brought boxed fruit drinks, oranges, and apples from home and had them with lunch and in the evenings.

An enthusiastic hiker could spend several weeks in the park. Guides and camping equipment are available for hire and camp sites in the jungle are strategically placed. In four days we hiked only a few of the trails and the two boat rides gave us a small taste of life on the river. Some trails had more leeches than others, and several hikers we talked with had given up a trek because their shoes had been covered with leeches within a few minutes.

We skipped the bat cave. The guidebook for the park said the cave was dark and narrow and in places we would be crawling on hands and knees through several inches of bat guano. Evidently the book's description was accurate and because of all the rain, there were places where the water was knee deep. It was interesting to hear about but we know we made the right choice to leave that off our itinerary.

We enjoyed our stay in spite of the primitive lodging and cold showers. The jungle sounds—particularly the variety of bird calls—were mesmerizing and we had the added bonus of seeing some wildlife. Our guides told us most animals and birds stay deep in the jungle to avoid contact with humans.

We saw more wildlife going down-river than we had seen on the trip in. The trip back to KL in a non-air-conditioned van was hair-raising. The driver drove Malaysian style—about 70 mph on a poor two-lane highway, passing on hills and curves with no regard for the no-passing zones. We were relieved when we got to KL. Aziz was waiting for us with the car in seemingly good repair although he had put over 550 miles on it in four and a half days.

We should have known better than to leave our car in the care of a 21-year-old Malaysian maniacal driver!

By 1993 new lodging facilities at the park provided visitors with modern comforts, blended well with the environment and, according to friends who stayed there, were clean and well maintained. The quality of the food had also improved. The privatized management of the park was making an effort to maintain the wilderness while at the same time providing a sheltered environment for visitors.

CRAB ISLAND

Crab Island—Pulau[18] Ketam—is reached by a ferry that leaves from Port Klang. In exchange for 30 sen the owners of sampans, unseaworthy looking flat-bottomed boats, will row the short distance from the pier to the ferry. The ferry winds through islands of mangrove swamps for a little over an hour. Crab Island is just as advertised—a village built on stilts.

We were there at low tide and we understood why it is not on the list of recommended sights for tourists. The amount of refuse is unbelievable. Malaysians have a relaxed attitude toward trash. The possibility the country will eventually be covered with pink plastic bags is increased by the scarcity of trash cans, and people seem to think trash thrown in the water will disappear.

The owner of the restaurant where we ate said the population of the island, mostly fishermen, was 20,000. The large collection of shacks connected with wooden boardwalks includes a school, a temple, a hospital, a snooker parlor and a theater. The natives ride around on bicycles so we were in danger of being run down or bumped off into the muck.

The delicious fresh fish or crab dinners available at any of the restaurants are well worth the investment of time getting there and back.

The boatman who took us back to the ferry wore a costume similar to the gondola owners in Venice!

PULAU PANGKOR LAUT

Some of the most beautiful islands in the world are located off Malaysian coasts. Parts of the movie *South Pacific* were filmed

---

[18]Malaysian word meaning "island." See glossary.

on Pulau Tioman. If lying on the beach, snorkeling, scuba diving, or a wide assortment of other water sports are your idea of a perfect vacation, you can experience paradise on the islands. The South China Sea, off the east coast, is bathwater temperature, whereas the Indian Ocean and the Straits of Malacca on the west coast are slightly cooler.

Pulau Pangkor Laut Resort, off the northwest coast, offers a quiet, Malaysian-style vacation. The drive up the coast to Lumut to get the ferry was one of our many adventures with the Malaysian highway and map system.

At Telok Intan we bought gas, after being detoured by a long Chinese funeral parade with at least three fairly large school bands, and asked about the route. We had to backtrack about five miles to find an unpaved private side road, through a company town and a palm oil plantation, leading to the ferry landing. Nearby, a large bridge under construction was far from finished. On the other side of the river we drove a long way on poor gravel road through oil palm groves. At one point we had to retrieve a piece of the car's tailpipe that had been shaken loose and were relieved to finally find a highway intended someday to connect with the bridge. It was new and good and had little traffic, but about 20 km later it suddenly ended and we were on the worst road we had seen in Malaysia, with large potholes and sections where paving had completely disintegrated.

We got to Lumut just in time to catch the 2 p.m. ferry. It took a little under an hour to get to the PanSea Resort on the island. We were greeted by a girl in a sarong who hung leis around our necks and gave us a fruit juice drink. There was also a small combo playing Hawaiian music.

Our second day started out with rain. Travel hint: never leave home without a book to read on rainy days or when the plane, train, or bus is delayed. After lunch we took the boat around to Emerald Bay on the west side of the island. It is a truly beautiful white-sand beach lined with palms. We swam and lay in the sun (and the shade after a while). We walked back, up and over the hill in the center of the island. Dinner was a poolside barbeque and very good. The cooks had been trained in France and the food was closer to an international buffet than a barbeque.

Back on the mainland we studied the map carefully with the intention of finding the main highway south to KL. We never did find the highway. We eventually figured out where we were but not how we got there. At one point the road took us across a river using a one-lane railroad bridge. I don't think we had ever driven across a railroad bridge before.

KUANTAN

Resorts on the east coast attract European and Australian tourists to Malaysia. Palm tree lined, white sand beaches and warm waters of the south China Sea offer visitors picture postcard vacations varying from thatch huts on the beach to Club Med luxury. "It rains on the just and the unjust" is surely true on the east coast, and during monsoon season even the Club Med Resort is uninhabitable.

Kuantan is a bustling city but, aside from scheduled folk festivals, hasn't much to recommend it. Outside of town are numerous cave temples. The one we visited has 235 steep steps to the mouth of the cave and many more up and down once we were inside. The trails are slippery with bat guano produced by thousands of bats hanging from the ceiling. The cave, a Buddhist shrine with several paintings and altars, also has a 33-foot reclining Buddha carved into the rock. A drive north provides a look at kampungs and fishing villages untouched by modern life.

A piece of hand-drawn batik, now framed and hanging on our bedroom wall, came from Kuantan. The artist, who works in a few shacks in the middle of a cane field, drew the bunga raya (hibiscus—the Malaysian national flower) and butterfly design and dyed the piece while we watched.

At a rest stop on the way to Kuantan I missed a step and did a belly flop, resulting in loss of dignity and broken sunglasses but no broken bones. We stopped in Maran for something to drink and a kind man in the eyeglass shop there managed a temporary repair with a rubber band. Being without sunglasses in the tropics is disaster so I appreciated his efforts.

On returning home we called "Jumbo" who took us to an optician in Klang. It required several tries to get the new glasses tinted dark enough because the technician thought I was going to wear them indoors as well as outdoors.

IPOH

The road between KL and Ipoh was better than the one we were on going to Pangkor Laut, but traffic was extremely heavy

Mosque at Kuala Kangsar.

for a two-lane highway. Finding this road on the way home from Lumut would not have improved our trip much.

Our walking tour of Ipoh included the memorial clock tower, the main mosque, the new and old post office, and the railway station. Ipoh has the reputation for being a clean town and on the

Restored sultan's palace from the 1800s.

main street they were in the process of converting open drains into a closed, underground system covered by sidewalks.

A small Japanese garden is an island of tranquility in contrast to the large city park crowded with family gatherings. Our guidebook listed the park as the site of the city's only surviving ipoh tree. Although the city is named for the tree, we never found it and have no idea what an ipoh tree looks like.

Our trip to Ipoh was near the Christmas season. As in Shah Alam, PJ, and KL, stores and restaurants were playing Christmas music. Traditional decorations, including artificial snow which looked peculiar on tropical plants, were everywhere. We decided our bodies must have acclimated more than we realized because even with the room unit turned off, enough cold air seeped in to make us wish we had brought sweaters. We had no trouble imagining the snow draped on the palm trees was real!

Ipoh, surrounded by limestone monoliths similar to those near KL where Batu Cave is found, has many ornately-decorated cave temples nearby. Most have large turtle ponds that look as if they have never been cleaned, but evidently turtles thrive on algae. In a cave temple north of town we finally found the golden Buddhas I'd mistakenly thought would be at Batu caves.

Kuala Kangsar, west of Ipoh, is the capital of Perak state. A four-lane, limited-access highway has been carved through the mountains. It will eventually be extended to connect KL with Butterworth, but at that time only went from Ipoh to Taiping.

Begun in 1913, the Kuala Kangsar mosque is built from red, green, and black marble brought from Italy. The large gold dome, slender minarets, and red glass windows combined with the marble makes it one of the most beautiful mosques we saw in Asia. An old man who spoke excellent English told us about the mosque and asked questions about the students studying in the Indiana program. It is unusual for a woman to be allowed inside the main part of a mosque but he invited me in because I was modestly dressed. The Perak state museum is housed in an intricately carved and delicately decorated wooden palace that was the home of past sultans. Nearby is the splendid new palace, where the current sultan and his family live. It is not open to the public.

Ipoh, a town made wealthy from tin mining, has many large, stately homes. The British colonial influence is evident in the buildings with thick masonry walls and large porches to take advantage of the shade and breezes. They contrast with the carved wood openwork of Malay structures. There are also many "temporary" wooden buildings left over from the war years, one of which is the main city hospital.

EAST MALAYSIA

Tales of "wild men" and headhunters are part of the myth and reality woven into the historical fabric of the Island of Borneo. Divided into four parts, the largest is Kalimantan, belonging to Indonesia, and the smallest is the independent, oil-rich sultanate of Brunei. The remaining two, Sarawak and Sabah, make up East Malaysia and are altogether different from peninsular Malaysia. In fact, we had to go through passport control in both Sabah and Sarawak! The officer in Sarawak kept our white immigration cards and we were not given new ones when we returned to peninsular Malaysia. In May, when we traveled to Sumatra, the officer at the Subang airport gave us a stern lecture since the card is to be kept with the passport at all times and turned in when leaving the country. We felt we had no control over its having been taken away from us and took the lecture as another indication that the two parts of Malaysia don't communicate.

In East Malaysia there are few roads, and those outside the towns often are not paved. Travel is mostly by boat or plane. The terrain is mountainous and the jungle endangered due to years of indiscriminate logging. From the air we could see rivers brown with topsoil runoff and if logging is not controlled, the jungle will soon be destroyed.

Kuching is a busy market town and has the best museum we visited in Asia. From Kuching we flew to Miri where we changed to river transport that took us almost 200 miles into the jungle. The boat ride was long but we were fascinated with the river traffic and the number of logs we could see floating downriver. Boats, the lifeline for villages along the way, carry food and provisions from Miri.

The Mulu Park guesthouse was primitive but clean. A generator provided electricity for lights and a fan in our rooms from dusk until bedtime. The people in charge were from several different tribes but all spoke English. The cook provided excellent meals and picnic lunches.

We explored two caves during the two days we were there and came back each day covered with mud and bat guano! The low water level prevented boats from going very far. We had almost two hours of level hiking on poor, muddy jungle trails before we reached Deer Cave. We crossed several streams and all but one had a log footbridge; for that one we took off our shoes and socks and waded.

When we got to the cave entrance, we ate a sandwich snack. A concrete sidewalk winds through a large chamber where the river flows through the mountain. Enormous openings on each side of the mountain provide light, keeping us within sight of one end or the other and therefore never in total darkness. Halfway through, the sidewalk ends and a ladder provides access to the bottom of the cave. In a few places there were ropes to pull up or rappel down, and we crossed the stream several times. It took us about an hour, climbing up and down over huge boulders, to work our way on to the other entrance. There we rested, ate lunch, and enjoyed the cool breeze coming out of the cave before retracing our route.

As we emerged from the cave entrance, it started to rain. The muddy trail quickly turned into a quagmire and by the time we got back to the guesthouse, we were a mess. We washed ourselves, clothes and all, in the river before leaving the dock.

At a native village we were met by the chief who wore only a loincloth. The women wore sarongs from the waist down and their earlobes were stretched by wearing large, heavy earrings. The children were filthy and covered with terrible sores. After seeing a real longhouse we were glad we had opted to sleep in the guesthouse. A longhouse opened to sleep tourists would surely be in better shape, but there was a limit to how native we wanted to be.

Added in 1993: a modern hotel and an airport, which now provides access to the park. Only time will tell whether the jungle will withstand the onslaught of tourists.

Mount Kinabalu, in Sabah, is 13,455 feet high and is Southeast Asia's highest mountain. It was disappointing not to climb it but since we had not fully recovered from Nepal, we were content to look. We only saw the mountain in the early morning when it dominates the rugged landscape. During the rainy season it is shrouded in clouds for most of the day.

Sandakan was almost completely destroyed by the Japanese as part of the "scorched earth" policy, and then finished off by the Allies. There are no old buildings in town. One of the Japanese

Richard and Maria at Buddhist temple in Sandakan.

death marches started here, and from what we have seen of the jungle, it is easy to understand why only six survived. Our guide was from one of the headhunter tribes but assured us he didn't practice.

Nearby, an orangutan sanctuary cares for orphans and in four or five years rehabilitates them to jungle life. The orangutan are the "wild men of Borneo." They are playful and cute but strong and heavy and tend to bite. Richard came away with bruises from "love bites." They were muddy from playing in the water and soon cleaned themselves off on our clothes. The sanctuary also has a baby elephant and one of the few Sumatran white Rhinos left in the world.

Sabah is an island paradise for snorkeling and scuba diving. The reefs aren't as spectacular as the Great Barrier Reef in Australia, but are still beautiful.

We learned Muslims bury their dead without a coffin. The body is wrapped in a shroud and buried head down at a 45° angle. Two stakes are placed at an angle in the ground, one pointed toward the head and one toward the feet. When the wooden stakes have decayed, the plot can be used for a new burial.

Maps in Malaysia are a "controlled substance" and we had to sign for those we bought at the surveyor's office. If Sarawak is invaded, our names will be on the list of suspects.

We were served baked beans each morning with our eggs and toast. Baked beans on toast must be considered a delicacy in Asia; it is an item on most breakfast menus.

TRAVEL IN MALAYSIA UPDATE

The second time around we traveled less by car simply because driving was unpleasant. Houseguests were treated to the standard tour of the Klang Valley and a day or two in Malacca as time permitted. Each time we tried to add something new to the tour. In Malacca, we saw the finished Stadthuys Museum for the first time with Sue and Jeanette Gustat. When Richard's cousin Rachel came for a long weekend, we finally found the Thean Hou Temple in KL.

Sue and Jeanette Gustat in our house in PJ.

140

The Agricultural Park in Shah Alam had developed into a successful tourist attraction. This park opened in 1989 before we left but closed within a week because of the inadequate facilities. The gardens were beautiful and the rice paddies produced enough harvest to pay for maintaining the park. One of the more ambitious displays was an All Season House. An Englishman was in charge of regulating the environment to trigger the change of seasons. The Sultan of Selangor wanted the seasons to match those in Australia. In June of 1991, he asked for an early, hard winter. They succeeded in causing an early snow but the winter was too severe and several of the trees and shrubs died. Visitors viewed the changes by walking through a glass tunnel, and therefore did not experience the temperature change. The King visited and was allowed inside to get the full impact. They have also succeeded in getting trees to produce beautiful fall colors. The park has become so popular with local people it has had to close several times since to expand facilities and widen roads.

My cousin Charles visited Malaysia soon after we arrived in 1991. Charles, a very adventurous traveller, stayed in US$4 a night hotels in Indonesia and in KL managed to find a hotel for under US$10 a night. We could not offer him bed and board because we were still in the Holiday Inn. He was interested in trying the local food so we took him to Lotus, an Indian banana leaf place, and Titian Mas (Golden Bridge), a Malaysian restaurant on the lake. Then, for contrast, we took him to The Sails, at the Genting Highlands Resort. We couldn't walk around the lake because it was pouring so the three of us explored a Chinese Temple. The custodians of the temple evidently thought no one would be out in that horrible weather because when we got down (the tower had more steps than Batu Cave) we found the door locked! It wasn't a very good lock or we'd still be there!

We spent the first August vacation settling into our house. For recreation we planned several day trips with Phil and Dooie Gillett to explore the area around KL. The first adventure was a drive to Nutan Lipur Kanching, a beautiful waterfall (more like what we call a cascade). Because of the rain we had a muddy hike getting to it. The road was pretty bad and we finally gave up and parked because we didn't want to get stuck. The mud was so sticky that we would have lost our shoes if they hadn't been tied on firmly. There was a trail beside the cascade but we decided against climbing to the top. We came across several orang asli settlements in our search for the falls, southeast of KL on roads with hardly any traffic. The next stop was Semenyih Dam. It had a breathtaking view. We stopped at the Taman Rekreasi Sungai Tekala (Tekala River Recreation Park) and hiked up to the cascade there. The park was poorly maintained, which was sad because it would take so little effort to keep it beautiful. We watched a family enjoying one of the shallow pools in the river while the mother and oldest daughter washed clothes on a rock. We thought it was a quaintly primitive sight. When we came back from our hike they were assembled in the parking lot, and got into a very NEW van and drove away!

Another special outing was a night boat ride to see the fireflies. Their synchronized flashing was a lovely sight. They were attracted only to certain kinds of trees so clustered together in trees all along the river. It looked like Christmas time on Michigan Avenue in Chicago.

▼

Friends from Kansas, Joan and Paul Shull, visited us in October 1991. We took them to Jeruntut where we stayed in the government resthouse. The Chinese-style motel had air-conditioned rooms, was relatively clean, but badly needed a paint job. We made contact with Steven Ng and he took us to an orang asli settlement about an hour's drive into the jungle. We were in a van along with four of Steven's friends or relatives plus one child. On the way into the jungle, we stopped at the village store to buy sweets for the children and cigarettes for the men. The last few miles was on dirt road. We sat on mats on the floor of the main hut and bargained for carvings with the whole village looking on. Joan and Paul bought three medium-sized carvings and a stringed musical instrument; we bought a totem-like carving with five figures that stands about four feet tall. It started raining shortly after we arrived at the village and by the time we left was dark, so we gave up on going to visit the second village. We'd run out of money anyway! On the way back we got stuck in the mud but Richard and the two young men who were with us pushed us out. We ate in village restaurants along the way to and from PJ and found an open air Thai stall in Jeruntut for our evening meal. We took a different way back over the mountain. The road was more winding but at least there was less traffic. We stopped at the orang asli museum. Joan and Paul thought the satay we had for supper was delicious but they weren't enthusiastic about the ais kecong we had for dessert.

▼

When Franck Ybert visited us we took a day to drive out to Klang. We found the istana (palace) and a mosque we had never seen before. After lunch we went to the 19th century capital of Selangor. The town was gone but there was a mausoleum for sultans on a high hill with a good view of the straits, another mosque and another istana that was in the process of being restored.

▼

Richard had no classes on Wednesday during the 1993 spring semester so on March 3 we took a day trip to Fraser's Hill. The expressway was open past where we had to get off onto two-lane highways so the traffic wasn't bad. The last part of the trip was on a winding, narrow road that was one-way up on odd hours and one-way down on even hours. We had to wait about forty-five minutes to go up since the trip to that point took less time than we expected. The older buildings at the top were charming and it was cool. A new golf course and club house were being built and the silt runoff was clogging what used to be a lovely swimming area at the base of a waterfall. So far the new condos that have been built were fairly inconspicuous but we could see Fraser's Hill would soon be over-developed. A lot of the large estates were owned by corporations and some were better cared for than others. We had an excellent lunch at a restaurant in one of the old British buildings.

TRAVEL OUTSIDE MALAYSIA: 1987-1989

OVERVIEW

In deciding to accept the assignment in Malaysia, we felt that one of the attractions was the opportunity to travel in Southeast Asia. Including Malaysia, we visited fifteen countries in two years. Richard carried a teaching overload the first spring so only taught half time the summer of 1988. That allowed us a large block of free time between May and August to visit five countries: Thailand, Singapore, China, Australia, and New Zealand. After satisfying the residency requirement keeping us in Malaysia for all except fourteen days of the first five months we were there, we vacationed in Hong Kong, Burma, India, Nepal, Sumatra, and East Malaysia. Our sons, Michael and John, spent Christmas of 1987 with us and in addition to sightseeing in Malaysia, we all went to Australia. On our return trip home to the U.S. at the end of our Malaysian assignment in July 1989, we saw a little of Germany, Belgium, Luxembourg, and The Netherlands.

During those two years we were up before the sun more times than in all our accumulated years before that. Airline and train schedules governed our itineraries, and our willingness to travel in the middle of the night enabled us to cover a lot of territory.

Protecting ourselves from tetanus, typhoid, cholera, and malaria was important, so we made regular visits to the Chief Medical Officer at Subang Hospital since he was in charge of dispensing shots and pills. On one of our first visits, the cashier looked at our bill and said, "Oh, I see you're going overseas?" Richard's first thought was, "But, we ARE overseas!"

In each country we bought stamps for our collection. Our increased awareness of history and geography has also broadened our appreciation of the collection. Since returning to the U.S., Richard has spent most of his spare time cataloging stamps.

We learned a lot about planning trips and considered opening a travel agency. We spent an amazing amount of time in airports and getting to and from them. Singapore and Hong Kong are hubs for Southeast Asia. We lost count of how many times we made connections in Singapore and began to feel about that airport the way we feel about Atlanta or O'Hare.

Failure to factor in the International Date Line can cause havoc with the best laid plans. It's hard to believe, but not all travel agents know about the IDL! Package tours often promise five countries in as many days but an experienced traveler knows he will only see the route between the airport and the hotel in each place. We often planned our own itinerary and had our travel agent arrange tours in each city. We didn't insist on first class hotels, but opted for clean with no frills because we spent most of our time sightseeing. In the next chapters we will take you on an armchair tour of Southeast Asia and the South Pacific.

BURMA

March 19,1988—March 24,1988

Rangoon, Burma, reached through the gateway city of Bangkok, Thailand, is in a time zone 1-1/2 hours earlier than Malaysia. We sat in the airport for over two hours while Charlie, our Thai guide, took care of getting us and our baggage through customs. Ours seemed to be the last flight of the day and the airport gradually closed down as we waited. The airport is small and resembles airports depicted in old movies we had seen. Picture taking is not permitted although we did manage to get a shot of the Burmese-style drinking fountain, a wooden keg of water with a tin cup for communal use on top, and of a father and daughter waiting for the plane. At least the building is air-conditioned; it was 100°F when we landed.

The hotel we stayed in had been built by the Russians and operated for many years by the Israelis before being taken over by the Burmese government. Once elegant, it had lost a good deal of its splendor to neglect.

The road from the airport to the hotel was guarded by soldiers and a few tanks, and soldiers were stationed at the hotel gate. The bus passed through extremely poor neighborhoods, and driving on the right side of the road seemed wrong to us after seven months in Malaysia!

There was a 6 p.m. curfew, and we were told of students riot-

Burmese-style drinking fountain.

ing and the military reaction, but were assured we were safe. After returning to Malaysia we learned soldiers had forced thousands of students into a lake, where they drowned. The situation was critical.

Except for soldiers and police, men wear a longee, the Burmese version of the sarong, instead of pants.

Ranked in importance with Angkor Wat, the archeological ruins of 5000 temples at Pagan are scattered every hundred yards or so on the plains in the surrounding countryside. Some are in good repair and others in varying stages of erosion and neglect. The temples were built from the 11th to 13th centuries when Pagan was the royal city and everyone wanted his own pagoda just outside the palace grounds. The palace was built of wood, but the stone pagodas withstood the ravages of time.

After the rainy season the countryside is lush and green, but in drought the hot, barren soil yields barely enough to sustain a people held captive by a government "protecting" them from the evils of modern life.

Burma is ranked the poorest of United Nations third world

147

countries by any standard of measurement. We had stepped fifty years back in time. There are almost no cars on the road and converted trucks, with a wooden bench on each side of the bed, serve as public buses. Most people travel on foot or by bicycle, oxcart, horse and buggy, or trishaw. Black market money-changers are everywhere but Charlie warned us not to deal with them.

The barter economy encourages tourists to bring cigarettes, liquor, new or used clothes,(especially t-shirts), and cosmetics to trade for local crafts. One little girl even wanted to trade post cards for the used handkerchief out of Richard's pocket. The children are dirty and even the smallest begged for liquor, cigarettes, lipsticks, and perfume which could be resold at enormous profit on the thriving black market. The street children sing French songs learned from tourists and also speak remarkably good English.

Gold leaf, lacquerware, woodcarving, and embroidered tapestry are among the cottage industries that support the meager economy. Local guides insist carved ivory pieces are made from tusks of elephants that died naturally. Prices are often quoted in terms of packs of cigarettes or bottles of whiskey. Their money (kyats) comes in 1,5,10,15,45, and 90 kyat bills. The 45 and 90 kyat denominations struck us as particularly odd.

The tourist hotels we stayed in were clean but very run-down. The furniture looked forty years old. The hotel in Rangoon is large (six stories), but limited to selling forty bottles of beer a day; when that was gone they said, "no more beer." A limited supply of bottled water, available sometimes in some places, and a lemon-flavored soft drink, sweeter than 7-Up, offered occasional change from the plentiful supply of bottled, carbonated water which provided most of the liquid we drank during the six days.

In Pagan we stayed in a resort complex with four-unit bungalows. The main building has a pagoda-like structure on top. There is a swimming pool with a view of the Irrawaddy River and the hills beyond. For lunch we had Burmese food—soup, curried chicken, braised bean sprouts, and banana dessert. It was not spicy like Thai or Malaysian food, but we suspected they toned it down for the tour group.

Burma is a golden land with thousands of temples and pagodas glowing in the sunlight, a reflection of the people's devotion to their Buddha. Temples are the main sightseeing attraction. During our six days we visited the finest, the biggest, the oldest, and the highest, and saw statues of Buddha standing, sitting, sleeping, and dead. One of the temples had over 1400 Buddhas and we saw several 50 to 60 feet high, covered with many tons of gold leaf. We climbed the tallest temple to watch the sun set over the Irrawaddy River. Each temple was more beautiful than the last but toward the end of the week, we began to be templed out. Of course we took our shoes and socks off at each one.

The quantity of gold leaf covering the temples is overwhelming and statues are often encased enough to have lost their shape. Burmese buy gold whenever possible and after death, jewelry is turned over to the temples and melted down to adorn buildings. Seven hours of pounding is required to make each small sheet of gold leaf. The work is done in stifling heat, the windows of the huts closed since the finished leaf is so fragile even the slightest puff of air will carry it away. Pay for 1000 packets a day was 30K, or US$5 at the official exchange rate and less at the real rate. To keep track of time, workers use an hour glass made from a half coconut with a hole in it floating in a bucket of water. Sinking 18 times equals one hour.

A city of half a million with almost no cars, the streets of Mandalay overflow with thousands of bicycles. It was dusty, dry, and hot. We revised our estimate: we had stepped 100 years back in time. Some of the houses, built of bamboo frame with woven mat walls and thatched or corrugated tin roofs, have electric lights; virtually none has running water. The general aura of poverty is everywhere. Women carry heavy, bulky loads on their heads, and families live in appallingly primitive conditions. Cooking and bathing are done outside; the "stove" is often a bed of coals in a hole in the ground and the village pump the only source of water. The eyes of old people reflect a calm acceptance of hardship; their wrinkled faces reveal an inner beauty.

We watched water buffalo drag two-ton teak logs out of the river and maneuver them onto trucks to be hauled to the sawmills. There was a modern forklift nearby which we assumed was no longer functional because of the scarcity of parts. Maintaining any type of machinery is difficult due to government policies of isolation. We thought conservation of parts was carried too far when drivers kept headlights turned off at night, flashing them only when meeting an oncoming car. With all the bicycles and pedestrians on the road, it is a wonder more people aren't slaughtered.

In Mandalay we stayed at the second best hotel in town, the Myamandala. The new wing of our hotel was clean but the old

Children in front of pagoda in Mandalay.

wing looked dreadful. The Jumpers, friends from Malaysia on a different tour, were in the best the government had to offer. It was spartan, with no hot water and a thin pad laid on plywood for a mattress. They shared their room with strangers the night all the tourists staying at the downtown Strand Hotel had to be evacuated because of student riots. Burma is considered an "adventure" tour, and flying on their planes gave us a new understanding of the word. While standing in line for our first flight, the man behind us said to his companion, "Well, thank goodness this is our last flight!" The companion said he thought that was a poor choice of words. Just before takeoff the pilot's voice came on the loudspeaker with the usual information. He ended his announcement with "and NOW for the TAKEOFF" as if this were his first attempt. We were terrified. Rumors about a recent plane crash didn't help our state of mind.

We never traveled by train in Burma but did see signs listing fares. We understood first class costing more than second and third, but were puzzled by top class which cost only a few cents. Top class fare bought space on top of the train!

On the way to Inle Lake we stopped at a monastery built in 1870. The building is of intricately carved wood but the image of antiquity was spoiled somewhat by the monk sitting beside the altar with his AM/FM/shortwave radio-cassette player running off a 12-volt car battery.

150

Monk with battery powered boom-box.

The "highway" to Inle Lake is a narrow, one-lane road and when our bus met another vehicle, both had to get off on the shoulder. Passing another vehicle, usually a truck since there are almost no cars on the road, is a thrill. We crossed a fairly rugged ridge of high hills to another large flat valley. The hairpin curves and the lack of guardrails added another facet to the excitement of the trip.

We cruised up and down Inle Lake for about three hours. The motor on the boat Richard was in kept stalling and the boat I was in had a leak. The cool water I was sitting in was refreshing but filthy! We passed several small villages and floating gardens (all sorts of vegetables, not flowers), and saw the leg-rowing fishermen. They row their boats while standing, pushing the oars with their legs instead of their arms. They have a unique way of catching a fish in a large cage and net.

Fisherman on Inle Lake.

Taunggyi, on top of a high ridge, was a British hill station in colonial times and is cool—almost chilly in the evening. We saw many soldiers on the roads, and tight security at the hotel was an indication of fighting nearby. The bus engines must not have liked the cool weather because when we were ready to leave, one of them had to be pushed before it would start.

Markets are similar to those in Malaysia but fruits and vegetables are of poorer quality. Rice and meat, scarce and also poor quality, some fish and prawns, and a few scrawny chickens were available. Heho has a livestock market with zebus, oxen, and water buffalo. The animals looked well cared for.

Charlie kept telling us his horoscope was lucky and nothing

would happen to him or us. He was right. We returned to Rangoon in good health and since the "disturbances" were under control, our tour of the city could go on as planned.

One afternoon we rented a taxi and called on Daw Khin Mu Aye, a Burmese friend of a friend, and retired after eighteen years in WHO[19]. Mu Aye asked many questions about the student riots. The government was censoring all newspaper articles and radio programs. As outsiders we knew more than she did. She is blind, and friends abroad had offered to pay for cataract surgery but she is virtually a prisoner. If she left the country for the surgery, she could take nothing with her and wouldn't be allowed to return.

After a short visit the cab driver took us downtown where we spent some time walking. It was depressing. A beautiful city with large, elegant buildings, built primarily by the British, had been allowed to deteriorate. There had been no maintenance at all. Everything is dirty, broken, and badly worn. There are piles of garbage in the streets. It is probably the only city in the world with a population over three million and no building over eight stories tall.

The student riots had ended and the curfew lifted, but everyone was leery of what might happen next. The papers reported one student killed, but the rumor was 35 were killed; months later we learned that the figure was closer to 3000. There were almost no traffic lights downtown because the students had torn them all down, but traffic was orderly, stopping and yielding to pedestrians and other vehicles at intersections.

The phone book is small considering the size of the city. Daw Khin wasn't listed in the book so she probably didn't have a phone. Our cab driver said he was allowed 1-1/2 gallons of gas per day at about U.S. 35¢ per gallon. Black market cost for additional gas was US$11 per gallon. Rice also had to be bought on the black market and even then was extremely poor quality. Burma used to be known as the rice bowl of the world. Food had been rationed until January 1988.

The Shwedagon Pagoda is a large complex with many temples and stupas[20] in it and is the focus of family and religious life in the community. The central stupa has a 76-carat diamond as well as many other jewels in the top, and is covered with 14 tons of pure gold.

---

[19]World Health Organization. See glossary.
[20]A hemispherical or cylindrical mound or tower serving as a Buddhist shrine. See glossary.

Shwedagon Pagoda in Rangoon.

Several months after we were there, Ne Win's government was forced from power. Pictures in our *TIME* magazine showed armed soldiers who had followed rioting students into the Shwedagon Pagoda. As a sign of devotion to Buddha, the soldiers had taken time to remove their boots.

Our tour group was taken to dinner at a fancy restaurant built in the shape of a boat on a lake in the middle of town. We later learned this was the lake where the students were offered the "choice" of walking into the lake or being shot. The restaurant, built sixteen years ago to entertain government VIPs, has three large halls decorated with marble and carved wood. The interior was dirty and covered with cobwebs. After dinner we watched a show of native Burmese dancers. The final dance was a skillful acrobatic exhibition using the cane ball.

We spent our last kyats on a package of Burmese stamps. At the airport Richard went to the Post Office window and bought one of each stamp they had. It came to Ks2.30 but the postal clerk sold them to Richard for Ks2 to simplify change making. Can you imagine the U.S. Post Office "having a sale" and selling you $2.30 worth of stamps for $2.00?

Travel in Burma was indeed an adventure, and Charlie kept us from getting permanently trapped in bureaucratic red tape. At each town we had local guides from Tourist Burma who provided insight into the lives of a gentle people who are frozen in time. They spoke of "their" Buddha in a tone of voice that touched the heart. It was hard not to sympathize with the government's closed-door policy. We did not miss neon signs, jam boxes and MacDonald's, and we knew Pagan would be spoiled if it was over-run with tourists. However, it was heart-breaking to see a people denied simple comforts.

SINGAPORE

December 28-30, 1987
May 8-11, 1988

We passed through Singapore in transit many times but only twice arranged to sightsee or shop. Our sons were with us the first time when we were on our way to Australia in December of 1987. The train, supposedly a good way to get to Singapore, is one part of our trip we would not repeat. We discovered if we checked our luggage, it would arrive in Singapore after we had left for Australia! Fortunately we travel light. We also found out why most people carry food and snacks. The train has a "dining car," but the food is poor and the non-air-conditioned car extremely dirty. The rough road bed has a single track with sidings for passing. We spent a lot of time waiting.

During the two-day layover, Richard and I nursed cases of 24-hour flu. During his short stay in Malaysia, John discovered a talent for bargaining so, in between trips back to the hotel to check on their dying parents, the boys enjoyed the delights of shopping. Street vendors selling watches were a nuisance until Michael offered to sell them his watch!

The second day we recovered enough to tour Sentosa Island, taking the monorail and exploring the coral museum, the history museum, and the fort. The coral museum has a pool full of sea cucumbers with signs encouraging visitors to handle them. A sea cucumber is a tube shaped creature and when taken from the water, it turns limp in your hand as water pours out of it. Considered a delicacy by Chinese, we never developed a taste for it.

Our second trip to Singapore was in May of 1988. Singapore is a shopper's paradise as well as a good place for R&R when we wanted some peace and order in our lives. People actually obey laws, wait patiently in lines without pushing, and the sidewalks are clean enough to eat off of. The subway and bus system took us anywhere we wanted to go for only a few cents. Bargaining for food and merchandise from all over the world is part of the fun.

The Goodwood Park Hotel serves three high teas with a choice of English, Nyonya, or Western. A fantastic Russian restaurant and Mexican food, which we missed having in Malaysia, are among the international dining experiences available. And of course there is Swensen's! What can I say about Swensen's except that their "Topless Five," five scoops of ice cream without any toppings, is the best deal in this part of the world. We should know. We've been to Swensen's in Malaysia, Sumatra, Thailand, Singapore, New Zealand, and India.

We managed to find shoes to fit our big feet (big by Asian standards, that is) but I was mortified to discover extra large-sized running suits were too small in the hips for me. Surely I must have been in a store selling clothes cut and sized for Asian figures!

St. Andrew's Cathedral is spectacular and the Raffles Hotel complex, closed from 1989 to 1990 for restoration, had an interesting museum featuring all the famous people who have stayed there. Singapore Zoo is outstanding, with natural settings and almost no fences or cages. When we visited, there were two magnificent white tigers on loan from the Cincinnati Zoo.

THAILAND

May 14-21, 1988

Our first visit to Bangkok was a half-day layover on our way back from Burma. We hired a cab to take us to the Jim Thompson house: six Thai houses put together to make a large, rambling building filled with Thai silks, paintings, carvings, furniture, etc. Jim Thompson was an American businessman responsible for developing the silk industry in Thailand.

Bangkok has incredible traffic problems. At one time called "Venice of the East," the city filled in many of the canals to make wide main streets. Older side streets are narrow and winding, like any Asian city. With only the beginnings of a few expressways, there is too much traffic everywhere and our cab spent long periods of time bogged down in traffic gridlock. We did manage a drive through the grounds of Chulalongkorn University where Dr. Edwin Hadlock, Richard's major professor in graduate school, taught years ago. Janet Hadlock, his widow, had kept in touch with us so we had a special interest in seeing where they once lived.

Our second trip to Thailand was in May of 1988. Thailand is hot in May—much hotter than Malaysia—until the summer monsoon starts. The heat and oppressive humidity resemble the summer climate in Florida.

In Bangkok, we stayed at the Ambassador, a lavish hotel complex with twenty-two restaurants. While there, we contacted friends of my parents. Mr. Jayanama, who had been ambassador to Italy in the 1950s, was not well, but Mrs. Jayanama and two of her sons picked us up and took us to the Princess Restaurant for a multi-course Thai meal of rice cakes, fish, vegetables, beef curry, wild boar, tam yam soup (an extremely spicy fish soup), and a jellied rambutan (a fruit similar to lycee nuts) dessert.

Mrs. Jayanama passed away in May 1989 at the age of seventy-eight years. In keeping with their tradition, the official cremation ceremony took place on February 3, 1990. Mr. Jayanama still lives in Bangkok where one son is a Deputy Director General in the Ministry of Foreign Affairs. Two other sons are in diplomatic service, one in Malaysia and the other in Singapore.

We spent one day sightseeing in Bangkok before going to Chiang Mai. Only 30 of the 80 rooms in Vimanmek Palace are open to the public, and this intricately carved teak building is filled with antiques reflecting the life style of royal families 100 years ago.

The "City and Temples" tour took three hours plus the thirty minutes getting from the hotel to the starting point. We saw the golden Buddha temple, the reclining Buddha, and finally the marble Buddha in the Royal Temple, and spent about two hours sitting in traffic or getting from one temple to the other. The golden Buddha, covered with five tons of solid gold, is displayed in an extremely small temple overcrowded with tourists. We saw little of the reclining Buddha because it was in the process of being refinished in gold. The temple itself is decorated with ornate tiles. The Royal Temple, Italian marble with stained glass windows from Italy, has interior walls handpainted to look like wallpaper.

Thai Buddhists forbid shoes in the main part of the temple, but allow tourists to wear shoes in the rest of the temple grounds. The soles of our feet were pretty tough by this time, but we appreciated being allowed to keep our shoes on in public areas where streets and sidewalks were filthy.

We rode in "tuk-tuks," three-wheeled open Cushman cabs, for most of our sightseeing. The small vehicle is easier to maneuver in heavy traffic but gives no protection from dirt and exhaust fumes or serious injury in case of accident. Water taxis are available but crowded, and we fought our way aboard for a ride to the Grand Palace. Seeing the Grand Palace, magnificent with gold, colored glass, and hand-painted tile everywhere, made sitting in all the traffic jams worthwhile; it is truly breathtaking. We spent a little over an hour there.

Chiang Mai, in northern Thailand, resembles Bangkok without the traffic. A tour of the craft industries took us to a lacquer-

Grand Palace in Bangkok.

ware factory much like those we saw in Burma, and to a furniture factory where carving was similar to that done in Malacca. The silverware, bronze, and nickelware is beautiful, as were the gems, but it is all expensive. We stopped at a leather goods store which sold items made from elephant hide. At the umbrella factory we bought five frames to make a Christmas tree. Our tree, a copy of Tina and Bob Hvitfeldt's umbrella tree in Malaysia, was probably the only one in Munster and, as far as we know, one of three in the world.

158

The English spoken in Thailand is fairly good, but we were often misunderstood. Not all that many English speaking tourists visit Thailand. Only a few signs were in English and their alphabet is so different from ours that we couldn't pronounce anything. We visited in the year 2531! We didn't find out whether that was a Buddhist calendar or something strictly Thai.

Our tuk-tuk driver offered to make an appointment for Richard's evening entertainment and, as an afterthought, said similar arrangements could be made for me! No wonder the AIDS epidemic is spreading in Thailand.

Instead, we chose to attend a Thai dinner and dance program. The food was excellent, but sitting cross-legged on the floor was uncomfortable. The dancing was a mixture of classical Thai and folk dances. One of the tourists in the audience was taking pictures of a large roach walking across the floor before the program began. Being used to roaches that size, we hadn't noticed it.

Elephants bathing in Thailand.

At an elephant camp north of Chiang Mai, we fed the elephants and watched them bathing in the river. Elephants are used to move and stack the huge teak logs cut in the forest. Four elephants, each carrying two passengers and a driver, took a group of us for a ride through the jungle. The hour's journey was rough, up and down the hills on muddy trails with lots of slipping and

159

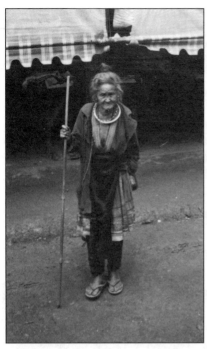
Hill tribe woman.

sliding. Our particular elephant was more interested in investigating the jungle than following the trail, and his lumbering, uneven gait made us feel insecure.

After a Thai lunch at the Mae Sa Valley Resort, we were taken on up the mountain to a hill tribe village, the second we had visited. The first involved a long miserable ride on an exceptionally poor road, but was close enough to Chiang Mai to be overrun with tourists. This second village, newly opened to the public, had a few handicrafts for sale, but the people were as curious about us as we were about them. The houses are of mud or woven mat walls with thatched roofs. Families sleep on raised wooden platforms with no padding and cook over a wood fire in the corner.

Back in Bangkok we decided to spend the day doing odds and ends of sightseeing we had missed before. We rode the hotel bus into town where we hired a tuk-tuk to take us to Wat Saket on Golden Mount, where we had a beautiful panorama of the city spreading as far as we could see in every direction.

Our guide book lists The Royal Barge Museum as an attraction, but our driver had to ask directions several times and then led us to a rickety, elevated sidewalk through a slum neighborhood of houses on stilts above a cesspool! The museum, a huge, corrugated steel roof building, houses war barges with cannons, powered by 36 oarsmen. The ceremonial barges, with covered seating for royalty, are decorated with gold leaf, have room for 50 oarsmen, and are approximately 150 feet long.

The Suan Pakkad Palace is now a museum displaying furniture, lacquer panels, and a variety of antiques. The small library behind the palace is one of the most ornate and delicately carved and decorated buildings we saw in Bangkok.

Hill tribe man with grandchildren.

Often, our only luggage on trips was a small suitcase and one carry-on bag. To save weight I did not take an extra pair of shoes to Thailand, a foolish decision since my sandals literally fell apart because of all the walking we did. The only reasonable way to see Bangkok is to ride a bus or tuk-tuk, or to walk. However, as the result of spending so much time breathing exhaust fumes, we both spent several weeks recovering from severe lung congestion.

CHINA

June 13-23, 1988

My Dad spent time in parts of China during the war and I'd often dreamed of going there. The long list of places we wanted to see had to be pared down in the face of reality. Our time and money were limited. We were fortunate, however, because only a year later China would not be welcoming foreigners.

Our itinerary was arranged by Sanie, our Malaysian travel agent, through China Travel Service in Hong Kong. Malaysians of Chinese ancestry had not been allowed to visit China until they turned sixty-five, but the age limit is now lower and there are indications of a softening in political relations between the two countries. Because we have U.S. passports, our visas were approved without question.

In Hong Kong, three hours before our flight to Shanghai, we checked at the CAAC[21] ticket counter as instructed. They had never heard of us. They did not have our tickets, vouchers, etc. We showed them the papers proving we had prepaid the whole trip. They didn't doubt us, but there wasn't much they could do except call China Travel Service. There was no answer, and since it was a public holiday (the Queen's birthday), it wasn't surprising the office was closed. Finally, shortly before flight time we bought two new tickets to Shanghai. We were lucky the plane wasn't full but those two empty seats we bought tickets for were probably the ones we had reserved! We did eventually get a refund for the extra tickets.

We now realize how foolish it was to think we could arrive in Shanghai in the middle of the night and easily contact our tour. We planned to call China Travel Service or find their booth at the airport. We had no idea that in Shanghai we would go through passport control and be out on the street. We didn't know what hotel we were supposed to be in or the name of the guide who was supposed to meet us. We could easily have been camped on the sidewalk outside the airport all night, and when a young man named Wang approached and asked if our name was Yates, we were so relieved we almost hugged him.

At the Jin Sha Hotel, Wang bought us a light meal even

---

[21]The Civil Aviation Administration of China. See glossary.

though we had eaten dinner on the plane, announced that our wake-up call would be at 4 a.m., and sent us off to bed.

Even tour groups can't make hotel or train reservations ahead of time. At each town all arrangements were made after we arrived. A lot of last minute shuffling went on, but we relaxed and let the guides do their job. We never had to sleep on a park bench. Getting a room is difficult if not impossible for travelers not with a tour. As tourists we stayed only in international class hotels and our meals were served in dining rooms not open to local clientele. Food was excellent and abundant, but we were served beer and orange soda instead of hot tea to drink. Tea, available on request, would usually be one small pot for the group to share.

Arranging for train, bus, or plane travel involves standing in line to get a chit for permission to stand in line to buy a ticket. The ticket windows are open certain hours and close on time, no matter how many are still in line. There are four different prices: 1) Chinese, 2) Hong Kong and Macau residents, 3) overseas Chinese, and 4) everyone else. We compared notes and were paying sixteen times what a Chinese would pay for the same tour. If we ever return to China we hope to tour with an English speaking group of Chinese so we could have the opportunity to experience life there as it really is.

The next morning we left the hotel at 4:30 a.m. in order to be on a 5:10 a.m. train to Suzhou, which is about 90 km from Shanghai. We were in "soft class" with padded seats and a table for the tea they served us. Local Chinese could buy cheaper seats in "hard class" and had to bring their own tea.

We arrived about 6:30 a.m. and were taken to the Gusu Hotel for a Chinese breakfast, which included a wide assortment of dishes. We never managed to identify specific ingredients. As with everywhere we ate, the meal was excellent and there was more food than we could possibly eat.

Suzhou, the silk producing capital of China, also has many tranquil gardens. Although teeming with people, all of China is relatively quiet with virtually no automobiles or motorcycles. There are trucks, buses, and millions of bicycles. The cities appear clean and relatively free of trash, maybe because people have little to throw away.

The silk factory we visited, where cocoons are processed into thread, is large compared to the small cottage industry shops in Thailand. Chinese silk is much softer than Thai silk and is almost gossamer in weight. After being woven, the cloth is dyed with vivid colors.

Tiger Hill Park boasts a 1000-year-old leaning pagoda. We had climbed the leaning tower in Pisa but this one was closed to the public. Nearby we stopped by a canal and watched the boat traffic. There are miles and miles of canals, including the Great Canal that goes all the way to Beijing and is the longest internal waterway in the world. Suzhou competes with Bangkok for the title "Venice of the East."

Barge-load of hay on the Great Canal.

On the plane to Guangzhou, a box lunch included a package of dried curried beef, a cream puff with a bit of jam, a muffin, crackers, a dinner roll, a sausage roll, and a packet of coconut jam. We were served tea and a warm soft drink. Three pieces of chocolate redeemed it somewhat. CAAC has a long way to go in the food service department.

In Guangzhou, as in every town, we had a local guide and caught up with Wong, the CTS tour guide who accompanied us for the rest of our trip. The number of our group varied since people had planned their own itineraries. We liked having this kind of flexibility.

The Chen Clan Classical Learning Academy, a compound of beautifully decorated buildings and courtyards, is a museum with incredibly beautiful carvings and embroidery on display. The exquisite jade carvings were particularly intriguing since we had watched the artisans at work in a local factory. The price discouraged us from buying any.

Many Chinese have studied English and are eager to practice. With their limited vocabulary they often run out of anything to say after the first few phrases. Our guides all spoke excellent English but had trouble answering questions about subjects not covered by the tour.

The 27,000 karst mountains/monoliths in and around Guilin are represented in many Chinese paintings we have seen and admired. The weather in June was warm and extremely humid, with no sign of a breeze. We were more uncomfortable there than anywhere else in China. Reed Flute Cave, one of the largest caves in the area, is filled with fancifully named limestone formations. Our guide encouraged us to "use our imaginations," a phrase we have heard from cave guides all over the world. Exhibits at the Limestone Research Center cleared up many of the questions we had about the geological background of the karsts.

Monoliths near Guilin.

The summer monsoon had not started yet. Low water levels on the rivers, combined with dependence on hydroelectric power, meant electricity was rationed. Our hotel was new and air-conditioned but, with electricity only available a few hours each day, our room was a sauna.

We spent an entire day cruising down the Li River through mile after mile of karst monoliths. We were hypnotized. At each

Sign near the Great Wall.

new bend in the river the boat slipped us deeper into a mist-shrouded fantasy world.

Beijing is not China. As the centerpiece of efforts to compete with the free world, the city receives a large portion of industrial profits. The amount of new high-rise construction underway was amazing, and residents had begun calling it the city of cranes.

Tiananmen Square, the largest public square in the world, is bordered by the Great Hall of the People, Chairman Mao's tomb, and several other massive government buildings. Less than a year later, this peaceful square would be the scene of bloody riots that changed the way China is viewed by the rest of the world.

In Beijing the Holiday Inn, built and administered in a joint venture with Japan, can compete with international class hotels all over the world. At a flick of the switch the TV in our room provided a taste of home with a broadcast of CBS news! Some of our fellow travelers opted for hamburgers and western barbecue instead of the Chinese meal offered by the tour.

The Ding Ling Tomb is the only one of the thirteen Ming Tombs, about 50 km north of Beijing, that had been excavated and

The Great Wall of China.

opened. The emperor, who died in 1620, the empress, and the concubine who bore his only son, are buried there. The mausoleum contents are a mixture of authentic original and replica.

Another 35 km on winding mountain roads brought us to the Great Wall where we spent two hours climbing and hiking on one section. We were surprised at how steep some of it is, but a wall built in the mountains is not likely to be flat. The Wall is wide enough to accommodate chariots, but with many sections of steep steps, we wonder how the horses managed. We had wisely followed our guide's advice to wear sturdy walking shoes and to bring jackets. Even on a warm day it is chilly and windy on the Wall.

Our sightseeing tour of Beijing included a stop to see the three pandas because the Chinese know Americans are crazy about pandas. Nothing was said about efforts to conserve their natural habitat.

We spent several hours enjoying the Summer Palace on the outskirts of the city. Built as a retreat, it has long, covered walkways lined with benches to give royalty access to cool breezes and allow a place to sit while admiring the painted ceilings and columns.

The Empress Dowager's marble boat, one of the more unusual sights, is moored at the dock on an artificially created

The Empress Dowager's marble boat.

lake and was built by the Dowager with funds originally intended for the Chinese navy.

We toured a cloisonné factory. Neither one of us had realized before just how it is made. The long, complicated process produces exquisite results.

From the pagoda on the top of Jade Hill in Beihai (Coal Hill) Park, we looked down on the Forbidden City. Since the park is centrally located, magnificent views in every direction reinforced our impression that Beijing is a large, modern metropolis.

The Forbidden City was all we expected and more. Even with all the pictures we had seen, we hadn't realized how extensive it is and how massive the walls are. We spent about two hours inside and only saw a few of the over 9000 rooms. Many of the courtyards and reception halls were familiar from the movie, *The Last Emperor,* which we had seen in Singapore with Chinese subtitles! Copies of Pu Yi's autobiography were on sale. The two-volume book is rather dry reading, probably because language always loses in translation, but we did learn a great deal about life in China during those times.

Wandering in the neighborhood while the rest of our group went to a shopping street designed for tourists, we came across a stamp show and exchange. We hunted up our guide who bought tickets for the three of us, but even with him along we were turned away because we were foreigners. We did get our money back.

Inside the Forbidden City.

Beijing's underground city is a massive system of tunnels built as a bomb shelter when the government feared a Third World War with the U.S. and/or Russia. In reality it would have provided little protection from modern day warfare. Some of the larger areas are now used as factories and shops.

The flight to X'ian on a Russian-built plane, a totally different design than we are used to with the interior resembling a military transport, made Burmese planes look like luxury aircraft. Seats had almost no padding and backs folded forward flat at the touch of a finger. On takeoff the plane lumbered down the runway and we seriously doubted it would ever get far enough off the ground to be airborne. We tried to make ourselves as light as possible and held our breath. It was a long flight and we were thankful to be safely on the ground again.

CAAC also used American built 737s, which weren't in such good shape either. On one of our flights, Richard's seat belt wouldn't latch, but the stewardess had him hold the ends together during takeoff! There was a waiting room for departing passengers in X'ian but on arrival we collected our baggage from an open shed and stood in the street until our local guide arrived with a bus to take us to the Tang Cheng Hotel.

The Banpo Museum is an excavation and reproduction of a village 6000-7000 years old. When we visited the dig, a local eth-

Carved stairway at the Forbidden City.

nic group, probably Mongolian, was performing, with several people in costume and many exhibits of their culture.

The Qin Shi Huang mausoleum, the site of the famous terra cotta figures, is overwhelming. Workers have only excavated about 1/6 of the total and expect to take at least fifteen years to do the rest. Recent changes in the political situation no doubt will add years to that prediction and in fact, work may stop completely since funding was already a problem. We debated buying a small reproduction and decided we didn't need something else to dust. Now we are kicking ourselves for not getting one. Photography is not allowed inside the dig so we bought lots of postcards. Maybe someday we will go back.

In 1992 a friend visited X'ian and hand-carried a statue of a kneeling warrior back for us.

Each city has special memories. We saw one woman whose feet had been bound, and we were captivated by the beautiful faces. Babies wear open pants rather than diapers, but in general the sidewalks and streets are clean and unlittered. We saw no open drains. We saw piles of cabbage in the markets but weren't served a lot. We went into a "Chinese only" food market and a clothing store. The food market was not self-service and the meat mostly fat; the clothing was of poor quality material and workmanship. People from the north still wear the blue Mao jackets and pants.

The free market in Guangzhou, where the locals shop, was similar in many ways to those in Malaysia. It had all sorts of different meats on sale—frog, snake, eel, cat, pigeon, and others we couldn't identify. We wonder what has happened to the free enterprise system that had such enthusiastic support when we visited.

Daniel, our guide, told us it was easier to change money at the hotel than at the border, but when Richard tried the hotel bank, three tellers refused to do it and said it had to be done at the border. One of the other men in the group, assigned to our embassy in Hong Kong, went back with his diplomatic passport and the bank made the exchange right away. Rank hath its privileges.

HONG KONG

June 24-25, 1988

On our way back to Malaysia from China, airline schedules gave us a layover in Hong Kong. The train we took between Guangzhou and Hong Kong was comfortable and air conditioned. We arrived about ten minutes late but customs was easy. A special enterprise zone on China's side of the border is crowded with hundreds of high-rise, modern apartment buildings. Young people selected from all over the country live and work there, and Wong said they make a lot of money. The New Territory development on the Hong Kong side, also wall-to-wall, new, high-rise apartments with many more going up, is low income housing for workers commuting to Kowloon or Hong Kong. A fence marks the border. We wonder what is going to happen when Hong Kong becomes part of China.

Our room at the New World Hotel in Hong Kong was the smallest we had ever seen, about eight feet wide, but the beds were comfortable. We had enjoyed a large, luxurious room in the same hotel for our one-night layover on our way to Malaysia in 1987. When we made reservations for this trip we had been puzzled by the lower price for this room in the same hotel. Perhaps price is computed per square inch!

Hong Kong guide books list Victoria Peak as one of the sightseeing highlights but as far as we know the Peak doesn't exist. In fact, we think it always rains in Hong Kong! We have seen pictures and of course post cards, and someday we hope to take the tram and enjoy the view not veiled by fog or rain.

Even in the rain, the one-hour sightseeing cruise on the Star Ferry is worthwhile. We never found the big public park in Kowloon where the historical museum is housed. After walking around the several blocks containing the park and finding all the entrances bricked up, we gave up. The construction work going on inside made us suspect the park was being eliminated, no doubt to make room for more housing.

Hong Kong skyline.

Almost anything you can name is for sale in Hong Kong if you have the time, energy, and money to spend. However, as in Singapore, it is wise to do your homework. Not everything for sale is a bargain.

AUSTRALIA

December 31, 1987 - January 7, 1988
July 24 - August 6, 1988

We made two trips to Australia: the first in January of 1988 when our sons, Michael and John, came to visit us, and the second in July of 1988. Michael and John chose Australia as the country they wanted to visit in addition to Malaysia. Had we realized how far Australia is from Malaysia, and that December/January is the height of summer and therefore their tourist season, we wouldn't have promised. Including the round trip from Chicago to KL, Michael and John logged 30,500 miles (Richard and I a paltry 12,000) in three weeks. It was no wonder we started the new semester a bit jet-lagged.

Our second trip "down under" included New Zealand: two weeks (July 11-23) touring the north and south islands followed by two weeks in Australia (July 24-August 6). July and August are winter months south of the equator and the change from tropical temperatures was a shock. The United States and Australia are similar in size, so even though we covered a lot of territory, there are whole regions we haven't seen.

Australia has figured out how to make family travel easy. Motels have reasonably priced two-room units available and a breakfast tray, ordered the night before, is delivered at the time requested.

Our first visit to Australia began in Cairns, and one of the high points of our lives was the day we spent on the Great Barrier Reef. Between Cairns and Port Douglas, rugged hills on one side of the road contrast with calm sea on the other. The 30 mph catamaran ride from Port Douglas to the mooring platform on the eastern edge of the reef took an hour and a half. The reef is closest to the mainland at Cairns. A line of low breakers was the only indication of the reef as we approached in a calm sea, and the 40 x 90-foot platform looked like a postage stamp in the vast expanse of water.

Underneath is an observation room and on the side, a diving platform for snorkelers. Glass walled subs make trips around the reef. There is also a boat for scuba divers and a helicopter for aerial viewing. The kaleidoscope of color and the visual memories of the hundreds of fish that inhabit the reef simply didn't come through in our photographs. At low tide the reef is only about two feet below the surface but standing or walking on it is prohibited and not advisable. It is extremely sharp and cuts from it often become infected. Walking on the reef also damages or destroys it.

Our guide book had nothing good to say about the road between Cairns and Brisbane; among the locals it has the reputation of being "murder highway," but we are glad we ignored the dire warnings. Parts of the two-lane road have been rebuilt or resurfaced, and outside of Brisbane it becomes a four-lane expressway. We could see the "remains" of the old road where it had been abandoned and it was in dreadful condition. There was hardly any traffic and the few cars we did encounter had courteous drivers. The terrain between Townsville and MacKay is desertlike with scrub trees. From MacKay to Maryborough it changes to flat valleys between mountains and rolling hills that reminded us of Maryland and Virginia. We saw lots of sugarcane and pineapple being grown under irrigation. It took us a while to realize the signs advertising "fresh pines" weren't trying to sell Christmas trees, but were advertising pineapples!

Wildlife sanctuaries are a big attraction for us. In addition to the expected koalas and kangaroos, the large assortment of animals included wallabies, wallaroos, emus, wombats, cockatoos, crocodiles, dingos, skinks, echidnas, and many varieties of birds. Koalas are ugly/cute, and their kinky fur feels more like a Brillo pad than anything we wanted to cuddle. Wombats are just fat, furry blobs with black noses. Kangaroos love to be fed and petted. One mother kangaroo had a joey, young enough to be almost hairless, who kept falling out of her pouch. Pythons are rather nice to pet, and pelicans are aggressive and rambunctious when offered food.

We ate counter meals in taverns and enjoyed the hearty food and Australian beer. We had a terrible time understanding local patrons. One old man went away in a huff after repeating his remark three times. We never did figure out what he was trying to tell us and asked the waitress to explain that we really weren't being rude.

We visited Gladys Stephensen, who prefers to be called Steve. She had been an associate of my father in FAO[22] in Rome, Italy and had retired to Brisbane. It had been thirty years since we had lived in Rome so we caught up on old times. Steve keeps busy looking after a sister who is confined to a nursing home, and works as a volunteer making recordings for the blind.

---

[22]Food and Agriculture Organization of the United Nations. See glossary.

174

Koala bear.

Sydney was our first stop on our second visit to Australia. We took a two-hour cruise which gave us a good idea of the layout of the city and impressed us with the magnificence of the harbor and its many coves. It was chilly out on the water and even with our coats, we were just plain COLD. Daytime winter temperatures run in the 50s or 60s and we did not adapt quickly to the change.

The Opera House caused heated controversy during the planning, design, and building stages. In its completed form this building is outstanding. The lobbies and the interiors of the various auditoriums are unique, but the look at the backstage world of sets, lights, costumes, and dressing rooms was a special treat.

The church we attended had recently been rebuilt following a disastrous fire. The priest and his wife had returned to Australia last year after living in the U.S. for several years. The priest's wife, who was born in the U.S., talked about how difficult life was for her in Australia when she first moved there years ago as a new

Sydney Opera House.

bride. She had never had milk tea before being served it by her in-laws, and she found this combination particularly distasteful. Having been schooled to take "small bites" she was appalled by what she considered a lack of manners, as Australians also use the British style of holding the knife and fork and manage to pile an amazing amount of food on the back of a fork.

The Blue Mountains, west of Sydney, are a curious formation—not really mountains, but a high plateau with deeply eroded valleys leaving high, sheer cliffs with dramatic views and many waterfalls. We explored the area around Katoomba and we rode the skyway gondola car at the falls. With a gale force wind (45 mph), the ride itself was exciting and scary. The few times I dared open my eyes I could see for miles across the valley. The skyway operator took great pleasure in the obvious fear of his passengers. He knew we weren't in any danger!

The strong winds followed us to Canberra. On the Telecom Tower at the top of Black Mountain we walked all around the enclosed viewing lounge, but when we went out on the open balcony, the wind was so strong we could hardly stand up. Soon a guard came to tell us the observation platform was being closed until the wind died down.

Canberra is a dream city that took fifty years to build. The government buildings are attractive combinations of marble, inlaid wood, structural steel, and glass. The High Court building and the new Parliament building, which only opened two months before we visited, is extremely modern and striking, but doesn't have the mellow beauty of older buildings. We wonder what people will think of it a hundred years from now.

Two churches attracted our attention. One was an Anglican church built long before the city of Canberra was thought of, and the other was originally built as a mortuary station for funeral trains. A fire destroyed the mortuary, and the surviving stone structure was moved from its original location and converted into a church.

The highest mountain in Australia, Mt. Koscuisko in the Snowy Mountains, is under 7300-feet high. The surrounding mountains are just large hills covered with eucalyptus trees, which don't lose their leaves. Except for the snow on the ground, we could have been out for an afternoon ride in the summer. The "Skitube," a cog train which goes through a tunnel in the mountains, takes skiers to two different resorts, Blue Cow and Perisher. The snow was slushy but there was plenty of it. On the other side of Mt. Koscuisko, the landscape turns to lush, green pasture with sheep grazing everywhere, and there was no sign of snow.

Jimmy Watson's Wine Bar in Melbourne, recommended by our guide book, only serves lunches and was just closing up from the "after work trade" when we arrived wanting dinner. As we started to leave the barman asked us to stay and have a glass of wine on the house. We sipped wine and talked with him and a waitress (who turned out to be seventy-three years old) for a while. Soon everyone else left and he got out a bottle of champagne for the four of us to share. Then he invited us home for "tea." Home was a long drive to a northwestern suburb of Melbourne. "Tea," prepared by his thirteen- and sixteen-year-old sons, was fried chicken, baked potato, salad and dessert! We thoroughly enjoyed talking with Edna and Julius, and were particularly impressed with their sons. Both were attending private school and the older boy, who was starting his fifth year of Chinese language courses, had spent two months studying in China.

Several years ago we read Neville Shute's book *A Town Like Alice* and also watched the PBS TV series based on his story. The beginning is set in Malaysia and the "Alice" of the title refers to Alice Springs in Australia. Alice, the site of the telegraph station and a fresh water spring, was never a town. A nearby settlement took the name of Alice Springs after the telegraph station closed.

The flat valley, surrounded by red rock hills, hidden canyons, and dry river beds, is a hiker's dream.

Standley Chasm, resembling a miniature Grand Canyon, cuts through the mountains and is about 15 feet wide with 200-foot vertical red-rock walls. During the "wet," floods are awesome and destructive. During the dry season the land bakes under temperatures often reaching 120 degrees. John Flynn, who established the Flying Doctor Service, is buried near Alice Springs. The Flying Doctor network frequently means the difference between life and death for people in the outback.

During our walks through town we saw evidence of the aborigine struggle with the white man's culture. Many aborigines have not adapted well, and alcohol abuse is a significant problem with repercussions affecting the entire community. We were told not to walk near dry river beds after dark because aborigine families camping there would consider us trespassers.

Ayers Rock is a sacred place for the aborigine, and an agreement with the Australian government allows visitors except during inviolable religious celebrations. The five-hour bus ride from Alice Springs across the seemingly endless outback includes stops at a camel farm, a salt lake, and a cattle station which operates a

Camel in the outback.

tea room and souvenir shop. Swarms of flies overwhelmed us at each stop. The lake is like the rivers in the outback—no water in them unless there has just been rain. Since no water ever flows out of the lake the salt accumulates and, reflected in the sun, looks like water.

Near Ayers Rock, the Olgas are large rock domes (thirty-six in all) standing out in the middle of the plains. We hiked in Olga Gorge and just before sunset were taken to a viewing area west of Ayers Rock to watch the color changes on the rock formations.

The next morning we were up before daylight to start the climb up Ayers Rock. The first part is the steepest and most difficult but we pulled ourselves up with the help of a chain provided for that purpose. It was cold (about 40°) and the wind got stronger as we climbed. When we reached the top of the chain, which is most of the way up vertically, but only about half the total distance, we were both shivering. After considering the wind and the narrow, steep ridge without a chain we would have to negotiate to reach the rounded top of the rock, we decided the view was good enough from where we were. The climbers who reached the summit confirmed the wind seemed worse and the view wasn't much different. On the way down we couldn't believe we had come up such a steep slope. Each year several climbers fall to their deaths, so the Rock is not an adventure for the foolish or the faint-hearted. I admit to coming down mostly on my bottom and ruining a pair of jeans!

Perth would be an ideal place to live were it not so isolated. We took a walking tour of the downtown and admired the old buildings that have been restored to create a picturesque shopping mall. New, modern skyscrapers seem to harmonize rather than conflict with the historical district.

On the west coast north of Perth, through arid coastal dune country, are the pinnacles in Nambung National Park. In a yellow sand desert these rock pillars, varying in height from a few inches to over thirteen feet, cover several acres. Coming on them is a surprise since there is no sign of these unusual formations from the park entrance or the road leading to them. A few miles east, a lush, green valley with wheat farms at the northern end changed to vineyards with many wineries as we approached Perth.

We spent two days exploring the coast south of Perth, including Cape Naturaliste and Cape Leeuwin. The coast has some nice beaches, but the rugged, rocky terrain is more suited to hiking than swimming. Inland are lush, green rolling hills with

Richard at Nambung National Park.

lots of sheep and cattle pasture and some wheat fields resembling Maryland farmland.

In addition to three main meals a day, all our tours included morning and afternoon tea with scones, clotted cream, and delicious jam. The evening tea we were invited to share in Melbourne was what we would call dinner. One example of the counter meals we ordered was a seafood platter with vegetables. The vegetables included carrots, potatoes, broccoli, peas, AND brussels sprouts. The Australian people are hearty eaters.

NEW ZEALAND

July 11-23, 1988

Our photgraphs don't reflect how much of New Zealand looks like a John Constable painting with rolling green hills and sheep peacefully grazing. New Zealand landscapes have been described as a combination of Puget Sound, Wisconsin farmland, and the Rockies.

As our plane approached Christ Church, we had a splendid view of the Southern Alps to the west with the rising sun shining on them. Having the sun low in the northern sky disturbed us.

Our first chance to observe the kiwi, a very shy, nocturnal bird, was in an artificial habitat on the North Island. By reversing daylight and darkness, the birds are fooled into becoming active in the daytime. The kiwi fruit with its fuzzy, brown skin is named after this unlikely looking bird. We bought kiwi fruit in large quantities, paying as little as 50¢ a dozen. Restaurants were willing to let us carry in our own fruit to eat with the bowl of soup or the sandwich we would buy.

The seven-hour drive to Queenstown took us through truly extraordinary scenery. After two hours of Canterbury Plain, very flat and arid with the New Zealand Alps off to the right, we turned

Lake near Twizel.

into the mountains for most of the rest of the way. The mountain-
tops were snow covered and the lakes an unbelievably vivid
blue-green.

In Queenstown we took the gondola ride to the top of the
mountain west of town. The 1988 ski season had been disappointing. There was no mention of snow-making machines, perhaps
because they aren't used. We missed the roughest country to the
south because our rental car would not be covered by insurance
on those roads. Several roads into the mountains around
Queenstown are marked with signs warning us our car insurance
was void if we had an accident while driving on them. The rental
company gave us a chit for a free bus ride which we didn't have
time to use.

Our room in Queenstown was frigid. The manager pointed
out two supplementary electric heaters and explained the main
heat, controlled by the town, would come on about 5:30 p.m. when
the demand for electricity dropped, and would run for about six
hours. A metal box about three feet high and a foot square stored
heat in some sort of chemical bed which gets hotter and hotter.
Then it exudes heat all night. Electric blankets or more commonly, electric mattress pads, are standard in motel rooms, but windows or doors were often open in lobbies and restaurants!

The cold air was probably good for our health, but we lacked
the proper clothing. One motel clerk told us we would be warmer
at night if we kept the bathroom door closed. One look at the
bathroom told us why: the louvered windows are permanently
open.

Northwest of Queenstown the road across Haast Pass is
paved in some places, but much of it is "metal," their word for
gravel, and one-lane with occasional passing bays. Even the main
highways have many one-lane bridges, no problem at all considering the lack of traffic. In the two weeks we only had to wait once
at a bridge because the other car had the right of way. The mountain scenery with snow covered peaks and deep blue lakes
changes from arid to lush, semitropical rain forest on the west
side of the pass.

The road on the west coast of the South Island must be one
of the great scenic highways of the world. It follows the high cliffs
that hug the beach, and we could see snowcapped mountains east
of us in the distance. Lush rain forest with huge tree-ferns gives
way to a rocky coast with patches of sandy beaches.

Punakaiki National Park protects deposits of pancake rocks,

West Coast of South Island.

alternate layers of hard and soft material with the soft eroded away, leaving formations resembling huge stacks of pancakes. The surf crashes against high cliffs with vertical vents making spectacular blowholes at high tide. Naturally we were there at low tide.

Businesses in New Zealand close at 5 p.m. We were wandering around the back country one afternoon when we suddenly realized the car's petrol gauge was almost on empty and we were far from civilization. We had a few anxious moments wondering if we were going to find a town and a gas station before the witching hour. We were lucky, but the attendant was in the process of closing up and we were his last customer for the day. Blue laws are also in effect and virtually every business is closed on Sundays.

The North and South Islands are connected by ferry between Wellington and Picton. We'd checked schedules but discovered on arrival in Picton that the ferry we planned to take had been discontinued the day before! No problem lah. We ate lunch, wandered around town and read during the four-hour wait. We also turned in our car since companies don't allow rentals to be taken on the ferry. We were afraid to ask why. During the three-hour trip we never lost sight of land, but the choppy sea made us both a little queasy. From reading newspaper accounts of recent storms, we knew the channel could be rough.

In Wellington, Old St. Paul's used to be the Anglican cathe-

Marakopa Falls on North Island.

dral and is now a government-operated, historic place with occasional church services and concerts. We attended a special non-denominational service sponsored by the Stroke Society. The speaker and most of the readers were recovering stroke victims, and we particularly enjoyed music provided by girls from a local Catholic college.

The Orakei Korako Thermal Area near Taupo is similar to Yellowstone with geysers, hot baths and boiling mud pots. The geothermal power project there generates 20% of North Island's electric power. As we drove on north, stopping at many more thermal areas, we were reminded of our visits to U.S. national parks 40 years ago. New roads are being built but in August of 1988, excursions off the beaten path, often on unpaved roads, provided us some of our most memorable views. We hiked many of the trails suggested in our guidebook and were rewarded for our efforts with sights of natural bridges, hidden canyons, and high waterfalls.

The Glowworm Cave at Waitomo is small compared to other caves we have been through, but the glowworms put on an enchanting show. We floated down an underground river in the dark and the walls and roof were covered with little dots of light.

Auckland, with two harbors surrounded by green hills and extinct volcanos, has an historical museum with informative exhibits on New Zealand and the Maori culture. The nearby greenhouse conservatory, which they call a "wintergarden," has an excellent display of flowers and semitropical plants. It was WARM inside!

The Waipona Forest, north of Auckland, has an impressive growth of kauri trees. Of the largest, similar to redwoods and sequoias in size, one was 165 feet high and another 18 feet in diameter.

We found it easy to travel in New Zealand and could have filled another week or two with sightseeing. There is a wide variety of accommodations available, and we managed to keep expenses down by eating in pubs. As in Australia, food is good and servings generous. Lamb is always on the menu. The New Zealand national dessert, pavlova, is a rich confection made from meringue, whipped cream, and fresh fruit.

NEPAL

October 15-23, 1988

Nepal, in the Himalayas, presented a solid wall of incredible snow-covered peaks, soaring high above the clouds as far as we could see as our plane approached Kathmandu. Eight of the fourteen mountains in the world over 26,400 feet are in Nepal. The Tibetens call Everest "Chomolungma" - Goddess Mother of the World - but the sacred aura extends to the whole range. All the photos we had seen hadn't prepared us for the impact of those mountains.

Nepal is two and a quarter hours behind Malaysia. Their money-changing, customs, and passport control are incredibly slow and inefficient, with visas issued on arrival. A fee of $10 in United States currency applied to visitors of all nationalities. (Update 1993: the fee is now US$20.) The local money changer, who refused to accept Nepalese currency, was doing a brisk business.

Kathmandu, on a high plateau ringed by mountains, is one of a cluster of three towns, including Patan across the river and Bhaktapur a little further away. The population is a racial mix —Tibetan, Indian, and some who have Arab features. The Bagmati River is sacred and the Hindu Temple on its banks is a place of sacrifice and cremation for the devout as well as where the faithful bathe and drink the water! Many Nepalese live in incredibly cramped and dirty conditions, not as poor as Burma, but Nepal is definitely a very poor, third-world country. There is a strong Indian influence although we were told there are as many Buddhists as Hindus here.

Hindu temples and merchants selling everything under the sun enlivened the atmosphere in the main squares. Many of the buildings are ornamented with intricate wood carvings. In preparation for the approaching festival, people carried animals they had bought for sacrifices.

Durbar Square in Kathmandu.

Kathmandu street scene.

The "Living Goddess," chosen as an infant, is an object of veneration until she reaches puberty, when a new goddess replaces her. In the past a retired living goddess led a pretty miserable life since myth dictated that any man who married her would die soon after the marriage. In recent years several have married and since

Kathmandu vegetable vendor.

187

Typical Kathmandu house.

these grooms have avoided untimely death, the future for a living goddess is less bleak.

Our guide's yearly wage was US$720! He was content with this income, but had no hope of owning many of the things we take for granted.

A four-day trek around the Kathmandu rim tested our stamina, gave us insight into village and country life, and each day filled our minds with a permanent image of God's glory on earth—The Himalayas!

Nima, our trekking guide, a cook, and two porters carried all the gear (including duffel bags, tents, sleeping bags, a complete kitchen, food, and fuel for four days) in large wicker baskets on their backs braced with a strap across their heads. Meals were delicious—western breakfasts and lunches and Nepalese dinners, all cooked over a wood fire or a gasoline pressure burner. Richard and I each carried only a day pack.

Our four-day trek began at Nargakot, on a narrow winding mountain road which had been paved once, a long time ago. From there we started walking—uphill and down for about an hour and twenty minutes. At lunchtime, from a kitchen set up beside the road, our cook and porters served us hot orange drink, tea, fried sliced bologna, fried potatoes, a tomato, lettuce and onion tossed salad, bread and butter with honey, jam, and peanut butter, an omelet, and an apple. They and Nima ate huge mounds of rice with boiled squash. As we ate we were watched by a large group of children and several adults who refused the food we offered them. One child wore a sweatshirt with a Mickey Mouse that squeaked appliqued on it. We made friends by making Mickey squeak.

The first night we camped in a pasture at 7000 feet. Days were sunny and pleasantly warm, even a little hot in the sun, but nights were cold. We hiked most of the time on high ridges with indescribable views of incredibly high mountains, a solid wall with snow covered peaks, to the north.

Our tent was small, six-feet square, and we slept on inch-thick foam pads. The nights were long—the ground was hard, we were cold, and we missed having a pillow. After the first night, when we wore only pajamas, (seasoned campers will laugh at that), we used them as long underwear and slept in our clothes. We were somewhat warmer, but the sleeping bags were made for Nepalese who are generally a little over five-feet tall and about 100 pounds. Just turning over was a major effort. But we must have slept better than we thought because we felt fine and we didn't have sore muscles.

Each evening we were served tea, coffee, or cocoa with cookies as soon as the cook could heat water. The first evening we ate a Nepalese dinner of rice, vegetables, and dal sauce, with tea and bananas for dessert. Nima and the crew again ate only enormous mounds of rice topped with a little vegetable. No wonder they are so thin, considering the energy they expend each day. We were pleasantly surprised by the variety of food. One lunch was fried Spam, cold baked beans, a tomato and cucumber salad, a cheese sandwich, a tomato and onion sandwich, and an apple.

Breakfast preparations began about 5:15 a.m. At 6:00 they woke us with tea and cocoa followed soon by eggs, toast, jam, honey, peanut butter, and another round of tea, coffee, and cocoa. We drank every drop provided since it is easy to get dehydrated at those elevations.

Part of the second day we hiked on a road being built through the mountains north from Kathmandu. The crew was living up there with their families, and their lean-to village almost filled the road. A buffalo had just been slaughtered for a festival. The road still had long sections even a four-wheel drive vehicle couldn't have driven on. Delivery of regular food supplies, much less a buffalo, would have been slow work.

The second night we found protection from the strong wind by camping in a farmer's front yard. His wife let our cook use her kitchen. Richard peeked in the house, but the family didn't want him to come in. It was one-room, thatched-roof, and windowless, with two doors about four feet high. A fire in one corner filled the room so full of smoke it was difficult to see.

The Nepalese chicken and rice we ate for dinner was made with a chicken the cook bought from the road crew we passed that day. We expected buffalo meat! We went to bed at 7:30 p.m. because we were tired and it was dark. Actually, Nima came to our tent each night, announced it was time for bed, and zipped up the flap! We decided he didn't want us wandering around and falling off a cliff. He and the rest of the crew stayed up much later but didn't make a lot of noise. They all slept together in a tent the size of ours!

Nine-thousand-foot-high Mount Shivapuri was our last campsite with an inspiring 360° panoramic view of the Himalayas to the north and the Kathmandu valley to the south. Sunrise was magnificent! At first, sunlight touched just the tips of the peaks and then gradually crept down over the mountainsides.

The last day, climbing down very steep, eroded gullies and over large rocks was tough on our legs and knees. Local people going to Kathmandu for a festival followed the same route, many either barefoot or wearing thongs! The "trail," about to become my Waterloo, was only a leisurely Sunday stroll for them. The women wore saris, the children's eyes were painted with kohl, and some of the men carried animals for sacrifice! Our porters practically ran down the mountain with their heavy loads, and when they were climbing uphill, they had enough breath left over to sing. Richard, with his long legs and good sense of balance, kept up a reasonable pace, but I began to wonder if Nima was going to have to carry me off the mountain.

It was a relief to reach a primitive road that would lead us to the town where the van was scheduled to pick us up. Nima kept telling us we were hiking faster than most of his clients. We didn't mind the two-hour wait spent sitting on the main street completely absorbed in watching life go by.

The "van" turned out to be a small car. With the exception of two large backpacks, all our gear fit in the trunk, back seat, or was tied on top, leaving room for us, Nima, and the driver. The crew had to walk or wait for a bus to take them into Kathmandu.

We survived sleeping in a tent, which I had never done before, but decided a real bed, a pillow, and a hot shower at the end of a day are **NECESSITIES**. During the four days we hiked a total of seventeen hours, both uphill and down. We were stiff and sore, had a few blisters and bruises and between us, lost three toenails, but avoided any major problems. Having a medical emergency in Nepal doesn't bear thinking about!

Babies and small children were naked from the waist down. While we were sitting in the square, waiting for the van to arrive, one little girl walked into the rice spread out for drying and winnowing and squatted there to urinate. We decided that was no problem since the rice would be cooked before it was eaten. Perhaps we had been in Asia too long.

On our walk near the hotel in Kathmandu one morning, we encountered—by sheer chance—a family from FAO who had known my parents, Ralph and Mary Phillips, when they were stationed in Rome, Italy. It is a small world.

The Royal Botanical Garden in Godawari could have been beautiful, but is terribly neglected. The ride there and back was fascinating. The way of life is similar to other Asian countries we have visited and yet it is unique. All of the houses have thatched roofs with brick or stone walls painted a terra cotta color. We decided Nepal is closest to "exotic" of any country we visited.

INDIA

December 11-31, 1988

We spent three weeks in India. It is a land of contrasts: rich-poor, beautiful-ugly, clean-filthy. Each area has people with distinct features, dress, customs, and traditions. The caste system is flexible in that all jobs are open — there are untouchables in parliament; however, socially it is rigid and hardly anyone marries outside his caste. There is only a small middle class; almost everyone is either wealthy or miserably poor.

Going to school is voluntary. Primary schools are in every village but secondary schools only in the larger villages. Girls, hardly ever allowed to leave their village, have their education cut short. Birth control is desperately needed but the people are not receptive. Children, especially male children, are looked on as a guarantee of immortality as well as security for parents' old age.

Sanitation is a major problem: large numbers of people either don't have indoor plumbing or choose not to use it. Garbage is simply piled on the sidewalk or in the street, and cow dung is everywhere in piles or patties drying in the sun. We were appalled by the number of people living in cardboard or cloth huts and even sleeping on the sidewalk, covered only with a piece of burlap or plastic.

Gateway to India and the Taj Mahal Hotel in Bombay.

The food was spicy but excellent, the guides interesting and gracious, and the drivers insane! Waiters invariably offered us hamburgers and French fries and when we ordered local food, we tried to remember to request it be "Indian" hot rather than "tourist" hot.

Our guide in Bombay was a tough, outspoken lady who bossed everyone around. She stopped people from boarding sampans when she thought they were overloaded, and she chased a man out of the Prince of Wales Museum because she thought his sleeping on the window seat made a bad impression on tourists. In each city we had a private guide and driver who took great pleasure in scaring us to death.

Travel by car in India makes similar travel in Malaysia look orderly. The streets are used by pedestrians, bicycles, scooters, bullock carts, cars, buses, cows, and water buffalo. The yellow line down the middle doesn't mean a thing. In fact, if the traffic jam is bad enough, the sidewalk is fair game. The horn is used liberally and often, and a two-lane road routinely has five or six lanes of traffic.

The Gateway of India in Bombay is a magnificent monument marking the old seaport entrance to the city, now a beautiful bay,

Topiary Garden in Bombay.

193

and we enjoyed a boat ride to one of the islands to see Hindu temples hewn out of solid rock.

New Delhi is a planned city. However, away from the wide streets and beautiful government buildings, streets and sidewalks were in poor repair. The narrow streets of the old city were jammed with traffic, and a pall of smog left us with sore throats and watery eyes. We did see the old red fort and a beautiful mosque, as well as the Gandhi memorial in a large park containing memorials to Nehru, Indira Gandhi, and Shastri. We were allowed inside the mosque, an indication that Muslims must be more relaxed in India.

For us, one of the pleasures of travel is being free to walk around on our own when the tours are over. Walking provides us with much needed exercise and a leisurely look at people and buildings, in addition to giving us contact with the local rhythm of life. In India it was impossible to walk without being pestered by vendors and beggars who did not respond to polite rejections. We persevered and were rewarded with sights and sounds that are among our most vivid memories. Down one fairly elegant residential street in Bangalore, there was a dairy barn full of cows jammed in between two houses.

While in New Delhi we saw preparations for several weddings, including one where the bridegroom was arriving on horseback. The horse was covered with jeweled cloth and the groom

Indian-style power lawnmower and manure spreader.

194

was in a white suit, also encrusted with jewels. We watched a wedding going on in the hotel one evening. Indian weddings are very public and anyone is welcome to watch. The saris are exquisite.

We saw several "power" lawnmowers; the mower is pulled by a bullock, probably a good way to cut and fertilize the grass simultaneously in a country where animals are considered more precious than people. We learned cows are not sacred in the way we thought. They are protected because the family depends on dung for cooking and milk for food. If the cow dies the family will starve. Cows are turned loose to forage in the daytime but at night, always find their way home.

Children were heartbreakingly undernourished and filthy but many spoke English. We talked with one fifteen-year-old boy touting for a rug store. He was paid 500 rupees (US$33) a month. Meals were provided, allowing the young man to send his salary to his family who lived 150 km away.

An encounter with a ragged entrepreneur gave us insight into how the locals work the tourist business. As we walked down the street a dirty young man pulled Richard's sleeve and said, "Excuse me, sir, you have "sheet" on your shoe. Let me clean it off." Richard looked down and saw a mess of watery cow dung on top of his shoe. He was sure the man put it there, so didn't let him clean it off and get paid for the job. The second time Richard got

Crematorium at Mehrangarh Fort.

195

the "sheet" on your shoe routine he let the man clean it off just to see what his game was. One cloth was used to clean off the cow dung and almost simultaneously shoe polish was applied. Now Richard had one shiny shoe and one dusty one. The natural thing was to have the other shoe shined! The young man asked for 60 rupees (US$4) but settled for the 7 rupees (US40¢) Richard offered!

In order to see as much of India as possible, we spent a week on the Palace on Wheels. The luxurious train, with an interior of polished wood and velvet, runs only during the winter months. It is not air-conditioned and would be unbearable in summer. The stewards treated us like maharajas. The tour took us to Jaipur, Chittaurgarh, Udaipur, Jaisalmer, Bharatur, Jodhpur, and Agra. Our particular "saloon" car, built in 1936 for the Maharaja Kumar of Jaipur, had four compartments for two people each, a lounge, two toilets, and a service area where our two cabin stewards lived and worked.

Our Palace on Wheels "saloon" car.

196

Our 26-year-old head cabin steward was Brahmin. Engaged to a girl his parents chose for him, he had seen only a picture of her. They would meet for the first time at the wedding. When we asked what he would do if they didn't get along his response was, "That is not possible. We would disgrace our parents." From a very young age an Indian girl is taught to take care of her father and brothers and do housework, and boys are taught they must earn money to provide for their family. If love enters into a marriage arrangement, it is considered a bonus.

The only really good night's sleep we had on the train was the one night it parked in the Udaipur station. The road bed was rough and the motion of the train meant tensed muscles to avoid being thrown out of the bunk. The train started and stopped a lot and each time we passed another train, we were jolted awake.

Everywhere we visited palaces and forts, each one more magnificent than the last. The Taj Mahal lived up to our expectations. It is simply exquisite. We spent an hour and a half walking around and taking pictures. Because of recurring vandalism, the monument can no longer be viewed by moonlight. We were surprised to find it is a large complex with several red sandstone buildings as well as the familiar white marble memorial itself.

During the train ride we were in the desert most of the time—one place hadn't had rain in five years—and the dry air and dust was hard on us after the moist climate of Malaysia. Clothes sent to the laundry came back a grey-brown color, no doubt a result of being washed in the local rivers.

Arranging travel and tours in India was easy and relatively inexpensive, even with a private guide and driver in each town. Because of an air controllers' strike, we went to Varanasi instead of Aurangabad, but we figured anything we saw would be new to us and the rearrangement was made by the tour office at no cost to us. We found out pilots were protesting against thirty airports in India that were operating without even minimal instruments necessary to ensure safe landings. They started flying again after the government agreed to install the necessary equipment. There were a few minor mix-ups along the way such as not having a hotel room in Bombay, but one was found for us without too much delay. In all our travels we figured if we were bothered by the problems we ought to stay home.

The plane from New Delhi to Varanasi was a Fokker propeller plane like the ones we flew in Burma but even smaller—it only seated forty-four people and we did not have assigned seats.

Taj Mahal.

The seats were small and our tall bodies felt very cramped. A box supper included a soggy fried vegetable cutlet, two slices of bread, and a small apple. We will never complain about the food on other airlines again.

Varanasi (Benares is the Muslim and British name) is a holy city for Hindus and the birthplace of Buddha. Everywhere in this holy city thousands of pilgrims bathe in the Ganges, considered bacteria-free by the faithful, and in two days walk a ten kilometer route clockwise around the holy part of the city. They make offerings and pray at many of the 1500 temples. Along the way are free guesthouses where they can stay up to three nights. At sunrise on the Ganges we saw a body being cremated. The government is trying to discourage disposing of ashes in the river but is not making much progress. The old town has streets so narrow two people can hardly pass. We were relieved most of the temples were closed to non-Hindus since floors were filthy.

The university in Varanasi is called the Harvard of India. Classes are in English and open to all who pass the entrance exams. The university, founded by a Hindu, has a temple in the center of campus, that was the cleanest of any we were in. We learned a lot about Hindu philosophy and were surprised at the many parallels with Christianity.

Calcutta is indescribable. We had read Dominique Lapierre's *City of Joy* but even then were not prepared for the level of filth. The city does have some beautiful buildings, the Victoria Memorial being the most notable, and our guide assured us that the new subway is clean and doesn't flood during the monsoon.

We thought the rest of India was poor and dirty, but this was a new low: huge garbage piles every few blocks; piles of dung waiting to be made into cakes; walls plastered with cow dung cakes drying in the sun; and incredible poverty everywhere. People urinate and defecate openly in the streets without any concern about privacy. A well and pump provide water for every block. The waste water runs down the gutters and had been dammed to form pools where people bathed and washed their clothes. It truly has to be seen to be believed. Even with unlimited funds and manpower, I'm not sure I could figure out a way to clean up Calcutta. I can't even imagine where I would start.

The trip to Mysore was supposed to take three hours. The highway was pathetic by U.S. standards, but was much better than those in Burma and Nepal. There was a great deal of pedestrian traffic as well as animal-drawn vehicles and herds of animals. We made pretty good progress until we got to Mandya, where we came to a complete halt in an impressive jam of traffic. The college students were on strike against the government and were "flatting the tyres" on all government buses and not letting anyone else through. After a little while we were told there was a narrow road we could use to bypass the problem. An old man got in the car and directed us down narrow dirt streets for a long way through the back parts of the town until we came to a group of students who wouldn't let us go on. We sat and waited and finally they asked us what nationality we were. When we said "American," they let us pass. The old man got out soon after that.

For the rest of the way we were on a winding, back road across the hills through all sorts of wonderful little villages. The road was at most one lane, sometimes paved and sometimes not. Finally, after a little over three hours, we got to Mysore. Our hotel, originally the palace of the Maharaja of Mysore, was elegant. It was like staying in a museum or one of the old Palm Beach estates. We found out later that Queen Elizabeth, Haile Selassie, and other royalty stayed here when visiting Mysore.

Bangalore and Mysore were cleaner with fewer vendors or beggars, but there was still cow dung and garbage everywhere. Mysore has the most exquisite palace we saw on the whole trip, and a garden of fountains that rivals Villa d'Este outside Rome. Our guide in Mysore was proud of the newly installed fountain controlled by computer. It was worth fighting the crowds to see and hear the excellent sound and light show.

In Madras we saw the San Thome Church where St. Thomas is buried, and St. Mary's, the oldest Anglican Church east of Suez. The Christian missionary effort in India has a long history. At the end of our tour, we were driven down the coast about 50 km to Mamallapurnam to see ruins of a city occupied from 600 to 850 A.D.

We experienced our first camel ride while in India. It was a success but Richard didn't feel too secure sitting behind me without stirrups. Our camel stuck his tongue out and made strange noises, no doubt a reaction to something he had eaten. The ride was fairly smooth once the animal picked up speed. We didn't get any pictures—too busy hanging on.

A different system for large numbers is used in India. The newspaper reports were confusing until we had it explained. They count by a thousand, a lakh (which is 100,000), a crore (which is 10,000,000), etc., increasing by hundreds instead of thousands. Rather than writing 12,345,678 they would write 1,23,45,678. A headline "0.5 LAKH KILLED IN EARTHQUAKE" confuses the casual tourist.

Christmas evening we were serenaded with carols by a group of children, mostly from Canada and the U.S., whose parents were missionaries in Bangalore. One of the fathers talked with us about his work. Missionaries, not permitted to enter the country to convert people, come to work with orphanages and to help the poor, hoping they can spread the gospel at the same time. Visa renewal is difficult so this family was going to have to leave in another four months.

SUMATRA

May 7-11, 1989

Lake Toba, the largest in Asia, was formed by the eruption of a volcano, and Samosir Island in the middle is about the size of Singapore. At 3000 feet the air is cool and the resort area an ideal place for a lazy, relaxed vacation. Batak tribes inhabit the island and in addition to learning about their culture, we enjoyed listening to the men sing music which has a South American sound.

The roads in Sumatra gave a new meaning to the word primitive. The few main highways were paved. Single-lane secondary roads were deteriorating paving or gravel.

We started out with a Chinese tour group of honeymooners, but were soon turned over to an Indonesian group. Both the Chinese and Indonesian guides spoke English and translated for us but we were surprised how much of the Bahasa Indonesia we understood. The first few meals we were shunted off by ourselves and served western food. When we expressed dismay, the guide seemed surprised that we would prefer to eat Indonesian food. Two of the young people spoke some English and we had many long conversations with them. The rest of the group smiled a lot and we think were pleased to have us join them.

We tried almost everything, but drew the line at durians. In our two years in Asia we tried durian ice cream, but the smell and texture prevented us from learning to appreciate the taste of the fruit itself. We will always remember the smell of rotten meat permeating the air in durian season. Because of the strong, lingering smell, signs saying "No Durian" were standard in hotel rooms.

In Parapat we were the first people to stay in the new wing of the hotel. The lights in the room were installed outside the electrical boxes with wires running across the wall; the toilet did flush, but took forever to refill; there was almost no flow of water at the sink, but the shower was fine; and a leaking pipe in the bathroom ceiling dripped a constant stream of water onto the toilet. Of course there was no hot water. The water, direct from the lake, was VERY cold. The pillows were about eight inches thick and hard as rocks—absolutely inflexible.

We were lucky to have a roof over our heads at Hari Raya. We came close to missing the trip completely. Fortunately Richard checked our tickets in time to discover we were due to leave a day ahead of when we had expected to!

View of Lake Toba at Parapat.

We bought a Batak perpetual calendar carved in wood and bamboo. Based on a 360-day year, it tells which days are favorable and unfavorable. Only the medicine man knows how to read which day is "today" and whether it is favorable or not.

Our first tour guide in Sumatra asked if there were any in the group, all Chinese except for us, who didn't eat beef. We were surprised when several held up their hands. A month later when Miss Lim took us to lunch she commented she had finally learned to use real butter. She explained it tasted like cow and Chinese often don't like the taste or smell of beef. Chinese restaurants in the U.S. have many beef dishes on the menu but this is evidently a concession to western tastes.

MORE ADVENTURES: 1991-1993

When we returned to Malaysia we agreed we would use our travel time to visit countries we had never been to before. We did visit Abu Dhabi, Sri Lanka, Tibet, and Japan. In defense of our return trips to Nepal, Australia, and New Zealand, we explored areas that were new to us.

NEPAL

October 4-12, 1991

Exotic Nepal, land of the Himalayas, lured us to return. We were uplifted by the power and splendor of the mountains revealed at sunrise, only to hide in clouds or mist later in the day. We trekked around Lake Begnas near the Annapurna range, where Annapurna I, over 26,500 feet, was the highest peak. Pokhara, lower than Kathmandu, was semi-tropical.

Our guide, Nima, said the Royal Trail (2,900-6,000 feet) was a good trek for "older" people! The "geriatric" route provided us with magnificent panoramic views of terraced valleys, picturesque villages, and glorious mountains. The Nepalese

House under construction near Pokhara.

lived in circumstances we couldn't begin to imagine. Fruits and vegetables were plentiful, but children were dressed in rags. Babies and very young children often wore no clothes at all. Women wrapped saris differently than in India or Malaysia. Some wore an elaborate turban with the end flipped over in front to give shade. Men wore a short sarong or long loose pants. Men and women carried wood, heavy loads of fodder for livestock, and other provisions on their backs. Houses constructed of bricks or stones shaped with hand tools to fit, were held together with mud. The resulting walls were works of art, often covered with red mud resembling the adobe dwellings of our southwest. Poorer families lived in thatch-covered bamboo huts.

SELECTED DIARY EXCERPTS

4 OCTOBER, 1991—Bangkok, a stopover on the easiest and most economical route between Malaysia and Nepal, was as congested and polluted as we remembered. It took well over an hour for the van to get us to the New Peninsula Hotel, and the amount of high-rise building construction, a sure sign of prosperity, was unbelievable. We went walking and did not buy the hand woven coat Maria admired, but we did find Dial soap in a little store and bought 16 bars! (Dial soap was not available in Malaysia.) Each 4-bar pack came with a free glass; we gave them to Nima. We had an excellent dinner at the hotel with our Thai Airlines chit—cashew chicken, mango kerabu, and Chinese sausage salad. The hotel provided a price list of <u>everything</u> in the room in case we might want to take something. The list included head board (US$75), water heater (US$255), toilet (US$130), toilet seat (US$30), carpet (US$22 per piece), wardrobe (US$90), and doorknob (US$15). We wondered whether thievery was a significant problem. The hotel also provided magazines with listings of local bars and massage parlors. They ranged from legitimate? to all sorts of male/female and same-sex pleasure houses and escort services. AIDS was a problem of epidemic proportions.

5 OCTOBER, 1991—We were a half hour late leaving Bangkok because of mechanical problems with the cargo door. It was cloudy and overcast most of the way, but we had a good view of Mount Everest. Nima and Siti Ram met us at the airport. Our hotel, the Marshyangdi, was clean and the staff seemed nice. When we tried to put film in the camera, it wouldn't wind at all, so we took it to be worked on. Bikrum, the owner of Himalayan Expeditions, offered to lend us his for the Everest flight. The electricity went off in a large area of that part of Kathmandu shortly after 6 p.m. We walked in the dark to the restaurant and the power came back on about 8:15 while we were still eating. We had an excellent dinner—Nepalese soup (tomato egg-drop and chicken mushroom), Tibetan dumplings [chicken momo and buff (water buffalo) kothey], marinated goat liver, soybeans in garlic and chilies, and cinnamon yoghurt for dessert.

▼

The "road" between Kathmandu and Pokhara was being rebuilt by a joint Japanese/Chinese effort. Approximately 80 km of the bone jarring, teeth rattling, 200 km route was under construction. The rest was deteriorating paving connected by potholes, gravel and mud. We averaged 17 mph in our "private" car, an ancient Toyota. Progress was slowed by huge traffic jams caused by one-lane stretches and broken down trucks and buses.

8 OCTOBER, 1991—Nima picked us up in a taxi a little before 8 a.m. We drove out east of town to the trailhead, but our porters weren't there. About 10 a.m. we started hiking without them. Nima said they knew where we were to go and they could catch up with us. The trail went steadily up and the air was cool, but the sun was hot so we were uncomfortably warm. After about an hour we came to a small village, maybe six houses, and there were the porters waiting for us! They had come from a different trailhead nearer to Pokhara. They served us a cold drink and also brewed tea before we went on. We walked another hour and a half—still uphill—until we stopped for lunch a little after 1 p.m. They set up camp for the night on top of a high ridge with a view south down into the Pokhara valley and north to the wall of snow-covered Himalayas. The Annapurnas rise up over 26,500 feet with virtually no foothills in front of them. It was magnificent! They served us tea, fried eggs, cucumber slices, cheese sandwiches, and bananas. They also set out jars of peanut butter, butter, and apricot jam, but there is a limit to how much we can consume at one meal.

We talked to a young man who looked 16 but was in the ninth grade in school. He wanted to go on to the local college. He went to school twelve months per year and paid tuition of 40 rupees (96¢) per month. Just as it was getting dusk a German couple with guide showed up. They had gotten separated from their group and had no idea where they were. They had warm clothes and a box lunch, but no tent, sleeping bags, or other food. One of our porters went back down the trail to see what he could find. It took him a long time to find the others but he returned to lead our visitors back to their group in pitch dark with flashlights. For supper we were served vegetable garlic soup (delicious!), kothey, cauliflower, fried eggplant, carrot-cabbage slaw, and for dessert an apple pie! We sat for a long time in the dark looking at the stars and the lights in the valley.

▼

Nima, a cook, and three porters took care of the two of us during our three-day trek. The ground was as hard as we remembered from three years ago but this time we had good quality, extra-long sleeping bags. Again, we were amazed at what delicious meals could be produced over an open fire. The cook served us a variety of western, Indian, and Nepalese dishes.

9 OCTOBER, 1991—We got up about 6 a.m. It was light but the sun hadn't risen yet. We had a reasonably good night—not nearly as cold as the 1988 trek. They had a table and stools so we weren't sitting on the ground, and a latrine tent had replaced the great outdoors. Breakfast was cooked cereal with shredded coconut in it. Our mid-morning tea had water buffalo milk in it. The taste was similar to cow's milk. The views continued to be incredible—steep valleys, lakes, rivers, streams, villages, and always the wall of snow-covered mountains to the north. We stopped for lunch about 10:15. They served us hot orange drink right away and then hot tea. Lunch was fried spam, french fries, chapatis with cheese, sliced cucumbers, and apples. We went on our way about 11:30. It continued up and down with a couple of very steep, long climbs. There was little breeze and it got steamy hot after noon. We stopped in one small village for a rest break and got to our campsite shortly after 2:00. They served us cold lemonade at once. (We have no idea how they manage to

Nima with cook and porters.

chill it.) Again we sat in the shade to read, write, and enjoy the scenery. We camped around a buffalo wallow, which was interesting, but not exactly scenic. If we squinted just right, the green scum looked like a lawn in front of the tent. Dinner was cream of vegetable soup, tempura fried cauliflower, eggplant, boiled cabbage, green beans with carrots and onions, noodles, and coconut cake for dessert. We went to bed even earlier than the night before because we were so tired.

There were times during the three days when we wondered why we were subjecting ourselves to such an ordeal. The trails were relatively easy but there were several steep climbs that seemed to go on forever, and those were particularly difficult considering the unseasonable heat and humidity. Nima assured us it was cooler in early October last year. Many of the downhill stretches had stone steps. However, much of the trail followed dry or wet stream beds. Maria had a walking stick to make coming down easier.

10 OCTOBER, 1991—We were up before sunrise again and the mountains with the sun on their peaks were spectacular. We asked Nima what the name of one mountain was and

Campsite by buffalo wallow.

he said, "Oh, that's not a mountain—only a ridge. It's only about 20,000 feet high." It's all relative. Breakfast was fried eggs and toast with a lot more options we didn't need. We started walking before 7:30 and the first 45 minutes was steeply downhill. They had set stones to make stairs so it wasn't too bad. Then we got to the head of a stream and followed the rocky stream bed down for another 45 minutes. We stopped for tea and from there we went uphill steeply for about 45 minutes. We got to a farmhouse at the top and we think we were lost, but, of course, we can't understand the Nepalese conversations. The farmer pointed us down a poor, very steep trail and in another 45 minutes we were down to the river again. We followed it and waded across it twice. Some of it was a good track along the river side and some went through rice paddies and got very muddy at times. [Added after we got home: When Maria started to do laundry, she discovered a pair of Richard's underwear with a large amount of blood at the back waistband. When she looked, he had a small round circle cut on his back. We think he must have gotten a leach out there, but by changing clothes in the dark he never knew it.] A little before noon we caught up with our porters who had lunch all ready for us. They immediately served us orangeade and hot tea. Then lunch was canned tuna, chapatis with cheese, boiled potatoes with a tomato-onion sauce, and oranges. We started on our way again about 12:50. We thought that it would be a gentle walk following the river, but we were wrong. We went up over a very steep, high ridge and down to the next valley. It was about 3 p.m. when we finally got to the trailhead and took a taxi to our hotel. We were not much the worse for wear—a blister apiece, sore feet, and sore muscles.

▼

The Pokhara area was more populated than the Kathmandu rim so we were never far from people or villages. At times we played "Pied Piper" with a following of children eager to practice their English skills, so Richard tested their knowledge of Nepalese and American political structure. They knew about George Bush and Dan Quayle! We saw few other trekkers. The second day we played "tag" with a German group that walked faster than we did but rested more often.

We were scheduled to fly back to Kathmandu but our plane had mechanical problems. With the shortage of planes no replacement was available, so Nima hired a taxi. We waited a half hour at the scene of a two-truck-breakdown that held up later travelers for as long as 2 1/2 hours. We drove in the dark only after reaching the outskirts of Kathmandu.

TASMANIA/NEW ZEALAND

December 8-29, 1991

Tasmania in the spring was an island of flowers. Private homes were surrounded by carefully tended gardens, public parks were showplaces, and the roadsides were thick with wildflowers. We didn't know roses could be so large or that colors could be so brilliant. We stayed in Hobart, Queenstown, Boat Harbor Beach, and Launceston. We had a rental car so we could explore the countryside between those towns. We hiked often, finding waterfalls, unique rock formations, caves and spectacular views. Hobart was built around a natural harbor in the shadow of Mt. Wellington. South of Hobart, Port Arthur, one of the original prison colonies, was being restored.

SELECTED DIARY EXCERPT

10 DECEMBER, 1991—Along the coast east toward Port

Arthur were high, steep rock cliffs with sandy beaches around the bay. One curious formation called "tessellated pavement" is a horizontal rock slab at the water's edge with a network of perpendicular vertical fractures that made the beach look paved with rectangular tiles. Several blowholes, Devil's Kitchen, and Tasman Arch were rock formations formed by wave action on rock that is vertically fractured and falls (or stands) in slabs.

Coastline near Port Arthur.

Port Arthur ruins.

Queenstown, Tasmania, is an old copper-mining town and the surrounding terrain has been almost completely destroyed by the open-pit mining. It was a surrealistic landscape and quite a contrast to the rest of the southwest that was well-forested and unspoiled, rugged, unexplored wilderness.

SELECTED DIARY EXCERPT

12 DECEMBER, 1991—The bathroom in the Queenstown motel was unique. Along one wall was a counter with the washbasin at one side and the toilet on the other. However, the handle to flush the toilet was a button to push mounted in the wall across the room from the fixture itself. If Richard hadn't said, "I wonder what this does," and pushed it, we might never have figured out how to flush the toilet.

North of Queenstown we saw many large fields of daisies and poppies. The poppy farms were sponsored by the international chemical and pharmaceutical industries (Tasmania is one of three places in the world doing this). The opium and its derivatives are used for medical purposes. They also sell poppy seed for baking. The farmer we asked said the fields of ripe pods were heavily guarded to keep people from stealing them for the illicit drug industry. Pyrethrum was extracted from the daisy flowers to make insecticide.

Boat Harbor Beach is a resort area, with several national parks along the coast and a large basalt rock (a la Gibraltar) called "The Nut," which we climbed and explored.

We made friends with a Tasmanian Devil. "Josephine" was tame and we understand that devils born in captivity make good pets; however, those in the wild can inflict a nasty bite and are best left alone.

Launceston has many historic buildings and Cataract Gorge that bisects the city. Stores were open on Saturday because of the holiday season but Christmas selling was low key in Australia.

SELECTED DIARY EXCERPT

16 DECEMBER, 1991—We woke to sunny skies but had a

few showers by afternoon. It hadn't rained for six months. We walked to the Launceston post office to mail letters and then to City Park to go through the conservatory. It was small, but had some beautiful floral displays. We drove across town to Cataract Gorge where we took the chair lift across the gorge and walked back on the suspension bridge. On the way out of town we stopped at Talbot lookout where we had a view in all directions across the city and valley to the hills. We took the Midland Highway to Hobart and stopped in all the National Historic Towns along the way (Evandale, Longford, Ross, Oatlands, Kempton, and Pontville). In most of them we saw interesting old churches, hotels, houses, and other buildings mostly of brown sandstone and ranging from 125 to 165 years old. We had lunch in Evandale in the 1830s Clarendon Arms Hotel. It was in marvelous condition and had some nice murals.

After arriving in New Zealand, we called to reconfirm our return flight to KL. We discovered our return reservations were messed up. New Zealand went on daylight saving time after we made our reservations so now we have only fifteen minutes between flights in Sydney. We talked to "Peter" daily for the remainder of our trip, and he finally managed to make satisfactory connections for us.

In New Zealand we concentrated on the south end of the south island. We stayed in Dunedin, Invercargill, Cascade Creek, and Queenstown, with overnights in Christchurch going and coming.

SELECTED DIARY EXCERPT

18 DECEMBER, 1991—We drove to Dunedin, with a stop at Moeraki Beach to see the boulders. Several dozen one-to two-meter diameter, almost perfect spheres were scattered in this one place. After we checked into our motel (which had no reservation for us because the FAX had been garbled, but had plenty of room), we drove to the City Center and walked around a little. We went into St. Paul's Cathedral and were jarred by the architecture. It was neo-gothic from the front up to where the crossing and transepts should be. It stood that way unfinished for over fifty years. When they added the chancel in 1971, they made it extremely modern, so the two parts seemed to sit there and shout at each other. We went to eat at Willoughby's because the Shulls had recommended the green-lipped mussels there, but they were out of season until after New Year's. We had an excellent meal anyway.

▼

Dunedin's Baldwin Street, the steepest street in the world according to Guinness Book of Records, goes straight up, while the one in San Francisco turns back and forth. We then drove out the Otago Peninsula with a stop at Larnach Castle, which

Signpost at Bluff..

213

was impressive. We went on out to the tip of the peninsula to the Royal Albatross Refuge. It happened to be a relatively warm, calm day so they weren't flying but we saw them nesting, incubating eggs, as well as seeing lots of shags and a few seals.

South of Invercargill, the town of Bluff is 46° 46' 54" south. It is over 4000 miles from there to the south pole which is about the same distance Bluff is from the equator. That's a long way to travel just to look at a block of ice.

"This is the end of the world and the beginning of paradise." This fiordlands claim was not exaggerated. Our motel in Cascade Creek was at the head of a valley surrounded by snow-capped mountains on three sides. From our room we could see the rugged peaks and snow—a truly magnificent setting. We drove on to the end of the road at Milford Sound. The scenery was indescribable. The mountains looked like one solid rock and the sides were almost vertical. There were literally hundreds of waterfalls and cascades falling from the top all the way to the bottom. With all our travel in the American and Canadian Rockies, Nepal, etc. we had never seen anything so spectacular as this. On the way back from Milford Sound we took a short walk to the Chasm where a large stream plunges down through a very narrow chasm. We also stopped to take pictures of a spectacular waterfall by the roadside. This is one

Road to Milford Sound.

214

Doubtful Sound.

of the wettest places in the world. They average over twenty-five **FEET** of rain per year. We were fortunate to have lots of sun mixed in with the rain. The rain just increased the number of waterfalls in the fiords and decreased the number of sand-flies. We took both the Milford and Doubtful Sound cruises.

SELECTED DIARY EXCERPTS

23 DECEMBER, 1991—In 1983 this area had over twenty-eight feet of rain. We drove out to Hollyford Valley and hiked to Humbolt Falls. It was spectacular—coming down the vertical mountainside in three large cascades. We stopped at the trail at the upper end of Homer's Tunnel but it was buried under several feet of snow. On the other side of the tunnel we did take the nature trail. After lunch we took the Milford Sound cruise. It was 1½ hours and took us down the fiord to the open ocean (the Tasman Sea) and back. Some walls were covered with trees and scrub growth, which had a minimal root system in moss that grows on the rock, so tree avalanches are common. The peaks were all snow-covered and one had the remnants of a glacier toward its top. It was windy and very cold, but we sat on the open top deck anyway to get the best possible view. After the cruise we walked to the base of Lady Bowen Falls and then drove back to our motel.

215

24 DECEMBER, 1991—We woke early to partly cloudy skies that turned to light rain all the time we were on our cruise and then back to sunshine when we returned. We drove down to Manapouri for the 8:30 Doubtful Sound cruise, crossed Lake Manapouri in a high speed jet boat and took a bus to tour the underground hydroelectric station and cross Wilmot Pass to the head of Doubtful Sound for a trip through one arm of the sound. We were twenty-five miles from ocean. The beautiful scenery was not nearly so spectacular as Milford Sound, but with the rain there were far more waterfalls.

25 DECEMBER, 1991—MERRY CHRISTMAS! What a beautiful day! All blue sky that developed a few high clouds—sunshine—cool air. We drove into Te Anau and went to Christmas mass at St. Michael and All Angels. It was a little church, but packed full. A couple invited us to their house for coffee and pie that turned out to be tea and cookies. We chatted for a while and then went to a park to eat our picnic lunch. We took the cruise across Lake Te Anau to the Glowworm Caves. A large stream running through is still eroding and forming the caves. And, of course, the glowworms on the ceiling were beautiful in an eerie sort of way. When we got back to the motel we called Michael to wish him a "Merry Christmas," but since it was midnight Christmas Eve in Eastern U.S. time, we thought any further calls would not be appreciated. Dinner at the motel was a Christmas buffet for all the staff and guests.

▼

December 26 was Boxing Day, a public holiday throughout the British Commonwealth. We asked a lot of people before we found someone who knew the origin of the term: Christmas Day was traditionally a religious holiday, therefore, the exchange of gifts was deferred until the day after Christmas. The post office, banks, etc. were closed, but most of the commercial places were open.

It rained all morning, but cleared off about the time we got to Queenstown. Even in the rain it was a beautiful drive up green valleys with mountains all around. We stopped for a picnic lunch but had to eat it in the car because of the rain. We spent the rest of the afternoon wandering around Queenstown. The dinner cruise on the *S.S. Earnslaw*, an old (1912) lake steamer, took us across the lake to the Colonel's Homestead at Walter Peak. Before dinner we walked around the barnyard.

216

Colonel's Homestead at Walter Peak.

In 1976, their shaggy highland cattle were counted among only 2000 in the world. We also watched a demonstration of sheep herding by border collies.

SELECTED DIARY EXCERPT

27 DECEMBER, 1991—Another beautiful sunny day. We drove to Wanaka and decided to climb Mount Roy. We almost bit off more than we could chew, but we made it and were very satisfied when we got back down. We climbed 5000 ft. vertically and walked five miles to the top, and another five miles down. The sign said it should take four to six hours. We took five hours and 10 minutes actual walking time, but 6¼ hours with all our rest stops and a stop for lunch. Actual walking time was 3 hours and 5 minutes up and 2 hours and 5 minutes down. On the way up we encountered several other climbers descending and each time when we asked about the top they said, "It's just a wee bit farther." We also were passed by a young man on a bicycle who went perhaps halfway to the top and then came roaring down past us. At the top the view was spectacular. It was the highest point on a thin ridge and on both sides there were broad valleys with deep blue lakes and then snow-capped mountains on the far side. The view justified the climb. When we got back down we went to The Maze. Besides all sorts of puzzles to demonstrate and sell, they had a three-dimensional maze we wanted to try. People spend hours trying to find the four corners. It would have been fun, but we decided we were just too tired to do any more walking.

When we bought gas in Queenstown, the attendant also washed the windshield. Richard told him he wasn't used to that kind of service. He said he had heard that in the U.S. people had to pump their own gas and wash their own windows but he thought that was "a bit over the top."

We saw a sign in a front yard out in the country offering "moo moo poos" for sale. We guessed at what they were, but weren't certain. Today we saw a similar sign for "horse poos" and we are sure we were right.

This was one of the best vacations we had ever taken. Much of our time was spent poking around the countryside. Both Tasmania and New Zealand have small populations and even though it was early summer and the beginning of the tourist season, we never felt overwhelmed. In driving around New Zealand we had to wait at one-laned bridges twice, compared to once when we visited in the winter of 1988!

SRI LANKA
Blessed Paradise

April 3-11, 1992

We visited Sri Lanka (Ceylon) during our spring break. The name means Blessed Paradise and the island was indeed beautiful in spite of the drought conditions that prevailed while we were there. The island depends on hydro power for electricity so, in addition to water shortages, government electrical power was available only between 9 p.m. and 5 a.m. Most hotels had their own generators.

Two-thirds of Sri Lankans are Singhalese, (translated "lion people") and theirs is the national language. Most are Buddhists and in general, cheerful, easy-going, generous, and welcoming to strangers. Between them and the rest of the population of Tamil, Muslim, and Eurasian backgrounds, harmony was ruffled by an undercurrent of social and political malaise over economic position.

The first days of our tour were spent hiking around ruins of various capital cities dating from about the 4th century B.C. to the 12th century A.D. Anuradhapura, the oldest, was a UNESCO protected site but tourists were allowed to climb on the ruins and enter the temples after first removing shoes and hats. Sigiriya was a 5th century fortress built on top of a 700 ft. stone mountain. The palace on top, now only foundations, had 128 rooms with gardens, bathing pool, audience hall, etc. It

Ruins at Anuradhapura.

was occupied for 18 years and then abandoned when the king was killed by his brother. It must have been a challenging engineering feat to transport materials up the sheer rock face. There were stone steps for the first part of the climb followed by an iron staircase that zigzagged up the rest of the way. In places it made use of the original toeholds and even though the climb was safe, it was hair-raising. Polonnaruwa, the most well-preserved of the three, was occupied from the 8th through the 12th century. Again, we were free to roam at will.

Statue at Anuradhapura.

"Ceylon" tea, known all over the world, was wilting in the drought. Picking had stopped but we toured a plantation and were given samples of the best grade. We decided we liked Malaysian tea as well or better. Sri Lanka batik, also known worldwide, had unique designs and we brought home a few pieces.

The British left their legacy of hill stations to escape the heat. We spent a night in Kandy and visited The Temple of the

Wood Carver.

Tooth (16th century) which housed one of Buddha's teeth. It was only open for one hour three times a day, at 5:30 a.m., 12:00 noon, and 6:30 p.m. when pilgrims made offerings of rice and thirty kinds of curry. There was a drum and horn concert first and then officials opened the silver doors and carried everything inside the chamber. Later the crowd filed by a doorway to look at the shrine. The tooth itself was housed in seven gold nested caskets. The next day we endured many

Toddy harvester.

hours of tortuous mountain roads to spend the night in Nuwara Eliya (over 6000 ft.) where it was cool enough that we slept under TWO blankets.

Roads were poor, slightly more than one lane wide, and near villages there was lots of pedestrian, bicycle, and other non-motor traffic, so we made slow progress. We saw toddy being harvested from the tops of coconut palms. The worker had a network of ropes strung from tree to tree so he didn't have to keep coming down and climbing up again. We also saw kapok, cashew, and all sorts of different spice trees and plants.

We went to Yala Game Preserve near Tissamaharama. The afternoon safari trek was more successful than we had dreamed possible. Soon after we started we sighted a large bull elephant with huge tusks. Many safaris don't see any elephants and few ever see a male. We drove for three hours from one waterhole to another. We saw about a dozen ele-

Maria enjoying elephant ride.

Old Dutch fort at Galle.

Stilt fishermen.

phants altogether including a family group with two little ones the guide estimated to be about six months old. We also saw a mongoose, a wild boar, deer, monitor lizards, crocodiles, and lots of water buffalo. There was also a large variety of beautiful birds—herons, egrets, storks, etc.

We visited an elephant park, watched them being bathed in the river by their trainers and then had a bareback ride. One, a male with large tusks, could only be ridden by shoeless men because a male elephant is considered holy.

Our first and last two nights were spent at beach resorts so we swam in the Indian Ocean. It was bathwater temperature. The hotels for the tour varied from new and modern or old and elegant, to slightly below summer camp (at Yala where we slept under mosquito nets and had to keep the doors of the room open to avoid suffocation.)

NEPAL/TIBET

May 10-24, 1992

We had dreamed of this trip for a long time. Along with Betty Gawthrop and Larry Reister, we submitted visa applications at the Chinese Embassy in Kuala Lumpur. Even as a group of four (individuals are not permitted to enter Tibet), we were turned down. The embassy required a letter from Richard's employer granting permission to take leave. When we submitted the letter, an itinerary from our guide was required. Next, we needed a letter from someone in Tibet inviting us to visit. As tourists who knew nobody in Tibet, that didn't make one bit of sense, but they wouldn't listen to reason. We decided the embassy was subtly telling us they would not issue a visa no matter what we did. We FAXed Nima to cancel everything. By return FAX he assured us he could get visas from the embassy in Kathmandu with no problem. Based on our faith in Nima, we went.

SELECTED DIARY EXCERPT

12 MAY, 1992—We met Nima's wife, Bimaya, and two children. They lived in one room on the fifth floor up a narrow, stone, unlighted staircase. They had a single faucet with a concrete catch basin on the floor. There was no closet or storage at all. They had one wide single bed and mats for the boys to sleep on the floor, a low table like a coffee table, four chairs, a shelf for dishes, and a small bookshelf. She had a wooden platform about a foot off the floor with a single burner gas plate to cook on. Whatever toilet and bathing facilities they had were elsewhere and obviously communal. They had two bare electric bulbs for light. Her dress had not been washed for

Bimaya and Pasang.

225

a long time but she, the children, and the room, looked clean. She first nursed the two-year old, Dipak, and he fell asleep on the bed. Then she fixed dinner for us: noodle soup, lots of rice, chicken, cauliflower, sliced tomatoes, sliced cucumbers, and apples for dessert. She refused to eat until after we left. She spoke no English, but we smiled a lot and Jwane, Nima's brother, translated for us. The eight-year-old, Pasang, was learning English in school. So far, he had learned the alphabet and how to count to ten.

▼

Our original plan of sleeping in monasteries as stopovers while being driven across Tibet with Nima, our Nepalese trekking guide, was not acceptable to the Chinese. Nepalese guides were only allowed into China in order to lead treks. We were not allowed to stay in monasteries if hotels were available and we were put in the hands of Tibet International Sport Travel (TIST) with a Tibetan guide and a Tibetan driver.

SELECTED DIARY EXCERPT

14 MAY, 1992—Jwane went with us to make sure we got to Chinese immigration at the border. We drove east and then north from Kathmandu on roads with only one center lane paved which got steadily worse as we went on. It was mostly uphill in increasingly mountainous country. There was a lot of farming on the terraced hillsides and the wheat harvest was going strong. It was strictly by hand with a sickle, and much of the cut wheat was spread on the highway as a means of threshing it. We went through checkpoints where the driver had to stop to sign a registry about every ten miles. We stopped for lunch about 10 a.m. and just ate a little of what we had with us. When we were ready to leave, they discovered we had a flat tire. They changed it fairly quickly and we went on our way. Soon after that it started to rain—a heavy, cold rain. After a while we came to a larger village and stopped to see about having the tire repaired. It was an agonizingly slow process of negotiation, conversation, and finally the repair. We were there a good 45 minutes and were becoming increasingly aware of the time. We understood that the border closed at 5 p.m. and we were going to lose 2¼ hours since all of China runs on Beijing time regardless of the sun. We could see that we were going to be cutting it very close even if things went well. From there the road was gravel and we understood that we would see no more paving on this trip. We went up very steeply and it got progressively cooler. We got to the Nepal exit point at Kodary about 1 p.m. (3:15 China time). They were slow, but finally got us checked through. They told us that many people checked out there, were denied admission at the China border (even with a valid entry visa), and had to come back to Nepal. Our mini-bus could go no farther and we had missed the last bus to Zhangmu. A five-mile "no man's land" separated the Nepalese and Tibetan borders. They said the only way to get there was to walk and it was still raining hard. The road was almost straight up. We had a huge pile of luggage with all our heavy clothes, food for lunches, several bottles of water, and sleeping bags, but porters were available to carry. The trail was very steep and would take over an hour and a half. That was the epitome of our discouragement!!! We finally bribed a freight bus to take us. It was worth the US$10 apiece not to have to walk in the rain. The bus was loaded with freight and had a few seats for local workers, but could not legally take other passengers. The road was a poor mountain trail and very steep with lots of hairpin curves, but we finally made Zhangmu (about 7500 ft.). They stopped to unload freight on the edge of town and then took us on to the border checkpoint. We never did figure out what the no-man's-land between the two checkpoints is all about, except that it is so rugged that they probably can't set up posts at the actual border. We were relieved to find our tour guide waiting for us. We filled out several different forms and they checked things pretty carefully but finally cleared us. They even looked through our two paperback novels to see if they were acceptable. They confiscated our bag of fresh apples, but the raisins passed.

Customs was all part of the usual hassle in this part of the world and when we had finished we walked a few hundred yards to our hotel. For the next five nights we would stay in hotels that would not pass even the lowest inspection standards. They had not been cleaned in years, there was no running water, toilets didn't flush, no heat.... At least the sheets were clean and we didn't encounter any bedbugs. Boiled water was supplied for drinking. The last four nights in the Lhasa Holiday Inn were pure luxury. It even had hot water for showers!

SELECTED DIARY EXCERPTS

15 MAY, 1992—We loaded the 4WD land cruiser and, after a stop at the bank to change money, headed up. We went up a steep, narrow gorge on a road that was better than yesterday's. (This cut in the Himalayas can be seen from outer space.) We stopped at Nyalam (12,375 ft.) for gas and a break. From there the road was surprisingly good, for gravel,

Western Tibet village.

Yaks grazing near village.

most of the time. The terrain changed to very dry and almost without vegetation as we got up to the high plateau which averages over 14,000 ft. It was extremely windy and cold. A temple, built by the 5th Dalai Lama in the 17th century, has a throne for the Dalai Lama. At every temple and monastery monks begged for his picture.

Nilam pass was 16,665 ft. The mountains all around were 24,000 ft. and more. Down on the plateau were little houses, occasional villages and, in spite of looking completely barren, many herds of sheep, goats, yaks, and a few cows, horses, and donkeys. Transportation seemed to be largely by horse and donkey carts. Women used shovels to cultivate the irrigated fields and seemed to work much harder than the men. The house where we ate lunch had one room with a little stove in the center, a bed at one side, and a huge pile of dried dung in one corner. They had no food to spare, but provided us with boiling water, bowls, and chopsticks to make the instant noodle soup we had with us. We took pictures and offered to send copies to the occupants, but they have no mail service. They essentially have no contact with the outside world.

Obviously, we had stepped into a dimension of living we had never dreamed of. Tibetans consider body oils to be sacred so they never wash. Babies are smeared with yak butter and allowed to run around naked so by the time they reach adulthood the dirt, yak butter, and skin have all become one. On the high plateau houses were made of mud-bricks painted white, with ocher and black patterns. The corners of each house were decorated with plumes of barley and prayer flags.

The land is mostly rock but during the short growing season it yields amazingly large vegetables that supplement the main diet of tsampa (barley flour) and yak butter. Trees grow only along streams or where there is irrigation.

Except around Lhasa, the roads were unpaved. A few spots were bad but mostly they were better than we had expected them to be. Dust was a big problem and even though we wore face masks, we brought home a lot of it in our lungs and in our clothes.

We were over 14,000 feet a good part of the time and went as high as 17,000 at Everest base camp. We had planned to stay the night at Rongbuk monastery, but Maria had altitude sickness and we had to come back down. The accommodations would have been basic: a 10X15 ft. room with rug-covered stone benches for sleeping and a small wood stove in the center. We carried our own sleeping bags. The privy was outdoors, with waist high walls and no roof!

Chomolungma (Mount Everest).

Richard with Cho Oyu in background.

16 MAY, 1992—The 70 miles from New Tingri to Rongbuk Monastery was a path over great fields of large rocks crisscrossing a river bed. After about 15 miles at the top of Pang Lu pass (17,325 ft.) the high range of the Himalayas suddenly spread like a wall of snow in front of us. There was Makalu, Lhotse, Nuptse, and Cho Oyu with Chomolungma

Shepherds near Rombuck Monastery.

(Mount Everest) rising above it all in the center—probably the most impressive mountain sight we have ever seen. We drove on to Rongbuk Monastery at 16,500 ft. The 70 miles took us five hours. The monastery, less than 100 years old, was completely destroyed during the cultural revolution. It was being rebuilt and restored and had 15 monks and five nuns in residence.

18 MAY, 1992—Today we stayed in Shigatse. Maria seems better, but still weak. In the morning we went to Tashilhunpo Monastery, which is the largest in Tibet and is the home of the Panchen Lama, second to the Dalai Lama. It covers several acres and has a multitude of temples, each dedicated to a different Buddha or Lama, but they look pretty much alike to us. Each has elaborate paintings, statues, and decorations with many wicks burning in large vats of yak butter, and monks chanting at the side. It was founded in 1447 by the first Dalai Lama. Of course, it is also a small town with all the housing, etc., for the monks. In the afternoon we went to a Tibetan carpet factory. All of the work is done by hand—carding, spinning, and dyeing the wool as well as actually knotting the carpet. We bought a small (about 30" square) brown and white carpet. It was shipped, along with a larger rug that Betty and Larry purchased, to Betty's house in Florida

Carpet factory worker.

Kitchen at the yak-steak restaurant.

with the understanding that we would pay for them after they arrived. The owner of the factory insisted he had never lost any money by doing business this way. We then went to the town free market where they were selling everything imaginable. For dinner we went back to last night's restaurant and had yak steak with mixed vegetables. The steak tasted like beef and was good, but tough as shoe leather.

Main street of Gyantse.

233

20 MAY, 1992—This morning we went to the Drepung Monastery, once the largest in the world with 10,000 monks. Founded in 1416 and enlarged in the early 1600s by the 5th Dalai Lama, it now has only about 400 monks. Besides a multitude of temples, it has 4 large dukhangs (assembly halls) with great courtyards in front. At one time these were used by 4 colleges to teach 4 different kinds of Buddhism to the monks. The monastery was built on a mountainside and had lots of stairs. We were sitting resting in one courtyard when a group of young monks gathered around Richard. They wanted to feel his beard and the hair on the back of his hands. Since they were nearly devoid of body hair, they were fascinated. In the afternoon we went to the Jokhang Temple, which is

Large hall at Drepung Monastery.

in the heart of the city. It was nearly destroyed in the Cultural Revolution, but the restoration was well along. It was full of pilgrims inside and walking the pilgrim circuit around it. The front pavilion had many pilgrims prostrating themselves repeatedly to the point that they had polished and worn the stone floor. Inside was a large courtyard with 20 chapels around it dedicated to Buddhist deities, Indian saints, and Tibetan kings and queens. We went up to the rooftop and had a magnificent view of the Potala.

21 MAY, 1992—The Potala, the Dalai Lama's winter

Pilgrims prostrating themselves in front of the Jokhang Temple.

Begging monk.

palace, was built on a hilltop, and we were driven almost to the top so we could work our way down. It was started in the 7th century, but burned in the 9th century and most of this was built in the middle 1600s. It is 13 stories high and has over 1000 rooms with 10,000 shrines and over 200,000 statues. The walls, over 16 ft. thick at the base and strengthened with molten copper, have no steel framework and no nails. They were built entirely of stone and wood. The Dalai Lama's private quarters are plush from a Tibetan point of view. The shrines and temples are very much like what we have seen

The Potala.

except cleaner and more elaborate. Some of the wood carving is intricate. But shades of tourism—in the center they were building a large salesroom with public toilets! We also saw the mausoleums where the 5th through 13th Dalai Lamas (except the 6th) were interred in chortens (a Tibetan stupa). They were salt-dried before burial. The chortens are covered with stupendous amounts of gold, diamonds, pearls, and semi-precious stones. The 5th Dalai Lama's chorten has over 4 tons of gold on it and stands over 65 feet high.

The Summer Palace, Norbulinka, is a large complex of small palaces and chapels within a walled garden. The oldest palace was started in 1755, but all we saw of it was a small temple. The newest palace was finished in 1956, but of course the Dalai Lama went into exile in 1959. It was in excellent

Shoe factory worker.

condition and modern for Tibet in the 1950s. His bedroom had an elaborate shortwave/AM/FM radio with record player in a beautiful wood console. The throne room has an elaborate electric chandelier that is completely out of place in the Tibetan decor. The modern bathroom looks more like the 1930s than the 1950s. It even had a heater sitting on a shelf.

22 MAY, 1992—We visited a shoe factory. We started with the raw sheep and yak hides with the wool or hair still on them and went through the entire cleaning and tanning process. Then we saw them making leather jackets and finally went on to the actual shoe factory. The employees (about 300) live within the factory compound. The company is old, but moved to this site in 1960. They had recently mechanized in a joint venture with Germany, so much of the work was being done on gleaming new machines. While we were there the electricity went off, so we only saw the first part in actual production.

23 MAY, 1992—We left the hotel at 6 a.m. for our 10:00 flight since the airport was 60 miles from Lhasa. The road was paved all the way, but was very rough. It was all the usual

Drunken Celestial Beings Restaurant.

Betty, Maria, Richard, and Larry.

Street-side bicycle repair shop.

hurry up and wait routine, but it was a little perplexing to find that they wouldn't accept Chinese money to pay the airport tax. Taking off at 12,000 feet was disconcerting. There was so little lift in that rarified atmosphere that it took a long runway and the plane climbed very slowly. They served us a box lunch consisting of a salted, boiled egg, an orange, a package of rice and peanut munchies, a LARGE chocolate bar, and a large package of saltines.

▼

The mountains were glorious. It was worth the bad roads, the miserable hotels, and the altitude sickness just to be that close to Everest.

Tibet was beginning to rebuild the monasteries that were destroyed by the Chinese during the Cultural Revolution, and we could see how splendid they once were. The crowning glory was the Potala in Lhasa. Lhasa was very Chinese and the tension was palpable. We admired the industry and tenacity of a people struggling to free themselves from an oppressor. It was probably the most rugged, adventurous trip we have ever taken, and is certainly one we will never forget.

UNITED ARAB EMIRATES

ABU DHABI

October 20-24, 1992

During our October break we went to visit Emmy Wohlenberg in Abu Dhabi, United Arab Emirates. Americans can't enter the country without a "sponsor." We were rejected the first time but she finally got visas just about 12 hours before our scheduled flight time. The flight was NOT routine. We got to the airport a little after 9 p.m. for our 11:15 flight. We checked in, went through passport control, and were sitting in the departure lounge when the police suddenly swept through and rushed everyone out. There had been a bomb threat and they evacuated the entire terminal in a surprisingly short time. We stood across the street for nearly two hours before they began letting employees back in. After a while we were permitted in and went through passport control again. After a long wait they announced that our flight would depart at 1:30 a.m. They got us boarded and might have made the rescheduled time, but there was a problem with the nose wheel. That took half an hour to correct, so we took off about 2 a.m. We got to Dubai at 8:30 (4:30 a.m. local time) and Emmy was waiting patiently. The temperature was still about 77°. Even though the really hot summer was over, it was still well up in the 90s in the afternoon and humid. It reminded us of summer in Florida.

From Dubai it is a two-hour (100 mile) drive to Abu Dhabi on a lighted four-lane highway through bare desert. Without irrigation there was only sand and a little scrub. In the cities, greenery and small trees thrive where there is irrigation, but a few feet from water there is sand again. The buildings, beautiful Middle Eastern-Moorish architecture, are mostly extremely new. Everything was clean and well maintained—obviously there was plenty of public money. Except for running the government and managing large companies, nationals avoid work by importing a tremendous number of laborers (about 40% of the people). The Muslim weekend is Thursday and Friday.

Abu Dhabi, a beautiful city with broad streets, new build-

Emmy Wohlenberg.

ings, and irrigated gardens, has twenty-story apartment buildings mixed in with older four-story buildings. The latter were rapidly being torn down to be replaced with higher buildings. Emmy's apartment was on the 17th floor of a building located on the edge of the main downtown business area. There were still touches of the old city and bare sand wherever it was not irrigated. The Arab-Lebanese food, a completely new cuisine to us, was one we liked very much.

Al Ain, an oasis city, is about 100 miles from Abu Dhabi. There were lots of camels along the roadside and any minute we expected Lawrence of Arabia to come out from behind a dune. We climbed a little on one dune and were surprised at how fine the sand is. In Al Ain we went to the museum until it closed at noon. Much of what they had on display was from 2500 to 3000 B.C. Nearby was the livestock market; we walked through the sheep and goat shed since they seemed to be doing a lot of business. A man would pick out an animal, pay for it, and hoist it on his shoulders to carry it away. We visited a hotel/resort development by a natural spring and later walked around the gardens that had been designed

241

Camel crossing.

around the tomb area from which many of the museum arti-
facts were excavated. The trip back to Abu Dhabi was through
quite different looking desert, as the sand was varying shades
of red instead of light tan. Back in Abu Dhabi we wandered
around the souk (the old market) and for dinner ate some
shwarma sandwiches, which were much like Greek gyros, and
drank pomegranate juice.

Friday we drove southwest along the coast through what
they called "salt marsh." It is barren—absolutely no plant life—
brown, flat terrain periodically flooded from the gulf. Away
from the coast to the south is hilly, sand dune country dotted
with oil fields with a lot of gas being flared off. The Liwa oasis
is a crescent shaped region 65 miles or so long through a relatively narrow valley. All of the water was underground, but
with pumping they have managed to develop a large winter
vegetable farming area. They were harvesting winter crops, a
big part of which were grown under white plastic sheeting for
protection from the sun. Although they might get a little rain in
December, they have to irrigate to produce a crop. There was
a lot of corn and potatoes; the faster growing crops would be
planted later. We drove to both ends of the crescent on a
lighted, four-lane, divided highway that ended abruptly at
both ends. There were clusters of houses now and then, but
nothing that could really be called a town.

The Abu Dhabi Women's College where Emmy teaches was only five years old and had beautiful facilities with lots of new equipment. The UAE had just begun to educate women. Teaching was similar to tutoring grammar or high school students in the U.S.

JAPAN

December 13-29, 1992

The serenity of the temples, shrines, and castles of Japan is an impressive contrast to the bustle of the surrounding cities. In warmer weather we would have spent hours enjoying the carefully sculptured gardens. We certainly got our money's worth out of the Japan Rail Pass. The trains were clean, fast (the Shinkansen travels at 130 mph+) and they ran ON TIME. In two weeks only one train was late and then only by seven minutes. The stops at the stations were short and people actually waited in line to get on. We missed a couple of local trains because we were a few seconds late. Fortunately there were trains every few minutes and missing a train only meant we had to wait for the next one. Subway fares were reasonable and the Rail Pass was good on many of the buses.

Jeanette Gustat was our "tour guide" and she and her friend, Brian, planned the days we were to be on our own and provided us with detailed written instructions in English and Japanese in case we got lost. We found strangers eager to help and able to read and write English. They did have trouble understanding our verbal questions and we had trouble understanding their speech. Except for Japan Rail there were very few signs in English so we couldn't even read street names. Houses are unnumbered. The postmen are expected to know everyone in their area and otherwise directions are given by description.

SELECTED DIARY EXCERPTS

13/14 DECEMBER, 1992—We left Kuala Lumpur about 10:30 p.m., had a two-hour layover in Singapore, and left for Nagoya at 1:30 a.m. We arrived on time and Jeanette was there to meet us. It was 40°F with heavy overcast and seemed awfully cold to us. We took a bus into town and then a taxi on to her house. It is right in town on a busy street, one-room wide, low-ceilinged, and small. After we settled in and met Brian, we took a bus to the Atsuta Shrine (Shinto). Even though it is in the heart of the city, it was quiet and serene. We went by subway to the Nagoya Castle. It is wooden and was built in 1620, destroyed in WWII and reconstructed since. We stopped at a tea house for a sweet and the tea ceremony. The green, uncured leaves made a brew that tasted like cooked grass. We went all through the five floors of the castle and up to the observation deck for a panoramic view of the city. Nagoya has a population of 2.1 million and really sprawls. None of the buildings is very tall—probably because of earthquakes. We wandered around through the grounds and through a small pottery museum. We then took the subway to a main crossing that has a large area of several levels of stores underground. We had the Nagoya specialty (a miso, noodle, chicken, egg soup) and, after lunch, wandered around the streets looking at houses and stores. The gardens were lovely and everything was clean, neat, and orderly. A fruit store had the most beautiful fruit we have ever seen anywhere, but the prices were unreal. We actually saw a single muskmelon priced at US$80!! While Jeanette taught a class, Brian joined us for a tour of a large department store. Again the merchandise was interesting, but the prices were exorbitant. The entire basement was devoted to foods.

15 DECEMBER, 1992— Our unheated bedroom was frigid. We slept on futons on the floor with a down comforter and a heavy blanket on that. Once we got them warmed up we were toasty warm. After breakfast, we walked to the Horita station on the Meitetsu Rail Line and took a train to the Nagoya station. There we transferred to the Japan Rail Line, activated our rail passes for the next two weeks, and—on our own—took the train to Gifu where we changed for a train to Unuma. The trains run so perfectly on time that we could set our watchs by them. We often didn't look at the station sign; if the time was right, we knew that the station was right. Once when we asked about a train we were told that it would leave at 10:37:30 and they were right! It didn't go at 10:37 and it was on its way before 10:38. We walked across the bridge over the Kiso River to Inuyama and climbed the hill to the Inuyama Castle. It is the oldest castle in Japan (1528) and is built on a stone foundation with a wooden superstructure. It is four stories inside although the exterior is built to look like three. All the grounds were beautifully maintained as well as quiet and peaceful. There are several shrines around it. We strolled back to the main part of Inuyama and stopped for a meal. At 4:30 it was hard to know what to call it, but we had a curried pork cutlet with rice and salad for a very reasonable price. By then it was dark, so we walked back across the bridge to Unuma, found the JR station, and retraced our steps to Jeanette's house.

16 DECEMBER, 1992—On the way to the JR Nagoya station, the three of us stopped at a bank to cash some travelers' checks. The banker asked us to sit at a table and came over with the forms. Then he chatted with us, and tea was served while we waited for our money. It took quite a while, but was certainly a pleasant way to cash checks. We took the bullet train to Tokyo. At a little over 130 mph, we got there in less than two hours and we had wonderful views of Mt. Fuji. At the Tokyo station we got sandwiches and canned tea to take on the train. We took another bullet train to Utsunomiya where we changed to a local for Nikko. This is a mountain resort town and this time of year has snow-capped mountains around it. It is very old, full of shrines, and reputed to be the most beautiful town in Japan. We are staying in a Ryokan (Japanese hotel). That means no shoes, mats on the floors, sit on the floor at low tables, and sleep on futons on the floor. But it has central heat and both of the toilets have electrically-heated seats! Soon after we arrived we took the public baths (men's and ladies' are separate). It was an interesting experience, but we all looked like boiled lobsters when we got out of the hot water. We were served a fantastic Japanese dinner in the room and then waiters moved the table and spread our futons for the night. They noticed that one of the fluorescent lights was blinking and within five minutes a man was there to change the bulb. Of course, for US$200 per night we could expect good service. After supper we all went for another bath. We understand why Japanese are addicted to their hot baths. They are soothing.

17 DECEMBER, 1992—We had a Japanese breakfast—fish, pickled vegetables, rice, soup, tofu, and tea. We transferred to the Pension Turtle for the second night—their van came to get us—and after we had registered and left our bags, we set off on foot to tour temples and shrines. We spent the morning seeing two shrines and two temples. We had to remove our shoes at the temples so we were glad to have our wool socks on. Shrines are open-air and you don't really go inside. The first was Rinnoji Temple which had three very large statues of Buddha. Then came the Toshogu Shrine which is the most intricately carved and decorated, rococo temple we have ever seen. There we saw the original "Hear no evil. See no evil. Speak no evil." monkeys carved on the wall above a stable door. This was followed by Futurasan Shrine and the Daiyuin Mausoleum. By the time we had done all that it was lunch time. In the afternoon we took a bus about 18 km up to Chuzenji Lake and village. In Nikko it had been spitting snow off and on, but up there it was snowing much more heavily and there was some on the ground not melting. The road up was a one-way road that was almost continual hairpin curves. It was as close to going straight up the mountainside as they could do. We walked around the town, but most things were closed for the winter season. The lake was splendid in a cold, wintry way with the mountains and snow reflected in it. We walked to Kegon Falls. It was beautiful with all the ice frozen around it. We then took the bus back to Nikko. If possible the road down was even steeper. We walked over to the "Stone Park" which the girl at the Pension had recommended. It was disappointing to say the least—just huge stones sitting in a grassy area. You must have to be Japanese to appreciate such things. However, we discovered a long path lined with Jizo, stone gods, with bibs tied on to keep them warm in the winter. Back at the Pension, we enjoyed a Japanese dinner including trout caught in the mountain streams around Nikko. The room was small, but heated, and the futons on the mat floor were comfortable. The owners spoke reasonably good English.

18 DECEMBER, 1992—We had an early breakfast and the van took us to the station. It had snowed overnight, so the town was beautiful. We retraced our steps to Tokyo, and Jeanette took the express bullet train to Nagoya since she had an early afternoon class. We took the local bullet to Odawara and then changed to the Hakone Line. The train took us to Miyanoshita where we went to see the Fujiya Hotel—western-style built in 1878. It is elegant. We had lunch and took the next train on up to Gora. All this time we had been climbing steeply up the shell of a huge volcano that blew its top thousands of years ago and now has a lake and three small volcanoes in its crater. From Gora we took a cable railroad up to

246

Sounzan and then transferred to a cable car tramway. It took us to the rim of the crater and then swung out across a valley with steam coming from lots of fumaroles. The sulphur smell was strong. We could see Mt. Fuji but there were more clouds around the top than when we saw it before. We got off at the station on one of the volcanoes to take pictures. Then the tramway took us on down to Togendai on the shore of Lake Ashino. We boarded a cruise ship made up to look like a pirates' sailing ship and went the full length of the lake to Hakone Machi. From there we took a bus up over the rim and down to Odawara. Since it was only 4:30, we decided to go back to Tokyo (thirty-five minutes) to see what we could find. It was dark as we came into the city so we glimpsed the Ginza district with all its neon signs. We went out on the west side of the station to walk over to the Imperial Palace. We walked for several blocks and couldn't find it. When we were looking lost, a man stopped and offered help. He explained that we were actually on the east (Ginza) side of the station. So we went back to the station. It has a vast underground shopping area where we stopped for dinner. Then we walked on through to the other side and started looking for the Palace again. After a few blocks we came to the same corner where the man had helped us. We don't know what happened, but we think perhaps the station only has one side. In disgust we went back to the station and took the non-stop bullet train for Nagoya.

19 DECEMBER, 1992—We took trains, mostly locals and fairly slow, to Toba where the Mikimoto Pearl Company is located (via a walkway) on Pearl Island. This was founded by the man who discovered the process for making cultured pearls. They had a demonstration of women pearl divers in spite of the temperature, a museum showing the whole process from operating on the oyster to stringing the pearls, and a marvelous museum of jewelry using pearls. The signs had English translations and some of the demonstrators were able to give an English explanation. Naturally they had two large salesrooms, also. It was all so interesting that we spent quite a long while there. They chased us out (very politely) at closing time and we realized we hadn't had anything to eat since breakfast. We had dinner and then headed for the train station. Another slow trip back to Nagoya got us to Jeanette's about 9 p.m.

20 DECEMBER, 1992—We left about 11 a.m. for Kyoto

via the bullet train. From the main station we took a small line out northwest to walk to two temples. At the station we had gotten a request for directions to the temples written in Japanese. We stopped in a tiny restaurant for some lunch and used the note. The owner pointed to the map a lot and assured us we were going the right way. It had started to drizzle, but we went on anyway. We walked quite a bit further and stopped at another restaurant to ask again. A young man showed us on the map and then indicated "car." Apparently he and his friend were just leaving and offered to drive us to Ryoanji Temple. They had a really fancy sports car and soon had us there. The temple is known for its rock garden consisting of twelve rocks in a raked gravel area. It was designed about 1500 and has not been changed except to re-rake the gravel every day. The whole place is a delightful, secluded park (not spectacular, but peaceful), but it was raining more. Jeanette was giving a party at 7 p.m., so we had to be back well before that. We decided that we didn't have time to walk to the second temple, so we headed back to the station to retrace our steps to Nagoya. The walk back took us through an area of dozens of small shrines and large homes. We could peek in and see how pleasant they really were. We dried out on the train, but it was raining lightly in Nagoya so we got dampened again. The party was lots of fun. Six of their friends, one Danish and five Japanese, came with food and drink for a pot luck. They varied in English language ability, but we managed to converse reasonably well. After we ate we played some simple games, trying to choose games that didn't require language skills. One game involved thinking of popular song lyrics and we decided that English, Japanese, and Danish were all acceptable. They all seemed to have a good time and stayed rather late.

21 DECEMBER, 1992—Two of Jeanette's students, middle-aged housewives, invited us to lunch. Mrs. Kato met us at the subway with her five-year-old son and drove us to the house where we met Mrs. Katsuno. The house was unusually large for a Japanese house. Mrs. Katsuno's son, who is a pre-med student, was home studying for an exam. (Later we figured out that he was doing nothing but studying for a major exam he was to take in about six months.) Their English was good enough that conversation was no problem at all. They had ordered two pizzas and also had a tossed salad, roast pork,

The Golden Pavilion.

and fruit for dessert. We had brought some sweet desserts and they served those, too. After lunch we went back downtown, got some money at American Express, did a little shopping, and came back to the house. The rest of the afternoon was spent on routine things like laundry and shampooing. The laundromat was the smallest I'd ever seen and was a long walk from the apartment. In the evening we took a bus into the downtown area and met Jeanette for dinner. At the restaurant, we had a grill in the center of the table so we could cook our own meal. One of the things we cooked was thin-sliced pork, chopped vegetables, and egg all stirred into a batter which made a pancake about an inch thick and seven inches in diameter. We also had fried noodles with pork and a salad.

22 DECEMBER, 1992—The three of us took the 9 a.m. bullet train to Kyoto. In Kyoto, we took the subway and bus up to Kinkakuji Temple (the Golden Pavilion), the one we didn't get to on Sunday. It is a Japanese-style Buddhist temple with the outside completely covered in gold. We then took a bus to the Sanjusangendo Temple which has 1001 statues of the Kannon form of Buddha. He has 42 arms which symbolize his 1000 actual arms, and twelve heads to symbolize his wisdom. We were running late, so we took a cab to the Imperial Palace for the 2 p.m. tour. Japanese are not allowed to tour the palace, but a limited number of foreigners are allowed in. We had no problem since there are so few tourists this time of year. We had an English language tour guide, but her pronunciation was so poor that we caught only a small portion of what she said. We were not permitted inside any building, but we could see into most of them since they have open fronts.

23 DECEMBER, 1992—The four of us took the bullet train to Kyoto and then a local to Nara. Nara was the capital even before Kyoto and much of it was built in the seventh and eighth centuries. The city is smaller now than it was in the eighth century. We walked to the three-story pagoda and then the five-story pagoda. The compound is full of tame deer. We had bought some lunch to eat here, but the deer were such pests trying to steal what we had that we had a hard time getting it eaten. We then walked to Todaiji Temple. It is the largest wooden building in the world and houses the largest bronze statue of Buddha in Japan. This building was built in 1709 after many previous versions had burned, but the statue was cast in 749. We walked to the Kasuga Grand and Kasuga Wakamiya Shrines. The former has over 3000 lanterns hanging from the eaves and standing around on the grounds. It was getting late so we walked back toward the train station, going past some beautiful homes and several more shrines and temples. We reversed our tracks (pun intended) with a local to Kyoto and the bullet train to Nagoya.

24 DECEMBER, 1992—This morning was noticeably colder. We took the bullet train to Himeji. We went through some heavy snow on the way, but it was dry in Himeji. After lunch we walked a short way to Hakuro-jo Castle (White Egret Castle). It is five stories, with large grounds and 78 other buildings. We had an English language tour guide who spoke quite adequately and gave us an interesting tour. The castle was started in the 1500s, reached its present form in the early 1800s, and was completely restored in the 1960s. Very little of it is original. The exterior is impressive, but the interior is just large spaces completely undecorated. Even though they lived in it, it was largely a defensive structure since the shoguns seemed to be at war all the time. We then got back on the train for Hiroshima and got there about 7 p.m. We went to the same sort of "cook-it-yourself-at-the-table" restaurant as we did Monday night and enjoyed it just as much.

25 DECEMBER, 1992—MERRY CHRISTMAS! We considered

Hakuro-jo Castle.

going to a Christmas mass, as there are Anglican churches, but anything we could find would probably be in Japanese so we gave up on the idea. After breakfast, we took the local train to Miyajimagushi and then the ferry over to Miyajima Island. The principal shrine there was built in the 12th century out over the water and has a famous torii standing out in the water. It is

Restaurant waitress at Miyajima Island.

251

Kintai-kyo Bridge.

large and elaborate for a Shinto shrine. After that we went to a museum of folklore and culture. It is in what had been a wealthy man's home. Part of it is the home furnished as it would have been 100 years ago, and the rest is a museum of tools, household goods, art, etc. We spent a long while there. We strolled along in and out of shops until we got part way up the hill and found a restaurant. We had lunch and then strolled back down to the pier. We took the ferry back to the mainland and another local train to Iwakuni. We took a bus to the Kintai-kyo Bridge, a very graceful and unusual bridge of five arches. It was built in 1673, swept away by a flood in 1950, and restored in 1953. It has no nails, and the walkway up and down over the arches is so steep it is only practical as a footbridge. We took the bus on to the Shinkansen station to catch a bullet train back to Hiroshima.

26 DECEMBER, 1992—We spent nearly two hours at the Peace Park and the museum. The presentation was slanted from the Hiroshima point of view; they never mention the war at all, as if someone dropped the bomb for no reason at all. But the photos and exhibits of the destruction are unsettling. After lunch there we took the trolley to a train station. We planned to go to a scenic gorge, but found out that we could get there, although there was no train coming back until the next day. Needless to say, we didn't go.

Ground Zero at Hiroshima.

27 DECEMBER, 1992—We caught the 10:27 bullet train for Kokura on the island of Kyushu where we changed to a local for Beppu. We had a confusing time finding the second train; we were given conflicting information because the railroad had added an extra train for the holiday. We arrived in Beppu about 1:30. Our minshuku is charming—an old wooden building with a hot mineral bath. Again we are sleeping on futons on tatami mats and sitting on the floor. The town is built in a hot springs area and steam is everywhere—even coming out of the drains. There are mineral baths and hot springs called "hells" similar to Yellowstone. There are also mud pots and, if we had wanted to pay the price, we could have been buried in hot sand. Such a treatment was supposed to cure a large assortment of ills including gout, arthritis, high blood pressure, and stomach ailments. We decided that US$17 per person was too much to pay for the treat. We had a delicious dinner: Richard had chicken nuggets, rice, soup, and salad, and Maria had champon (noodles and cabbage soup) which is a typical Nagasaki dish. We made reservations for Monday's train to Mt. Aso and then on to Kumamoto and Fukuoka. Our taxi drivers have all worn a uniform and white gloves. The bus drivers are similarly dressed and this evening's also wore white spats.

28 DECEMBER, 1992—We were up early to catch an 8:30 train to Aso to see Mt. Aso. It was the largest volcano in the world when it blew its top thousands of years ago, and now has five volcanos in its crater, one of which is active. When we got to Aso, we found that the viewing area had been closed two days earlier because it had suddenly become dangerously active. We had four hours before the next train, so we decided to take the bus up part way to see the museum and to see what views we could get of the volcano. Shortly after we started up, the fog settled in so heavily that we couldn't see the other side of the road. At the museum we saw an excellent multiple-screen movie of the active volcano and the region around it. We hurried through the rest of the museum and took the next bus down without even a glimpse of the mountains. After lunch we took the train to Kumamoto and changed to another for Fukuoka (Hakata). We checked into the Hakata Miyako Hotel which is the fanciest we have been in for some time.

29 DECEMBER, 1992—Our flight was completely uneventful except for one passenger who caused some ruckus before we took off. He tried to get off and they wouldn't let him because he was being deported for traveling on a false passport. Once the plane took off, we never heard from him again. We had a two-hour layover in Singapore and finally got home about 9 p.m. in the pouring rain.

▼

By going to Japan in December we missed the cherry blossoms and the beautiful gardens, but we did get an impression of a clean, peaceful country with a gentle, orderly people. We would be glad to go back again sometime.

SINGAPORE

The Raffles Hotel restoration is spectacular. The cheapest room in the upscale complex rents for around US$300 per

Bob and Tina.

night and the prices in the courtyard shops are comparable. The old-world ambiance remains and there is a cafe off the main courtyard where we enjoyed a simple, reasonably priced lunch. The bar, famous for the Singapore Sling, has been moved upstairs to make room for an opulent lobby.

Bob and Tina now live and work in Singapore. During our visits with them we had a taste of life in a benevolent dictatorship. The strict laws favor the rich but life on the Island runs smoothly. There are no traffic jams, the city is clean (chewing gum is outlawed) and safe, and shopping opportunities abound. We came home with spices and Indian saris and another Oriental rug. We didn't discover rug auctions until our last visit just before moving back to the U.S. Otherwise, we would have added more than one rug to our collection.

NEPAL AGAIN!

March 23-April 3, 1993

SELECTED DIARY EXCERPTS

25 MARCH, 1993—Joan and Paul Shull's return visit to Malaysia marked the 45th day of their trip around the world. They planned their visit to coincide with our spring vacation so we could all trek in Nepal. It NEVER rains in Nepal in March but it was raining when we arrived on March 26th. Nima just

Nima with his family.

smiled at our worried questions about trekking in the rain. About 6:30 he took us to his room for dinner with his family. It is the same small, one-room abode that we visited before, but there are now five people living in it. They served us a delicious dinner and we gave them the gifts we had brought. About 8 p.m. he announced that it was time to go to bed, so we took the hint and went back to the hotel.

27 MARCH, 1993—We were up at 7 a.m. and had breakfast. As an example of Nepalese prices: The American breakfast with eggs, ham, porridge, toast, juice, and tea was US$1.70. We started about 8:30 in a bus with the four of us, a driver, helper, Nima, Jwane, and six porters with all our camping and cooking equipment as well as luggage. After we got out of Kathmandu the road was steadily uphill. It was really only one lane wide even though we occasionally met buses and trucks coming the other way. It had been paved at one time, but is more potholes than paving now. The countryside was mountainous, with steep sides terraced all the way to the top. The crops were wheat, vegetables, and rice, but most of the terraces were unplanted in March. Rhododendron forests—gorgeous bright red flowers—were in full bloom. We hadn't realized rhododendrons would grow into trees with trunks over a foot in diameter. We went through many checkpoints; at each one they had to register the bus and show all our papers. Part way up a mountainside we came to a place where a bus had gone over the side three days earlier. It had rolled down the hillside about 300 ft. and was a crumpled mess. They said that it had had 46 passengers: ten were killed outright and the rest were all hospitalized in Kathmandu. We got to Trisuli Bazar about noon and had a Nepalese lunch (rice with dal bhat and a curried potato and cauliflower mixture) in a dark, dirty restaurant. The ceiling was under six feet and the doorways were about five feet. While we were there Paul discovered that he had forgotten to leave the hotel room key at the desk before we left. Richard reached into his pocket and there was ours, too! From there the road was unpaved and very rough. It went steadily upward fairly steeply. It also got steadily colder. We got to Dhunche at 6500 ft. about 3 p.m. The views of snow-covered mountains on three sides were magnificent. Langtang II to the north of us on the Tibetan border was over 24,000 ft. It was windy and cold, so we stopped at a little shop and bought knitted wool caps and mittens. (Two caps and two pairs of mittens cost us US$6.40.) This trek we had a meal tent with a table and five stools, separate sleeping tents for us and for the Shulls, and a latrine tent, as well as tents for Nima and the others. Dinner was chicken/cilantro soup with papadams, buff momo, mixed vegetables, and fried noodles. For dessert they served us warm fruit cocktail with tea, cocoa, and coffee.

28 MARCH, 1993—We survived the night. It was cold and windy but we did fairly well in our sleeping bags on the hard ground. The worst thing was the dogs that barked most of the night. As we stepped out of the tent, we faced a magnificent view of the Langtang range with the Tibet border only about 20 miles away. We were up a little after 6 a.m., ate breakfast, and started walking about 7:45. The four of us were

257

Nima with Dhunche vendor.

Clinic in Dhunche.

Barefoot porter.

supported by a guide, assistant guide, cook, two assistant cooks, and five porters. We trekked until we caught up with our lunch crew about 12:15. The trek was exhausting. It was steeply uphill almost all the way. Our lunch stop was on a sort of mesa with mountains all around. We estimated that we climbed from 6500 ft. to over 9000 ft. The view of the Langtang range was utterly fantastic since we were now much closer than we were in Dhunche, but we were all very tired.

Three Blind Mice.

Lunch was hot lemonade, tea, sliced cucumbers, cheese sandwiches, spiced carrot/cauliflower mixture, scrambled eggs, sardines, and bananas. After lunch we rested and actually napped a little. We started out about 2:30 for Dhimsa, which was not as far as we had originally planned for the day. That even steeper climb, took us to 10,000 ft. As we went up it got colder, and after a while we were trekking in snow which was a little treacherous at times. It took us about 1 3/4 hours to get to Dhimsa and we were pretty tired by then. There we had tea and played with the children—letting them look through Paul's binoculars and teaching them to sing "Three Blind Mice." Soon we were served tea and crackers and settled into the dining tent since it got much colder as the sun set. Our dinner was vegetable soup with popcorn!, asparagus rolls, mashed potatoes, and cold cabbage salad with fruit cocktail for dessert. We went to bed immediately after dinner; we were all exhausted.

29 MARCH, 1993—We were up about 6 a.m. after a good night's sleep. We had been comfortably warm and the ground didn't seem quite so hard the second night. Again the view was magnificent as the sun came up. The ground was frozen and there was frost everywhere. We had breakfast and started trekking at 8:25. Again it was all uphill and pretty steep. There was lots of snow and it was melting where the sun hit it, so the trail was muddy and slippery in places. We got to Singompa (11,000 ft.) about 10 a.m. and spent the rest of the morning there. [Nima revised our itinerary after hearing from other guides about the heavy snow where we intended to go. The rest of our trek won't be nearly as strenuous as yesterday was.] We had tea, visited the local Tibetan Buddhist monastery, and went through their cheese factory. It was not operating now because the yaks hadn't come up to the summer pasture yet. We also watched a group of carpenters sawing logs into planks, planing, and chiseling to fit the mortise and tenons. All of their building was without nails or screws. We had an early lunch with pancakes, scrambled eggs, potatoes, hot dogs, baked beans, and a carrot/cucumber salad, with oranges for dessert. We started again about 12:30 and only hiked about two hours to Phulung where we camped for the night. We were on a ridge with a panorama of high, snow-capped mountains on three sides. However it was terribly windy (and of course cold) so we tried to stay in the sun but sheltered from the wind. Fortunately the wind died down before sunset. At one point today we were on a high, bare point with mountains very close on all sides. We ran out of adjectives; it was literally indescribable. The views we are enjoying on this trek are even more spectacular than on our first two treks. The trail here from Singompa was mostly level or downhill through marvelous pine forests. However it was fairly deep snow and wherever it was hit by the sun it was

Scene at Phulung.

261

Mountains west of Phulung.

melting. That meant we slogged through a lot of mud also. Richard's shoes were canvas so he ended up with very wet shoes and socks. We put them in the sun to dry, and Richard sat in the sun with his wool mittens on his feet. It looked a little strange with the thumbs sticking out, but was comfortable. They served us tea and cookies. The wet shoes and socks dried well in the wind and sun. Our dinner started with soup and popcorn again and then was based on their version of pizza. It was good, but bore little resemblance to what we know as pizza. We didn't wait long before we went off to bed.

30 MARCH, 1993—Last night seemed even colder, but we did all right. We were up before 6 a.m. and until breakfast we just stood and looked at the view. We started trekking about 7:40 and this time it was all downhill. We soon got down below the snow line. There were some muddy, slick spots, but most of it was dry and easy. The views continued to be fantastic. After a couple of hours we stopped for tea, then walked a little more and stopped for lunch about 11 a.m. We had the usual large lunch with egg sandwiches and sardines and lots of vegetables. We rested for a long time and then started down again. By now it was dry and pretty easy. Within two hours we were down to our campsite in Syabru. When they first pitched the latrine tent they had it at about a 30° angle from the vertical and facing against a wall so you couldn't get in. Nima had them re-do it as soon as he noticed it. After tea we walked through the village looking at all their handi-

Young monk.

crafts. We bought a Tibetan teapot made from brass and copper. The workmanship was relatively crude. We were at about 7000 ft. so it was noticeably warmer.

31 MARCH, 1993—We slept reasonably well in spite of the village full of barking dogs. Nima hurried us because he knew we had a long way to walk. We left Syabru about 7:15 and went uphill for a while and downhill the rest of the morning. There were some houses, teahouses, and a monastery along the way so we had lots of picture taking opportunities, especially of children. We stopped for lunch about 10:30 at a teahouse along the way. One of our porters sprained his ankle pretty badly. They readjusted loads so his was bulky but not as heavy, and he went limping down the trail with the large basket of luggage on his back. The disgusting thing was that he stayed ahead of us. Porters normally carry 30 kilos (66 lbs). We got to Bharkhu about 1 p.m. and from there had a gravel road to Dhunche. It went down a long way through a ravine and then up to Dhunche. We finally got there about 4 p.m., utterly exhausted. Nima estimated that we had walked about 28 miles in the four days. That's not much distance but so much was steeply uphill or down that we felt we had performed quite a feat. At tea-time we took our shoes off to see how our feet were doing. We had no blisters or damage of that sort, but we did have several badly bruised toenails. (Richard eventually lost two; Maria lost one.) That morning Maria had announced that she was going to stuff a sock into the toe of each boot to try to protect her toenails as we came down. She was also going to wear two pairs of socks to cushion her feet. When she took her first shoe off, she was puzzled.

Breakfast at Syabru.

264

Along the road back to Kathmandu.

She had two socks on that foot, but there was none in the boot. It seemed to have vanished. But when she took the other boot off, she discovered she had four socks on that foot. We sat there watching her peel them off and laughed so hard we had a hard time stopping. We were probably a little slap-happy from our extreme tiredness, but she certainly provided the trigger.

1 APRIL, 1993—Nima had a ten-passenger Land Rover and we (with six of the crew) got started at 7:05. It was a long, slow ride on the same poor road that we had come up on. About 10:30 we got to Trisuli Bazar and had lunch in the same restaurant we ate in on the way up (and essentially the same lunch). We didn't get to Kathmandu until after 2:30, so it took us a good 7½ hours for the trip. The engine on the Land Rover was overheating and we stopped many times to refill the radiator. We had our fingers crossed that we wouldn't have to push.

GOING HOME

1987-1989

Several options for our trip home were available to us. Our original plans were to take the trans-Siberian railway but the situation in China and the week on the train in India convinced us that wasn't a particularly good idea. The pick-up point for the Trans-Siberian is Beijing and even though the Palace on Wheels was a marvelous experience, we had not forgotten that a moving train isn't conducive to a good night's sleep. We decided this was our chance to say we had been around the world, so settled on short visits to Germany, Belgium, and The Netherlands.

We were required to use a government agent to make our travel arrangements. Siti was pleasant and tried hard but hadn't the foggiest notion what she was doing. We wanted to visit friends in Frankfurt on our way home, spend three weeks touring in Europe before flying to Washington, D.C., from Amsterdam, and then go to Chicago by way of Tallahassee, Florida. Admittedly not the most direct route, but Siti never really understood our plans. After comparing notes with others in the program trying to get home, we decided we were all training novice agents. It took us five months to get everything arranged, and a great deal of time was spent explaining what we wanted to Sanie, our agent at Paradise Travel, and having him call Siti. Then we would get an airline computer printout to see what she had actually done and we could start correcting the newest mistakes. The only consolation in all this was that Siti probably learned a lot about the travel business. Even with all our checking, when we picked up our tickets our departure date was one day later than we had requested. MAS had changed its schedule but Siti hadn't thought it necessary to tell us! Of course that meant we had to change all our hotel reservations in Europe.

▼

In 1991, when Bob and Tina Hvitfeldt's son, Justin, was planning to go home to start college, the program assigned Siti as his agent. His final destination was Iowa, but when his tickets arrived he had been routed through Frankfurt, Washington, D.C., and Chicago. We are certain Siti remembered our route and decided it could be used again. The program informed Siti that Justin would have to go home across the Pacific.

267

A checkout packet from the program included all the obvious things such as paying final water and electric bills and settling up with our landlady. We had Murugaie clean everything thoroughly the day before Miss Lim was to come inspect the house. The cleaning binge was wasted effort. Miss Lim's primary concern was to make sure all the furniture was still there and the keys accounted for. In fact, she was so concerned about the keys she made two trips to Shah Alam that last day. We assured her we would slip the last set under the door after we locked it, but she insisted we had to give them to her personally.

On June 30, 1989, Crown Pacific carefully packed all our household goods. The ramshackle truck was filled to bursting and as it backed out of our driveway, we wondered if we would ever see our precious possessions again. We left Malaysia on July 12th. Customs control hardly existed in Europe, but all hand baggage was carefully checked, especially at Heathrow.

Our first stop was Frankfurt, Germany, where we stayed with friends for four days. Kurt and Erna live near the small village of Heppenheim and as our tour guides, they took us to Heidelberg and Worms and for a cruise on the Rhine. The villages are beautiful and clean, and the older buildings have been well restored. The German countryside looks manicured and there are castles everywhere. We nearly OD'd on luscious German bread, pastries, and hot chocolate.

Franck, our French friend from Malaysia, met us in Brussels. In addition to renewing our friendship and reminiscing, we had the advantage of an interpreter as we struggled with finding our way around. We went to Ghent and Bruges and did a walking tour of Brussels. The buildings are exquisite, and we were captivated by the lace making.

The canal trip was the highlight of our stay in Amsterdam. We also toured the Ann Frank house. The "attic" her family hid in is a large, multi-room apartment. We drove over the large dike that makes the inland sea and made a loop of towns that included The Hague, Delft, and Muiderslot, where there is a restored medieval castle. Seeing the Rembrandt *Night Watch* was a special thrill.

After stops in Arlington and Tallahassee, we were met by Michael at O'Hare on August 1st. John had moved back into the house after the renters left July 1, and he had the yard in reasonable shape when we got home. It still needed a lot of work, so between that and getting the house settled, we kept busy. We bought two cars within the first two weeks: a shock all by itself! Going to the grocery store was traumatic—the prices were much higher than in Malaysia. Even with everything else that needed doing we found time to pick vegetables and freeze them for the winter. At least we live in an area that has good truck gardens, and August was the right time to stock up.

Our sea freight arrived, undamaged, on September 6 and we continue to be pleased with the way our Asian purchases fit in. About ten days after getting back we went to a reunion of IU/MUCIA/ITM faculty. Even though we didn't know everyone, we shared the same experience and it was encouraging to know they all managed to survive the move back. We particularly enjoyed the slide show for which everyone had contributed five or ten of their favorites.

RE-ENTRY

When we left family and friends in July 1987 we said we would come back barefoot and wearing sarongs. We came close to doing just that. A sarong is a wonderfully comfortable garment, well suited to the tropical climate. After two years we were so used to being barefoot it was hard at first to remember to wear shoes. Leaving our shoes outside the front door had become second nature to us, and the soles of our feet were callused from walking barefoot through the mosques and temples of Asia and from the square dancing. The arrival of cold weather brought an abrupt end to forgetting our shoes!

We reclaimed the day we lost and are now where we started from 730 days ago, in Munster, Indiana, half a world away in miles from Malaysia, and light years away in terms of culture. We struggled with culture shock and the realization we were suffering the confusion and frustration of being strangers in our own country.

Learning to drive on the right side of the road was an adjustment. The German autobahn has no speed limit and the cruising speed of conservative drivers is over 100 mph! U.S. speed limits are lower, but after two years of thinking "KEEP LEFT," we puzzled over which way to turn into a divided street and we **MUST** remember the octagonal red sign that says **STOP** means STOP, not YIELD as it did in Malaysia. Six months after returning we would still occasionally open the door on the passenger side of the car and wonder where the steering wheel had gone!

Malaysian money, in different sizes and colors to designate denomination, had become familiar. Our paper money is longer and narrower than we remembered, and checkout girls gave us strange looks as we shuffled through bills looking closely at the numbers in the corner. We even had to relearn the coins.

Getting used to the prices of food, and everything else for that matter, took time. For two years our grocery bills had been about US$25 a week. Dinner from the corner food stall was US$1 and if we wanted white table clothes and elegant service, we paid about US$4 in one of the fancier places in town. After our first restaurant meal back in the U.S., we thought we would never eat out again. Our tastes and eating habits have changed. We frequent the local Asian restaurants where prices are higher than we were used to in Malaysia, but lower than we would pay other places.

Dogs, considered unclean by Muslims and scarce in Malaysia, were everywhere in Europe, even in shops and restaurants. The Chinese in Malaysia owned dogs, but they were kept in fenced yards and one hardly ever saw a dog in the streets. Of course one did see cows and goats in the streets and those are missing in European and U.S. cities!

We have spent a lot of time people-watching. After two years in Asia spent mostly in a Muslim country, we had lost touch with the west. We were shocked to see so many immodestly dressed men and women. Occasionally in the past two years we had seen tourists who were skimpily dressed, but we had adjusted to modesty being the norm.

We lived without a TV in Malaysia and didn't miss it. Malaysians watch television and are hooked on programs produced in the U.S. "Dallas" gives the impression that all of us drink whiskey, are rich, and sleep around!! We export our very worst programs. We did listen to shortwave radio. We were disappointed in the programming offered by the Voice of America. Again, we are missing an opportunity to put our best foot forward. We also listened to the BBC and Radio Moscow and several local programs which played classical and pop music.

It's difficult here to adjust to students who don't seem interested in working, and are entering college with much less preparation than they had ten years ago. Recently we read in the paper that if a foreign power had imposed our current educational system on us, we would consider it an act of war!

It is hard to go back to the high-pressure life style. We used to joke about leaving notes to each other to make sure we still lived in the same house, but after two years of togetherness, going back to that way of life is not easy. Friends also back from Malaysia agree having the family together at the dinner table was wonderful, and a luxury they miss now that their children are once again involved in extra-curricular activities and part-time jobs.

Malaysians have a different sense of time than we do. No one is in a hurry and business is conducted only after pleasantries are exchanged. It is a gentle way of life and we miss it.

1991-1993

Our plans to return to the U.S. through Europe were approved by ITM. Syed, the Bumi agent assigned to us, not only spoke excellent English but understood what we wanted and agreed with the cost our travel agent had quoted. Getting the tickets issued was complicated. The MAS ticket agent said there was no such fare available. Syed talked to someone higher up who assured him there was such a fare. Syed did produce tickets a few days later. By the time we were making these plans, Richard had a working phone in his office! He couldn't call out but he could receive calls. Miracles do happen. Syed would talk to Maria but he wanted everything confirmed by the man of the family.

THE SECOND TIME IS EASIER

SELECTED DIARY EXCERPTS

6 MAY, 1993—Even though this was Wesak Day, Murugaie and Ghopal came to do the last cleaning of the house. The sliding doors at the front of the living room had a padlocked iron grill for which we had never found a key. We had a bag full of keys for the house, but none of them fit this padlock. Consequently we had never been able to go in and out that way. When Murugaie was ready to clean the glass, she went to the kitchen, took the key from the hook beside the refrigerator, and opened the padlock. We had never tried that key or wondered what it was! Needless to say, we felt rather foolish. Puan Faridah came by in the morning to settle our financial matters and return our deposits. She was impressed with how clean we had the house, much cleaner than when we moved in, and didn't quibble about anything. Larry came about six and took us to Shah Alam where we left all the final program forms and our give-away household goods with Pearl Zehr. We had a nice Indian dinner and then he dropped us at the airport. Our flight was at 11:55 p.m. and left on time.

7 MAY, 1993—We had dinner about 2 a.m. and then tried to get some sleep. We stopped in Dubai for over an hour but we stayed on the plane. We finally got to London about 8:15 a.m. local time (20 minutes late). Our baggage claim took a long time. They finally apologized and said that "due to a technical problem" they couldn't get the baggage off the plane. When we finally got out, Franck and his friend, David, were waiting for us. We had a voucher for our rental car, but realized that it didn't say which rental company. The girl at the Budget rental counter was very helpful and finally found out that our car was at Eurodollar. They took us by shuttle bus to their rental office where we found that they had confused us with another Yates and didn't have our car ready. They found our booking, but the dates were wrong. In spite of all that, they came up with a nice little Peugeot and we headed for Birmingham. Since most of the traffic on the motorway seemed to be driving between 90 and 100 mph, we stayed at a conservative 80-85 and got to Birmingham about 12:30. John was waiting for us. After lunch at a dining room on campus, we went on a walking tour of the campus. The Barber Institute of Art had a surprisingly good collection of paintings. We then went to the pub where Eva worked for the owners, and sat and talked until she was free to leave. Our excellent dinner was at a Spanish restaurant in the center of Birmingham.

8 MAY, 1993—We both woke up fairly early, but blamed it more on the early sunrise than on any jet lag problem. After breakfast, we took John to the grocery store so he could take advantage of the car to get a load back to his flat. Franck and David wanted to head for London this evening, so we agreed to go to Oxford in two separate cars and meet at the Bowden Library at 3 p.m. We picked up Eva, stopped for some sandwiches, and started out. The drive to Oxford was easy, but in the town traffic was terrible and parking was virtually nonexistent. By the time we found a place to park and got to the library it was 3:50 and there was no sign of David and Franck. We waited around there for some time and then started wandering off to see something and coming back to check for them. Oxford is a fascinating place with its well-preserved medieval buildings. We climbed Carfax Tower for a view of the town about the time it started to rain, and then went down to Christ College and Christ Church. The cathedral was closed, but we were able to wander through some of the buildings, and saw the Great Hall. After checking at the library again, we got the car, drove around more of Oxford, and then headed for Birmingham without ever finding Franck and David.

9 MAY, 1993—Franck called while we were having breakfast. They had gotten to the library on time, waited until 3:30, and then gone sight-seeing as we did. They came back twice to look for us, but always when we were off sight-seeing ourselves. At least they hadn't had a serious problem. After a picture-taking excursion on campus we went with John to Cadbury World. It has a large exhibit/museum of the history of chocolate as well as a tour of the factory to see the whole process. They kept giving us candy bars and chocolate samples. We finally got to the point that we stuffed them in our pockets and couldn't stand the thought of eating any more!

Next, we toured Aston Hall, a manor house that was built between 1612 and 1635. The huge, beautifully preserved building had been remodelled repeatedly over the succeeding 250 years, but parts of it are the original. We didn't see a figure, but it must have at least 60 rooms, some of which are large halls. One room, the Gallery, is 136 feet long and was built primarily as a place to stroll in bad weather. The house is three stories plus basement and attics. The gardens around it are also well-groomed and had wonderful spring flowers. We then drove in to the city center, toured St. Martin's Church, the oldest in Birmingham, and walked on to the cathedral. Both were beautiful old churches with nice stained glass, but the cathedral is a strange boxy architecture with Greek columns in the chancel and sanctuary but not down the nave. We walked on over to see the public library simply because Prince Charles had described it as "the ugliest building in Britain." He was probably right.

10 MAY, 1993—Warwick Castle was started in 1068 and the grounds covered many acres. We spent about three hours exploring the private rooms, state rooms, and dungeons as well as towers and fortifications and several rooms full of exhibits. From the towers we could see a large church in the center of town so we took time to visit it. One of the guides there turned out to be a retired math teacher from a local prep-school who had had several Malaysian boys in his classes. We then drove on to Coventry to see the cathedral. The bombed-out shell was reminiscent of visiting Hiroshima. The new cathedral is strikingly modern. They showed an excellent A-V presentation of the bombing and the parish attitude of forgiveness.

11 MAY, 1993—We were up early to make sure we made our flight. As it turned out, everything went smoothly and the plane was nearly an hour late leaving, so we had lots of time to sit in the terminal. We were nearly on time in Newark, and immigration/customs was very efficiently handled. For the flight to Washington they loaded us on the plane and then we sat there for almost two hours because of thunderstorms just west of Newark. We got to Washington about an hour and a half late, but Dad and Ellen were waiting patiently. After dinner we soon went off to bed. It's been a wonderful two years, but it was nice to be back in the U.S.

STARTING OVER

We were better prepared coming back this time and have had little trouble adjusting, perhaps because Richard is retiring in December, 1993, and we are busy getting ready to move to Colorado Springs. We feel displaced, but that feeling is due partly to our not wanting to make any long term commitments before we settle into our new home. A lot of this past summer has been spent catching up with family and friends.

Drastic cultural and environmental changes in Malaysia made our second experience there less idyllic. The changes in the United States are no less drastic. We are perceived worldwide as a violent, depraved society. At the same time, the American mystique is idolized and copied by young people everywhere. Nima, our Nepalese guide, told friends of ours who trekked with him that perhaps, if he was lucky, in his next life he would be born American.

Our four years overseas have been a life-changing experience. For better or worse we see ourselves as citizens of the world as well as Americans. Life anywhere can be good, and Asia will be part of us wherever we are.

274

GLOSSARY

Bahasa - Malaysian word meaning "language" used to refer to the Malaysian language, Bahasa Melayu

Bumiputra - Malaysian word meaning "sons of the soil" used to describe the native Malay population

CAAC - China's domestic airline: The Civil Aviation Administrtion of China

ESL - English as a Second Language

Expat - short form of "expatriate" used to refer to foreigners living abroad

FAO - Food and Agriculture Organization of the United Nations

HEP - Hal Ehwal Pelajar: Office of Student Affairs responsible for students' religious, social, and personal lives

Hide - a small, enclosed shelter often built on stilts, offering shelter to humans wishing to observe animals in their natural habitat. Some have primitive bed and toilet facilities.

Imam - a Muslim man who exercises spiritual and temporal leadership over a region

IU - Indiana University

ITM - abbreviation for the Malaysian name for "Mara Institute of Technology"

KL - Kuala Lumpur, territorial capitol of Malaysia. "Kuala" is a river mouth, or the junction of two rivers. "Lumpur" means muddy.

MAS - Malaysian Air Service

MUCIA - Midwest Universities Consortium for International Affairs, Inc.

Nyonya - a subculture in and around Malacca, formed by Malaysian men married to Chinese women.

PJ - Petaling Jaya, suburb of Kuala Lumpur

PPP - abbreviation for the Malaysian name for "Center for Preparatory Studies" which was the Malaysian administrative equivalent to our Indiana University administration

PUC - Purdue University Calumet, Hammond, Indiana

Pulau - Malaysian word meaning "island"

Ringgit - Malaysian word meaning "dollar." The $ symbol was officially the same as for U.S. currency until 1992 when RM was adopted instead. In this book we have used RM for all references to ringgits.

Sen - Malaysian word meaning "cent"

Stadthuys - Dutch word meaning "statehouse" which refers to the old city government building in Malacca.

Stupa - a hemispherical or cylindrical mound or tower serving as a Buddhist shrine.

WHO - World Health Organization